DEVOTIONAL

{ for women }

DEVOTIONAL

{ for women }

The Livingstone Corporation

ZONDERVAN®

ZONDERVAN

Once-A-Day Devotional for Women
Copyright © 2011 by The Livingstone Corporation

Requests for information should be addressed to:
Zondervan, *Grand Rapids, Michigan 49530*

ISBN 978-0-310-44072-7

Cover design: Faceout Studio and Jamie DeBruyn
Interior design: Sherri Hoffman and Jamie DeBruyn

Printed in the United States of America

11 12 13 14 15 16 /DCI/ 20 19 18 17 16 15 14 13 12 11 10 9 8 7 6 5 4 3 2 1

ABOUT THE LIVINGSTONE CORPORATION

Since our inception in September 1988, Livingstone has helped Christian publishers produce 169 specialty Bibles and more than 500 trade books, devotionals, gift and specialty books, studies and curriculum products. Each year we produce about 70 new titles, including Bibles, reference products, trade books, children's books, studies, and curriculum. Our products have won 11 Gold Medallion awards and have been Gold Medallion finalists more than 30 times.

OUR VISION

Our vision is to glorify and enjoy God in and through our lives, relationships and services and support the advancement of the Good News of Jesus Christ.

OUR MISSION

Livingstone's mission is to provide superior ideation, content, design and composition services for religious publishers worldwide.

OUR MOTTO

Ideas to Marketplace. This saying expresses our core brand promise to clients and reflects both the breadth and depth of our capabilities to deliver convenient and effective solutions for marketplace success.

january1

SOLOMON'S PRAYER FOR WISDOM

At Gibeon the LORD appeared to Solomon during the night in a dream, and God said, "Ask for whatever you want me to give you."

Solomon answered, "You have shown great kindness to your servant, my father David, because he was faithful to you and righteous and upright in heart. You have continued this great kindness to him and have given him a son to sit on his throne this very day.

"Now, LORD my God, you have made your servant king in place of my father David. But I am only a little child and do not know how to carry out my duties. Your servant is here among the people you have chosen, a great people, too numerous to count or number. So give your servant a discerning heart to govern your people and to distinguish between right and wrong. For who is able to govern this great people of yours?"

1 KINGS 3:5–9

Imagine Solomon, the heir to one of the wealthiest nations at that time, beginning his inaugural address with a prayer for God to help him—a mere "little child." Perhaps you feel like that sometimes, even though you have children of your own. Instead of looking to his resources—the enormous power of military might; the wealth of his kingdom—Solomon turned to prayer. Only God could help him be the effective leader he needed to be. Solomon honestly evaluated his own abilities in light of the magnitude of his responsibilities as the king of Israel. He concluded: "Who by himself is able to govern this great nation of yours?"

As you begin this new year, let Solomon's prayer for wisdom guide your own prayer. Seek God's wisdom first; let him counsel you as you pray. ✤

PRAYER

Dear Lord, I ask for your wisdom in my life this year . . .

HANNAH'S CRY FOR A CHILD

In her deep anguish Hannah prayed to the LORD, weeping bitterly. And she made a vow, saying, "LORD Almighty, if you will only look on your servant's misery and remember me, and not forget your servant but give her a son, then I will give him to the Lord for all the days of his life, and no razor will ever be used on his head."

1 Samuel 1:10–11

Hannah lived in a time when a woman was dishonored if she was unable to bear children. Her rival—her husband's other wife—took advantage of this situation. She flaunted her own children before Hannah. When the whole family went up to Jerusalem for the feast, Hannah found herself unable to join in the celebration. Instead, she went into the Tabernacle and expressed her deep longings to God and poured out her intense sorrow before the Lord. She knew to whom she should turn when she was down. She knew the Almighty was the only one who could help her up. She didn't arrogantly demand that God give her a son. Instead, she expressed her willingness to give herself for what she desired. She vowed before God that, if he would give her what she most desired, she would give her son back to God.

What is the cry of your heart? Have you brought it before God? Have you been willing to bear the "cost," should God ask for it? ✣

PRAYER

Dear Lord Almighty, if you will look down upon me and answer my prayer ...

CELEBRATING GOD'S FAITHFUL LOVE

> *Give thanks to the LORD, for he is good;*
>   *his love endures forever.*
> *Let Israel say:*
>   *"His love endures forever."*
> *Let the house of Aaron say:*
>   *"His faithful love endures forever."*
> *Let those who fear the LORD say:*
>   *"His love endures forever."*

PSALM 118:1–4

Dependable. Reliable. Faithful. All of us want such qualities in our friends—dependable when the going gets tough, reliable when you have to count on them, and faithful to the end. Let us celebrate God's faithfulness. God came to our rescue when we were most desperate and at the mercy of our ruthless enemies. Such faithful love is something to celebrate; so praise him by saying: "His love endures forever."

Each day, let us celebrate God's faithfulness. Whether it is a birth of a child, the start of a new job, unexpected financial provision, or God's continual blessing on your family, thank God for being faithful to you. ❖

PRAYER

Dear Lord, your faithful love for me endures forever . . .

REJOICING OVER GOD'S FAVOR

> *LORD my God, I called to you for help,*
> *   and you healed me.*
> *You, LORD, brought me up from the realm of the dead;*
> *   you spared me from going down to the pit.*
> *Sing the praises of the LORD, you his faithful people;*
> *   praise his holy name.*
> *For his anger lasts only a moment,*
> *   but his favor lasts a lifetime;*
> *weeping may stay for the night,*
> *   but rejoicing comes in the morning.*

PSALM 30:2–5

Although God prevented David from building the great Temple in Jerusalem, this prayer of David was sung when the Temple was dedicated. The prayer's words echo the experience of someone who had survived God's anger and rejoiced in God's mercy. Even a moment of God's anger created a night of weeping for David. But the darkness and sorrow of the night were always followed by a joy-filled morning—a restoration of David's relationship with his Lord. David could praise God for his holy, just, and convicting anger because he knew God didn't get angry without reason. The appropriate response to God's anger was repentance.

The night of painful waiting—the dark night when we turn our sins and sorrows over to the Lord—will surely be followed by a morning of joy. At that time, every tear will be dried and every wound will be healed. ♣

PRAYER

Dear Lord, I am so grateful that your loving anger lasts for a moment, but your favor lasts for a lifetime ...

CARRIED IN HIS ARMS

> *Praise be to the LORD, to God our Savior,*
> *who daily bears our burdens.*
> *Our God is a God who saves;*
> *from the Sovereign LORD comes escape from death*

PSALM 68:19–20

What do you picture in your mind when you pray to God? Do you picture a loving father, listening to his child? Do you picture a mighty conqueror with the power of a vast army of angels at his disposal? Your answer likely depends on what you're praying for at the moment. David's prayer gives an intimate picture of God carrying his loved one in his arms.

Meditate on this picture for a moment. Imagine yourself in David's description. As you begin to speak with God about your needs and concerns, imagine his arms surrounding you in a protective embrace. How does that affect what you want to say to the Lord, your savior? Throughout the day, whenever you feel the need for "saving," draw this picture in your mind. And let his embrace comfort you. ✤

PRAYER

Dear Lord, I long to be carried in your arms today as I tell you what concerns me right now…

january**6**

PRAISE FOR GOD'S LIGHT

You, LORD, keep my lamp burning;
my God turns my darkness into light.
With your help I can advance against a troop;
with my God I can scale a wall.
As for God, his way is perfect:
The LORD's word is flawless;
he shields all who take refuge in him.

PSALM 18:28–30

All of us have experienced times when our lives grew dark—when hope seemed futile, when confusion set in, when we felt alone. David knew how dark life could seem at times. When he wrote this prayer, the memories of fleeing in terror from King Saul's manhunt and hiding in dark, damp caves were fresh in his mind. Yet, he focused on God's light in his life—the light that dispelled the confusion of darkness. With this light, David saw clearly that God's way was perfect, even if it brought him through dark and dangerous valleys. God would always prove himself true to his promises. God would always be with him to protect him.

When you are traveling a dark road, remind yourself of David's experience with God—of how God led him through those dark places. Use David's prayer to remind yourself of God's light in your life. ✤

PRAYER

Dear Lord, thank you for lighting up my darkness . . .

PROCLAIMING GOD'S SAVING POWER

As for me, I will always have hope;
   I will praise you more and more.
My mouth will tell of your righteous deeds,
   of your saving acts all day long—
   though I know not how to relate them all.
I will come and proclaim your mighty acts, Sovereign LORD;
   I will proclaim your righteous deeds, yours alone.

PSALM 71:14–16

The psalmist had trusted God from his childhood and had continually proclaimed the Lord's goodness to others. At his peak, his life was a shining example to others; but as he grew older, people began to plot against him. In his old age, he started to feel abandoned by God. So in this passionate prayer, he appealed to the Lord and placed his hope in him. He prayed that God would give him the chance to proclaim the Lord's saving power among the people once again.

Do you have that same desire to tell others of God's goodness to you? Recall God's protection and guidance in your life and let someone know how much God has helped you. ✤

PRAYER

Dear Lord, I am overwhelmed by how much you have done for me, and I want to tell everyone . . .

EZRA'S PRAYER OF CONFESSION

I am too ashamed and disgraced, my God, to lift up my face to you, because our sins are higher than our heads and our guilt has reached to the heavens. From the days of our ancestors until now, our guilt has been great. Because of our sins, we and our kings and our priests have been subjected to the sword and captivity, to pillage and humiliation at the hand of foreign kings, as it is today.

But now, for a brief moment, the LORD our God has been gracious in leaving us a remnant and giving us a firm place in his sanctuary, and so our God gives light to our eyes and a little relief in our bondage. Though we are slaves, our God has not forsaken us in our bondage. He has shown us kindness in the sight of the kings of Persia: He has granted us new life to rebuild the house of our God and repair its ruins, and he has given us a wall of protection in Judah and Jerusalem.

EZRA 9:6–9

Although the Israelites' sins were "higher than" their heads, God had been merciful to them. He had allowed some of them to survive their exile to Babylon and had allowed them to return to Jerusalem. But the remnant of Israelites God saved had not learned their lesson. They immediately began disobeying God again. They freely intermarried with the pagan peoples. Ezra is embarrassed to approach God because of all the sins of his people. Yet in spite of their sin, God granted the Israelites "relief." He forgave and restored them.

Sometimes confessing sin is embarrassing and awkward. At those times, remind yourself that the Lord loves to restore and forgive those who approach him with a humble and contrite heart. ✤

PRAYER

Dear Lord, my mistakes embarrass me. According to your unfailing love, please don't abandon me as I confess my sins to you . . .

A PRAYER FOR RESTORED SUCCESS

> *Teach us to number our days,*
> *   that we may gain a heart of wisdom.*
> *Relent, LORD! How long will it be?*
> *   Have compassion on your servants.*
> *Satisfy us in the morning with your unfailing love,*
> *   that we may sing for joy and be glad all our days.*
> *Make us glad for as many days as you have afflicted us,*
> *   for as many years as we have seen trouble.*
> *May your deeds be shown to your servants,*
> *   your splendor to their children.*
> *May the favor of the Lord our God rest on us;*
> *   establish the work of our hands for us —*
> *   yes, establish the work of our hands.*

PSALM 90:12 – 17

In this prayer, Moses asked that God's unfailing love would greet him every morning. He prayed for his people to see the miracles of God's work in their lives; and he asked for God's approval on his life.

Ask God to bless your endeavors: "Yes, establish the work of our hands." But remember your requests reveal how you measure success. When you spend time in prayer today, ask God for his blessings on your efforts. But first ask yourself what true success is. ♣

PRAYER

Dear Lord, make my efforts successful in these following ways ...

EXPRESSING OUR FEARS TO GOD

But Moses said to God, "Who am I that I should go to Pharaoh and bring the Israelites out of Egypt?"

And God said, "I will be with you. And this will be the sign to you that it is I who have sent you: When you have brought the people out of Egypt, you will worship God on this mountain."

Exodus 3:11 – 12

After fleeing from Egypt to escape Pharaoh's wrath, Moses settled down to a quiet and predictable life as a shepherd in the peaceful, yet desolate, region of Midian. But God had different plans for Moses. He wanted Moses to return to Egypt, confront Pharaoh, and lead the Israelites out of slavery. When God revealed his plan to Moses by speaking from a burning bush, Moses hesitated. "Who am I?" he asked. He made a further excuse: "I have never been eloquent, neither in the past nor since you have spoken to your servant. I am slow of speech and tongue" (4:10) followed by the plaintive: "Please send someone else" (4:13). But for every one of Moses' excuses, God had an answer. God promised to be with him, to back up his message with miraculous signs, and even to give Moses the words to say. In the end, Moses was left with no excuses. God promised to empower Moses each step of the way.

What challenging situation has God given you? Freely express your misgivings and fears about the tasks God has given to you. Commit those fears to God, and remind yourself of God's willingness to empower you every step of the way. ❖

PRAYER

Dear God, be with me as I do your will. Who am I to do . . .

january11

A PRICELESS INHERITANCE

Praise be to the God and Father of our Lord Jesus Christ! In his great mercy he has given us new birth into a living hope through the resurrection of Jesus Christ from the dead, and into an inheritance that can never perish, spoil or fade. This inheritance is kept in heaven for you.

1 PETER 1:3–4

Prayer keeps our hearts turned heavenward, while our feet remain firmly on this earth. Peter prayed for Christians facing persecution and rejection by their neighbors. He prayed to remind them of the prize awaiting them in heaven—even as they struggled here on earth.

Let your own troubled heart soar with wonderful expectation of all the treasures awaiting you in heaven. Let this prayer take your mind off the cares and struggles of this world. Refresh your soul with thoughts of the pure, undefiled inheritance reserved for you in heaven—an inheritance that cannot be destroyed. ✤

PRAYER

Dear Lord, I praise you for reserving a priceless inheritance for me in heaven . . .

PRAISE TO THE LORD!

> *May the glory of the LORD endure forever;*
> *   may the LORD rejoice in his works —*
> *he who looks at the earth, and it trembles,*
> *   who touches the mountains, and they smoke.*
> *I will sing to the LORD all my life;*
> *   I will sing praise to my God as long as I live.*
> *May my meditation be pleasing to him,*
> *   as I rejoice in the LORD.*
> *But may sinners vanish from the earth*
> *   and the wicked be no more.*
> *Praise the LORD, my soul.*
> *Praise the LORD.*

PSALM 104:31–35

You'll never lack for ways to express yourself to God in prayer when you use Scripture in your prayers. This prayer provides a portrait of the Almighty that will jump-start anyone's prayer life. Immerse yourself in this beautiful prayer of praise to the Lord. Imagine the piercing power of his mere glance. His eyes alone make the entire earth tremble. The very mountains he created ignite at his touch.

What adversary are you facing? God's glance makes the earth tremble. What mountain stands in your way? The Lord can eliminate any obstacle. Commit your adversaries, your worries, and your cares to him. ❖

PRAYER

Dear Lord, may you be pleased by all these thoughts about you for I rejoice in you . . .

PRAISE FOR GOD'S WORKMANSHIP

For you created my inmost being;
   you knit me together in my mother's womb.
I praise you because I am fearfully and wonderfully made;
   your works are wonderful,
   I know that full well.
My frame was not hidden from you
   when I was made in the secret place,
   when I was woven together in the depths of the earth.
Your eyes saw my unformed body;
   all the days ordained for me were written in your book
   before one of them came to be.

PSALM 139:13–16

Any biology text can illustrate how wonderfully complex the human body is. From brain cells to blood cells—each intricate component of our bodies is carefully designed. It doesn't take a biology course to marvel at how our eyes can take in the bright blue color of the sky, how our ears can detect a pin drop, how our nose can enjoy the aroma of ground coffee or a freshly baked pie. How exciting it is to enjoy the body God has made for us!

In this prayer, David took time to time to stand in awe of God's creation. Set aside a few minutes today to praise God for his sovereign care. ✤

PRAYER

Dear Lord, thank you for making me with such marvelous workmanship . . .

BOWING BEFORE OUR MAKER

> *Come, let us bow down in worship,*
> *let us kneel before the LORD our Maker;*
> *for he is our God*
> *and we are the people of his pasture,*
> *the flock under his care.*

PSALM 95:6−7

This prayer is a grand call to worship—a summons to bow low before God, our maker. Like a shepherd, our almighty Creator looks after us. He guides us. He wants to protect us from danger. That's why we need to listen carefully to his voice and follow him.

The more we make psalms like these our own, the more prayer will become natural to us. We will learn what it means to bow before our Lord and trust him to care for us. Meditate on this psalm, and slowly pray it back to your loving Shepherd. Recommit yourself to listen to him and follow his direction. ✤

PRAYER

Dear Lord, you are my God and I am under your care ...

january**15**

PRAISE TO THE EVERLASTING FATHER

Grace and peace to you from him who is, and who was, and who is to come, and from the seven spirits before his throne, and from Jesus Christ, who is the faithful witness, the firstborn from the dead, and the ruler of the kings of the earth. To him who loves us and has freed us from our sins by his blood, and has made us to be a kingdom and priests to serve his God and Father—to him be glory and power for ever and ever! Amen.

REVELATION 1:4–6

"Who's in charge around here anyway?" we utter under our breath. Burdens and trials can become so overwhelming that we become discouraged. Our prayers become stilted and awkward. In those times, we can draw strength from what the apostle John observed while in exile on the island of Patmos. The book of his visions—Revelation—is like a grand coronation ceremony of God's Son, Jesus Christ. It pictures Jesus as the King over all kings, as the ultimate authority in heaven and on earth. This prayer exalts Jesus and proclaims his royal status.

Reflect on what it will be like to meet this glorious King of kings. Then with the apostle John, proclaim: "To him be glory and power for ever and ever!" Who's in charge? He is. ✤

PRAYER

Dear Lord, I want to give you everlasting glory! You rule forever and ever ...

THE OWNER OF ALL THINGS

David praised the LORD in the presence of the whole assembly, saying,

> *"Praise be to you, LORD,*
> *the God of our father Israel,*
> *from everlasting to everlasting.*
> *Yours, LORD, is the greatness and the power*
> *and the glory and the majesty and the splendor,*
> *for everything in heaven and earth is yours.*
> *Yours, LORD, is the kingdom;*
> *you are exalted as head over all."*

1 CHRONICLES 29:10–11

Most of us work long and hard to buy the things we have. It's all too easy to conclude: "I've earned all of this by my own efforts. It's all mine." Although King David was one of the richest men of his day—owning gold and silver, and governing the united kingdom of Israel—he didn't fall into the trap of thinking his possessions were his own. Instead he reminded himself that everything in the heavens and on the earth belonged to the Lord. That's why David gave up many of his treasures to build the Lord's Temple.

Remember how great the Lord is; then pray with an attitude like David's. ✤

PRAYER

Dear Lord, everything in the heavens and on earth is yours . . .

january**17**

THE DESIRE TO OBEY

May he turn our hearts to him, to walk in obedience to him and keep the commands, decrees and laws he gave our ancestors. And may these words of mine, which I have prayed before the LORD, be near to the LORD our God day and night, that he may uphold the cause of his servant and the cause of his people Israel according to each day's need.

1 KINGS 8:58–59

After spending seven years constructing the Temple, King Solomon led the Israelites in dedicating this magnificent structure to the Lord. First, Solomon praised the Lord for keeping his promises, for establishing the Israelites in the land, and for giving them the opportunity to build God's Temple. God had kept all the promises he had made to Solomon's father, King David. How should the Israelites respond to their God? King Solomon prayed that the Israelites would want to obey the Lord's commands. Why? So the name of God would be exalted: "so that all the peoples of the earth may know that the LORD is God and that there is no other" (8:60)

Is your prayer that your life will bring glory to God? Reflect on your motives for obeying God, then pray with a heart like Solomon's. ✤

PRAYER

Dear Lord, give me the desire to do your will in everything ...

CONFESSION BEFORE PETITION

Then I said:

"LORD, the God of heaven, the great and awesome God, who keeps his covenant of love with those who love him and keep his commandments, let your ear be attentive and your eyes open to hear the prayer your servant is praying before you day and night for your servants, the people of Israel. I confess the sins we Israelites, including myself and my father's family, have committed against you. We have acted very wickedly toward you. We have not obeyed the commands, decrees and laws you gave your servant Moses.

"Remember the instruction you gave your servant Moses, saying, 'If you are unfaithful, I will scatter you among the nations, but if you return to me and obey my commands, then even if your exiled people are at the farthest horizon, I will gather them from there and bring them to the place I have chosen as a dwelling for my Name.'"

NEHEMIAH 1:5-9

When Nehemiah heard how his people were suffering back in the devastated province of Judah, he mourned, wept, fasted, and prayed. Nehemiah knew that unconfessed sin was a barrier to prayer. Only after he confessed his own sins, his family's sins, and those of his people did he ask God to grant him success before the king. God answered Nehemiah's prayer. The Lord moved the heart of King Artaxerxes to send Nehemiah back to Jerusalem to rebuild its walls.

Are you concerned about the condition of your neighborhood or nation? Confess your own sins and the sins of your people; and then, ask the Lord to intervene. ♣

PRAYER

Dear Lord, I confess that we have sinned against you ...

A PRAYER FOR HOLINESS

May God himself, the God of peace, sanctify you through and through. May your whole spirit, soul and body be kept blameless at the coming of our Lord Jesus Christ. The one who calls you is faithful, and he will do it.

1 THESSALONIANS 5:23–24

As we grow up, our parents teach us how to become more and more independent. They teach us how to tie our own shoes or how to cross a busy intersection. And then one day, they trust us to do it all alone. By the time we've become adults, we start believing we can do anything and everything on our own. That type of attitude often spills over into our spiritual lives. Scriptures teach us to live a holy life, and we determine to become holy by our own efforts. At the end of this letter, Paul doesn't tell the Thessalonians to be holy. Instead he prays: "May God himself, the God of peace, sanctify you."

In our own strength and by our own striving, we're not capable of becoming holy. But how are we blameless before God? Paul reassures the Thessalonians that God "is faithful, and he will do it" (5:24). Take to heart Paul's message to the Thessalonians. Pray that God will make you holy. ✤

PRAYER

Dear Lord, keep me blameless until that day when you come again . . .

PRAISING GOD FOR WISDOM

Then Daniel praised the God of heaven and said:

> *"Praise be to the name of God for ever and ever;*
>   *wisdom and power are his.*
> *He changes times and seasons;*
>   *he deposes kings and raises up others.*
> *He gives wisdom to the wise*
>   *and knowledge to the discerning.*
> *He reveals deep and hidden things;*
>   *he knows what lies in darkness,*
>   *and light dwells with him.*
> *I thank and praise you, God of my ancestors:*
>   *You have given me wisdom and power,*
> *you have made known to me what we asked of you,*
>   *you have made known to us the dream of the king."*

DANIEL 2:19–23

Daniel had been taken as a prisoner of war from Judah to Babylon, where he and three other young men were chosen to be advisors to King Nebuchadnezzar. One night, the king had a disturbing dream. He was tired of listening to lies from his magicians, enchanters, and astrologers, so he demanded that they tell him first what he dreamed before they interpreted the dream. If they couldn't, he would condemn them all to death—including Daniel and his friends.

Daniel responded to this challenge by consulting God in prayer. He urged his friends to do likewise. They couldn't know the thoughts of the king, but the all-knowing God could. The Lord answered their prayers. In a vision, the dream and its meaning were revealed to Daniel. He broke forth into praise, thanking God for giving him this knowledge and the wisdom to interpret the dream.

The God who answered Daniel's prayer is also listening to you. ✤

PRAYER

Dear Lord, you alone possess all wisdom and power ...

REQUESTING CLARIFICATION

Moses said to the LORD, "You have been telling me, 'Lead these people,' but you have not let me know whom you will send with me. You have said, 'I know you by name and you have found favor with me.' If you are pleased with me, teach me your ways so I may know you and continue to find favor with you. Remember that this nation is your people."
The LORD replied, "My Presence will go with you, and I will give you rest."

EXODUS 33:12–14

God had already commanded Moses to lead the Israelites into the Promised Land. But since they had disobeyed him by worshiping the calf of gold, God had refused to travel with such "stiff-necked people" (32:9). That's why Moses prayed: "Teach me your ways so I may know you and continue to find favor with you." God didn't reprimand Moses for stalling. Moses knew that God wanted him to lead the people to the Promised Land. But Moses also knew that moving ahead without the Lord's guidance, presence, and power would be disastrous, so he sought out the Lord.

God will answer those who seek him. Patiently, almost tenderly, God said, "My Presence will go with you." Moses asked for understanding, and God gave himself. He promised to be with Moses to guide him every step of the way. ✤

PRAYER

Dear Lord, show me your intentions so I will do exactly what you want me to do . . .

COMPLAINING ABOUT RIDICULE

You deceived me, LORD, and I was deceived;
you overpowered me and prevailed.
I am ridiculed all day long;
everyone mocks me.
Whenever I speak, I cry out
proclaiming violence and destruction.
So the word of the LORD has brought me
insult and reproach all day long.
But if I say, "I will not mention his word
or speak anymore in his name,"
his word is in my heart like a fire,
a fire shut up in my bones.
I am weary of holding it in;
indeed, I cannot.

JEREMIAH 20:7–9

When the Lord chose Jeremiah as his spokesman, the young man resisted. But God touched Jeremiah's mouth and said, "I have put my words in your mouth. See, today I appoint you over nations and kingdoms to uproot and tear down, to destroy and overthrow, to build and to plant" (1:9–10). But in prayer, Jeremiah openly admitted to God that he was tired of being ridiculed. Even so, he couldn't stop speaking the word of God: "I am weary of holding it in; indeed, I cannot."

Speaking the truth for God is difficult and takes its toll. If you're frustrated with witnessing for God, tell the Lord. Admit that you're weak, and ask the Lord for strength. He will renew your zeal for the truth. ✤

PRAYER

Dear Heavenly Father, rekindle the fire in my heart to speak the words you've put in my mouth ...

january23

PRAISE TO THE SUSTAINER OF LIFE

And the Levites—Jeshua, Kadmiel, Bani, Hashabneiah, Sherebiah, Hodiah, Shebaniah and Pethahiah—said: "Stand up and praise the LORD your God, who is from everlasting to everlasting."

"Blessed be your glorious name, and may it be exalted above all blessing and praise. You alone are the LORD. You made the heavens, even the highest heavens, and all their starry host, the earth and all that is on it, the seas and all that is in them. You give life to everything, and the multitudes of heaven worship you."

NEHEMIAH 9:5-6

After rebuilding the walls of Jerusalem, the Israelites gathered for a time of dedication and worship. They expressed sorrow for their sins by fasting, dressing in sackcloth, and sprinkling dust on their heads. They confessed their sins and the sins of their ancestors. Then, they listened for three hours while the Book of the Law was read, followed by another three more hours of confession. Only after thoroughly confessing their sins did the leaders of the Levites command the people to stand up and praise their eternal Creator.

Approach the Lord the way the Israelites did. Confess your sins. Humble yourself before the Lord. Then, let your confession lead into exuberant praise. Stand in awe of the Creator and Sustainer of life, the one who has forgiven your sins. ❖

PRAYER

Dear Lord, I stand before you, praising you. You live from everlasting to everlasting . . .

january**24**

JESUS' PRAYER FOR BELIEVERS

And now, Father, glorify me in your presence with the glory I had with you before the world began.

I have revealed you to those whom you gave me out of the world. They were yours; you gave them to me and they have obeyed your word.

JOHN 17:25–26

At the Last Supper, Jesus prepared his disciples for the death he would soon suffer. He washed their feet, talked about his coming betrayal, predicted Peter's denial, and told them that the Holy Spirit would be their Counselor. Then, Jesus prayed for them, asking the Father to "protect them from the evil one" (17:15) and to "sanctify them by the truth" (17:17). Even as he faced betrayal, denial, crucifixion, and death, Jesus was concerned about his followers. He wasn't concerned that they be kept from every trial, hardship, or danger; but he was concerned that they remain in God's love.

We can take great comfort that Jesus included us in his prayer: "My prayer is not for them alone. I pray also for those who will believe in me through their message" (17:20). ✤

PRAYER

Dear Jesus, thank you for your concern for me that even in your last few hours on earth you prayed for me ...

THANKS TO GOD, MY SHELTER

The LORD reigns forever;
he has established his throne for judgment.
He rules the world in righteousness
and judges the peoples with equity.
The LORD is a refuge for the oppressed,
a stronghold in times of trouble.

PSALM 9:7–9

David certainly had times of trouble in his life. He had been a fugitive, fleeing from Saul, the most powerful man in his land (1 Samuel 23:25). At other times, even his son turned against him (2 Samuel 15:14). So when David praised the Lord for being a shelter for the oppressed and a refuge in times of trouble, he wasn't talking about abstract concepts. Putting his trust in God was a life-and-death matter, and God had never abandoned him. That is why David sang about the Lord's protection. He described the Lord as being his "shield" (18:2), "stronghold" (18:2); a "hiding place" (32:7); a "refuge" and a "strong tower" where his enemies couldn't reach him (61:3).

In times of trouble, remember that God protects us. He will never abandon those who call on him. ✤

PRAYER

Dear Lord, thank you that we can find shelter in you, knowing that you have never abandoned anyone who comes to you . . .

january26

PRAISE TO GOD, OUR MAJESTIC KING

Righteousness and justice are the foundation of your throne;
love and faithfulness go before you.
Blessed are those who have learned to acclaim you,
who walk in the light of your presence, LORD.
They rejoice in your name all day long;
they celebrate your righteousness.
For you are their glory and strength,
and by your favor you exalt our horn.
Indeed, our shield belongs to the LORD,
our king to the Holy One of Israel.

PSALM 89:14–18

This psalm uses many lofty and majestic words to praise God for who he is. It pictures the Lord as an impressive king sitting on a throne supported by two strong pillars — his righteous actions and his justice. Two attendants — unfailing love and truth — go before the Lord clearing the way for him. It's a joy for the Lord's subjects to worship him, for he alone does what is completely right. He alone judges with justice. He alone upholds truth.

What is most amazing is that this powerful King and righteous Judge faithfully loves his people, and they're allowed to walk in his presence. Oh what a joy to walk in the light of God's presence and celebrate the King of kings! ✤

PRAYER

Dear King of kings, with great joy I answer the call to worship you . . .

FINDING REST IN GOD

> *Lord, you have been our dwelling place*
> > *throughout all generations.*
> *Before the mountains were born*
> > *or you brought forth the whole world,*
> > *from everlasting to everlasting you are God.*
> *You turn people back to dust,*
> > *saying, "Return to dust, you mortals."*
> *A thousand years in your sight*
> > *are like a day that has just gone by,*
> > *or like a watch in the night.*
> *Yet you sweep people away in the sleep of death —*
> > *they are like the new grass of the morning:*
> *In the morning it springs up new,*
> > *but by evening it is dry and withered.*

Psalm 90:1 – 6

"Where has all the time gone?" we often wonder as the minutes, hours, days, and years slip by. We never have enough time to accomplish all that we desire to do. Moses pondered the brevity of life in the oldest prayer in the book of Psalms. Yet, he praised God: "A thousand years in your sight are like a day." God is not rushed or exasperated by the time constraints we have. He doesn't have a beginning or an end; he is the Creator of time itself.

When you become painfully aware of your own limitations, seek peace in the Lord. Give all your moments over to God's care. Pray that God may infuse your efforts on this earth with eternal significance. ♣

PRAYER

Eternal God, I know that a thousand years are like a day to you ...

JOY IN GOD'S PRESENCE

How lovely is your dwelling place,
LORD Almighty!
My soul yearns, even faints,
for the courts of the LORD;
my heart and my flesh cry out
for the living God.
Even the sparrow has found a home,
and the swallow a nest for herself,
where she may have her young—
a place near your altar,
LORD Almighty, my King and my God.
Blessed are those who dwell in your house;
they are ever praising you.

PSALM 84:1–4

Like the sparrows at Solomon's Temple, we have the privilege of building our lives and homes in the presence of the Lord, for the Spirit is with those who confess Jesus' name (John 16:7). Unlike the temple musicians of Solomon's day, we don't have to go to a specific place to be in the Lord's presence (1 John 4:13).

We can make our homes and our workplaces sacred places by consciously reminding ourselves of the Lord's presence and worshiping him. "Blessed are those who dwell in your house." ❖

PRAYER

O Lord Almighty, I faint with longing for your presence …

january**29**

PRAISE FOR OUR GENEROUS LORD

Better is one day in your courts
than a thousand elsewhere;
I would rather be a doorkeeper in the house of my God
than dwell in the tents of the wicked.
For the LORD God is a sun and shield;
the LORD bestows favor and honor;
no good thing does he withhold
from those whose walk is blameless.
LORD Almighty,
blessed is the one who trusts in you.

PSALM 84:10–12

Too often, we envy someone else's dream relationship, stunning appearance, or extravagant income. We too easily forget that such things will never satisfy us. Only a relationship with God can bring eternal joy. In this prayer of praise, the temple musicians sang, "No good thing does he withhold from those whose walk is blameless.... Blessed is the one who trusts in you." They praised God for the blessings he gives to the obedient—mercy, protection, favor, honor, and joy.

God won't withhold his riches from those who obey him. God generously satisfies our needs. ♣

PRAYER

Dear generous King, I know you won't withhold any good thing . . .

AN URGENT CRY FOR HELP

Hear me, LORD, and answer me,
for I am poor and needy.
Guard my life, for I am faithful to you;
save your servant who trusts in you.
You are my God; have mercy on me, Lord,
for I call to you all day long.
Bring joy to your servant, Lord,
for I put my trust in you.
You, Lord, are forgiving and good,
abounding in love to all who call to you.
Hear my prayer, LORD;
listen to my cry for mercy.
When I am in distress, I call to you,
because you answer me.

PSALM 86:1–7

When you're in distress on whom or what do you rely? In deep distress, David relied on the Lord. David didn't base his appeals for mercy on what he had done for God. No, he appealed to God's character instead: "You, Lord, are forgiving and good, abounding in love to all who call to you." The Lord is truly a merciful God; and he wants to rescue those who are in trouble.

Like David, we can call on the Lord—not only when we're distressed, but at all times, and in humility: We are his servants, and he is our Master. We are the trusting ones; and he is the Trustworthy One. Rely on the Lord's steady character and pray with confidence, for he will answer his faithful servants. ❖

PRAYER

O merciful Master, my life depends on you . . .

PRAISING GOD'S FAITHFULNESS

I will sing of the LORD's great love forever;
  with my mouth I will make your faithfulness known through all generations.
I will declare that your love stands firm forever,
  that you have established your faithfulness in heaven itself.

PSALM 89:1–2

Early in David's reign, God promised David that his dynasty and his kingdom would "endure forever" (2 Samuel 7:16). This prayer of Ethan reminds us how God had begun to fulfill his promises to David. This was evidence to Ethan of God's "great love"—a love that would last forever and forever.

Let the words of this psalm lead you in praising God's unfailing love, for Jesus Christ has fulfilled God's promise to David. Jesus Christ—a descendant of David through his earthly father Joseph—was raised from the dead so he could rule at the right hand of God the Father (Mark 14:61–62; Acts 5:29–32). The Lord has mercifully included us in his kingdom. Reflect on Jesus' faithfulness to you. ✤

PRAYER

Dear Lord, thank you for your unfailing love . . .

february1

PRAISE TO MY SUPPORTER

It is God who arms me with strength
and keeps my way secure.
He makes my feet like the feet of a deer;
he causes me to stand on the heights.
He trains my hands for battle;
my arms can bend a bow of bronze.
You make your saving help my shield,
and your right hand sustains me;
your help has made me great.
You provide a broad path for my feet,
so that my ankles do not give way.

PSALM 18:32–36

Having narrowly escaped King Saul's murderous schemes, David could have boasted of his military skill—his talent with the bow and his extensive knowledge of the mountainous terrain. He certainly had bragging rights; he had just escaped King Saul's grasp. But David was a man of God. David praised the Lord God openly because his strength and skill came from the Lord. No earthly shield could have protected him from the arrows of his enemies. Only God could protect him and strengthen him for battle.

Has God strengthened and supported you in the last year? Thank the Lord for his support, and commit all your impossible situations to him. ✣

PRAYER

Dear Lord, your right hand has supported me in these ways . . .

february**2**

MORE THAN WE ASK

Now to him who is able to do immeasurably more than all we ask or imagine, according to his power that is at work within us, to him be glory in the church and in Christ Jesus throughout all generations, for ever and ever! Amen.

EPHESIANS 3:20–21

Paul's prayer of adoration is perhaps best summarized with one word: "more." His praise rises to its feet in a standing ovation for the God he adores. To Paul, God not only is more mighty, he does more. We pray for a morsel, and he gives us a feast. We beg for the strength to get to first base; he answers with a grand slam. God answers our prayers with far more than we can ever dare, ask, or hope for.

Are your prayers characterized by the word, "more"? More praise than just "the usual"? More trust in the infinite and almighty God? Let the glory of God expand your prayer today. ❖

PRAYER

Dear Lord, I praise you because you are able to do more than I would dare to ask . . .

CONFESSING, INSTEAD OF HIDING

> *When I kept silent,*
> *my bones wasted away*
> *through my groaning all day long.*
> *For day and night*
> *your hand was heavy on me;*
> *my strength was sapped*
> *as in the heat of summer.*
> *Then I acknowledged my sin to you*
> *and did not cover up my iniquity.*
> *I said, "I will confess*
> *my transgressions to the LORD."*
> *And you forgave*
> *the guilt of my sin.*
> *Therefore let all the faithful pray to you*
> *while you may be found;*
> *surely the rising of the mighty waters*
> *will not reach them.*

PSALM 32:3–6

We find many ways to get around admitting our sin. We rationalize our sins away. We try to drown out the guilt with all types of distractions that keep us bustling from one activity to another. Over time, our sins deplete our will to even approach God in prayer. David was intimately familiar with all the ways one can try to hide sin. He had exhausted himself covering up his own sins. But everything changed when David finally refused to keep on running away from his sin: "Then I acknowledged my sin to you."

Like David, we can find our prayer life renewed when we freely confess our sins to God. Does your prayer life seem lifeless and ineffective? Examine your heart and confess your sin. And let God restore your prayer life to what it can and should be. ✣

PRAYER

Dear Lord, I don't want to hide my sins anymore; I want to confess them to you today ...

february4

LONGING FOR THE LORD

As the deer pants for streams of water,
so my soul pants for you, my God.
My soul thirsts for God, for the living God.
When can I go and meet with God? ...
Why, my soul, are you downcast?
Why so disturbed within me?
Put your hope in God,
for I will yet praise him,
my Savior and my God.
My soul is downcast within me;
therefore I will remember you
from the land of the Jordan,
the heights of Hermon — from Mount Mizar ...
By day the LORD directs his love,
at night his song is with me —
a prayer to the God of my life.

PSALM 42:1–2, 5–6, 8

When have you felt like God was far away? For the psalmist, being surrounded by his taunting enemies made him feel distant from God. His enemies expressed what the psalmist only dared to think: "Where is your God?" (42:3). Their taunts only made him yearn for God even more. It was as if he were spiritually parched, awaiting a refreshing drink of water. In this prayer, the psalmist freely admitted to God that he was discouraged. But he didn't let his discouragement be the final word. He refused to focus on the sarcasm of his enemies and instead began counting the ways God had poured out his unfailing love on him. In the end, he learned to praise the Lord with songs and prayers for God was the one who was graciously sustaining his life.

Does God feel far away? Express your desires to God. Then, start recounting the ways God has provided for you. ✤

PRAYER

Dear Lord, I thirst for you. Though I am discouraged, I will put my hope in you ...

february5

JEHOSHAPHAT'S PRAYER DURING A CRISIS

Then Jehoshaphat stood up in the assembly of Judah and Jerusalem at the temple of the LORD in the front of the new courtyard and said:

"LORD, the God of our ancestors, are you not the God who is in heaven? You rule over all the kingdoms of the nations. Power and might are in your hand, and no one can withstand you. Our God, did you not drive out the inhabitants of this land before your people Israel and give it forever to the descendants of Abraham your friend? They have lived in it and have built in it a sanctuary for your Name, saying, 'If calamity comes upon us, whether the sword of judgment, or plague or famine, we will stand in your presence before this temple that bears your Name and will cry out to you in our distress, and you will hear us and save us.' . . .

"Our God, will you not judge them? For we have no power to face this vast army that is attacking us. We do not know what to do, but our eyes are on you."

2 CHRONICLES 20:5 – 9, 12

When has it felt like everything was going against you? King Jehoshaphat felt that way when the armies of the Moabites, Ammonites, and their allies surrounded him. He had no place to turn. He was trapped, but he knew God could provide a way to escape. God could be his fortress—one that wouldn't give way under his enemies' assaults. Even though his situation was hopeless, Jehoshaphat started recounting the ways God had delivered his people in the past. Only after reassuring himself of God's faithfulness did Jehoshaphat ask for the Lord's help in his present predicament. Jehoshaphat's trust was well-placed for the next day the Lord answered his prayer. The armies that were assembled before him turned on each other.

When you face impossible situations, take time to remind yourself of the way God has taken care of you and your family in the past. You may be powerless, but through prayer you have access to an all-powerful God. ✤

PRAYER

Dear Lord, I am powerless so I am looking to you to help . . .

february**6**

A COMPLAINT CONCERNING INJUSTICE

Help, LORD, for no one is faithful anymore;
those who are loyal have vanished from the human race.
Everyone lies to their neighbor;
they flatter with their lips
but harbor deception in their hearts.
May the LORD silence all flattering lips
and every boastful tongue—...
You, LORD, will keep the needy safe
and will protect us forever from the wicked,
who freely strut about
when what is vile is honored by the human race.

PSALM 12:1–3, 7–8

Why is it that those who get ahead always seem to be the ones who lie, cheat, and steal? They not only get away with their evil deeds, their actions are admired and paraded around the world. Daydreaming about wicked people getting their just desserts may bring a smile to our faces, but thinking about revenge isn't healthy for the soul. Instead, we should commit the wicked and the evil they do to God in prayer. We can't stop others from speaking lies or taking advantage of us, but we can and should cry out to the Lord who takes care of his own people. God knows the truth about all people, and he hears and responds to the cry of his people. It doesn't ultimately matter what the wicked do, what matters is that God, our guardian, hears our cries. ✤

PRAYER

Dear Lord, I know you will protect me from the wicked ...

PRAISE FOR SAFETY

David sang to the LORD the words of this song when the LORD delivered him from the hand of all his enemies and from the hand of Saul. He said:

"The LORD is my rock, my fortress and my deliverer;
my God is my rock, in whom I take refuge,
my shield and the horn of my salvation.
He is my stronghold, my refuge and my savior —
from violent people you save me.
"I called to the LORD, who is worthy of praise,
and have been saved from my enemies."

2 SAMUEL 22:1–4

There's no greater feeling than getting home safe and sound, especially when doing so was doubtful. Such experiences produce stories that we love to tell to others; but all too often when we tell those stories we forget to give thanks to the Lord for protecting us.

When David was relaxing in complete safety, he remembered to praise the Lord for delivering him from King Saul. He acknowledged that God, not his military prowess or physical strength, saved him. God was the fortress that protected him from Saul's murderous plots.

When the Lord rescues us from desperate situations, the threats of others, or simply our own mistakes, we must remember to stop and praise him. God's strength and protection compel us to joyfully praise him in our prayers. Who else could deliver us from the messes we create? Who else deserves our hearty thanks? The Lord God is the only one who can save us. ❖

PRAYER

O Lord, you are worthy of praise because you saved me from ...

february**8**

A REQUEST FOR PROTECTION

> *Hear my cry, O God;*
> *   listen to my prayer.*
> *From the ends of the earth I call to you,*
> *   I call as my heart grows faint;*
> *   lead me to the rock that is higher than I.*
> *For you have been my refuge,*
> *   a strong tower against the foe.*
> *I long to dwell in your tent forever*
> *   and take refuge in the shelter of your wings.*

PSALM 61:1–4

David, as the commander of Israel's armies, was an expert at analyzing an enemies' defenses and planning his own fortifications. It was under David's leadership that the impenetrable fortress of Zion was captured from the Jebusites. And after he captured it, David oversaw the building of additional fortifications around Zion — the place where he would eventually build his own palace (2 Samuel 5:6–10). Although David had built his home in the well-fortified city of Jerusalem, he didn't place his trust in the fortress he had built. He knew God was his "strong tower against the foe." There was no safer refuge than living in the Lord's sanctuary — in the presence of the Almighty. In the same way, David knew that he couldn't protect the nation of Israel; but God could. So David appealed to the Lord for protection.

Although we might not realize it, we are just as vulnerable as King David was. We need to be led to God's rock of safety. Run to the Almighty in prayer. Ask him to protect you and bring you to a safe place. ✤

PRAYER

O God, lead me to the towering rock of safety, for you are my safe refuge . . .

february9

NEHEMIAH'S PRAYER AGAINST MOCKERS

Hear us, our God, for we are despised. Turn their insults back on their own heads. Give them over as plunder in a land of captivity. Do not cover up their guilt or blot out their sins from your sight, for they have thrown insults in the face of the builders.

NEHEMIAH 4:4–5

Nehemiah had come all the way from Persia to lead his countrymen in the rebuilding of the walls of Jerusalem. When the people of Jerusalem finally got to work rebuilding the walls, they were greeted by a band of hecklers. "What they are building—even a fox climbing up on it would break down their wall of stones," Tobiah jeered (4:3). Nehemiah's response wasn't the natural one. He didn't try to silence the hecklers with a barrage of insults. He didn't get angry or violent. Instead he turned to God in prayer. He asked the Lord to hear their taunts.

Mocking and provocation shouldn't stop us from doing God's work. Rather, they reminds us that God's work is best done through prayer. Physical effort isn't enough to get the job done. Invoking God's blessing and provision in prayer is as important to completing the task at hand as having physical resources. ✤

PRAYER

Dear Lord, hear those who are mocking and deliver your servant today . . .

february**10**

PRAISE FOR GOD'S RESCUE

Then my enemies will turn back
when I call for help.
By this I will know that God is for me.
In God, whose word I praise,
in the LORD, whose word I praise—
in God I trust and am not afraid.
What can man do to me?
I am under vows to you, my God;
I will present my thank offerings to you.
For you have delivered me from death
and my feet from stumbling,
that I may walk before God
in the light of life.

PSALM 56:9–13

Desperate people do desperate things, yet it is God who ultimately delivers them. When David fled to the Philistine city of Gath to escape the hot pursuit of King Saul, he quickly realized that his life was in danger. The Philistines didn't welcome David—an Israelite warrior who had killed at least ten thousand of Israel's enemies. To escape the king of Gath, David acted as if he were insane. The king of Gath allowed David to leave; and David quickly took the opportunity to find a safer hideout in the cave at Adullam (1 Samuel 21:10–15). It was probably in that cave that David had the time to write this prayer, praising God for delivering him from "mere mortals."

If you're facing a difficult situation, be careful to acknowledge your dependence on God. Rely on him for deliverance. When you place you trust in the Almighty, you'll have no reason to fear. ♣

> **PRAYER**

Dear Lord, why should I be afraid when I am trusting you today for ...

CALLING ON GOD'S NAME

> *I called on your name, LORD,*
> *from the depths of the pit.*
> *You heard my plea: "Do not close your ears*
> *to my cry for relief."*
> *You came near when I called you,*
> *and you said, "Do not fear."*
> *You, Lord, took up my case;*
> *you redeemed my life.*

LAMENTATIONS 3:55–58

Every parent takes great care in choosing the right name for his or her baby. A child's name is important, but how much more important is God's name? God's name reveals his character. Calling on God's name means remembering the type of Holy God we're calling upon. Jeremiah faced the anger of those who had rejected God's warnings of judgment. It was at that time that Jeremiah called on the name of the Lord. He asked God to represent him as both his lawyer and his redeemer. In prayer, he asked the Lord to take up his cause and save him from the predicament he found himself in. The Lord didn't ignore his call. The Almighty rushed to his defense and comforted Jeremiah with these simple words: "Do not fear."

What a privilege we have to be able to call upon the same God Jeremiah did! Our God is the one who answers those who call on his name. He calms their fears, defends their cause, and frees them from the prison that is often of their own making. ✤

PRAYER

Dear Lord, plead my case and redeem me from . . .

february12

DAVID'S PLEA FOR GOD TO RESCUE HIM

Save me, O God,
for the waters have come up to my neck.
I sink in the miry depths,
where there is no foothold.
I have come into the deep waters;
the floods engulf me.
I am worn out calling for help;
my throat is parched.
My eyes fail,
looking for my God....
But I pray to you, LORD,
in the time of your favor;
in your great love, O God,
answer me with your sure salvation.

PSALM 69:1−3, 13

David's prayer recorded in this psalm amounts to a simple, "Save me, I'm sinking." It's the cry of a desperate man who can't even think of helping himself. But at least David knew to whom he needed to ask for help. Although he was exhausted from crying to the Lord in prayer, he kept on shouting to his God. He didn't ask anyone else for help—not even his family nor his friends. He sought out the only one who could save him—the Almighty.

When waves of adversity threaten to drown you in despair, pray to God. Remember David's persistence, and keep on asking God for help. ✤

PRAYER

Dear Lord, I am exhausted from crying for help. But I will keep on praying to you anyway ...

REJOICING IN GOD'S PROTECTION

> *But let all who take refuge in you be glad;*
> *let them ever sing for joy.*
> *Spread your protection over them,*
> *that those who love your name may rejoice in you.*
> *Surely, LORD, you bless the righteous;*
> *you surround them with your favor as with a shield.*

PSALM 5:11–12

All of us want security. That's why we put up fences, install electronic detection systems, and lock our doors. We want assurance that no one can harm us.

In this prayer, David rejoiced in God's protection. As king of Israel, David commanded fortresses and armies to protect him, but he knew he couldn't count on those to keep him safe. Only God could surround him with a shield of love when wicked people tried to attack him — not only with armies of men but also with vicious rumors and lies. Even when he was under attack, David had nothing to fear for the Lord was his safe refuge.

Are you concerned about your future security? Commit yourself to God's care. Ask him to surround you with a shield of love. Then, rejoice in the Lord's protection. ✤

PRAYER

Dear Lord, surround me with your shield of love . . .

A PRAYER FOR WHEN GOD FEELS DISTANT

My God, my God, why have you forsaken me?
Why are you so far from saving me,
so far from my cries of anguish?
My God, I cry out by day, but you do not answer,
by night, but I find no rest.
Yet you are enthroned as the Holy One;
you are the one Israel praises.
In you our ancestors put their trust;
they trusted and you delivered them.
To you they cried out and were saved;
in you they trusted and were not put to shame.

PSALM 22:1–5

Trust is a precious commodity in any relationship — slow to build and all-too-easy to undermine. Faced by dark and hopeless circumstances, we can start feeling abandoned by God. We start losing our trust in God. It is comforting to know that we're not the only ones who have felt that way. In desperate times, David too felt abandoned and alone. "My God, my God, why have you forsaken me?" he cried. Jesus repeated these same words on the cross. At the moment he took the sin of world on his own shoulders, he cried out to God, "Why have you forsaken me?" (Mark 15:34). Such a straightforward question implies an intimate and trusting relationship between the petitioner and God in the first place. Even though David felt abandoned by God, he didn't give up waiting on God to answer him. He comforted himself with the marvelous truth that those who call on God are never disappointed.

Do you feel abandoned by God? Do you feel alone? Remind yourself of the way God has worked in your life. God never abandons those who call on him. ✤

PRAYER

O God, I will never be disappointed because I put my trust in you . . .

PAUL'S PRAYER FOR LOVE

Now may our God and Father himself and our Lord Jesus clear the way for us to come to you. May the Lord make your love increase and overflow for each other and for everyone else, just as ours does for you. May he strengthen your hearts so that you will be blameless and holy in the presence of our God and Father when our Lord Jesus comes with all his holy ones.

1 THESSALONIANS 3:11–13

When Paul wrote to the Thessalonians—his love and concern for them were apparent in every word. When he prayed for them, he asked that their love for one another would increase to the point of overflowing. Paul prayed that the Thessalonian church might become a loving, supporting community of faith. The strong, silent, loner Christian didn't fit into Paul's understanding of how God works among his people. Each of us needs each other. God uses other believers to strengthen us and make us holy.

Do you want to be spiritually strong? In this prayer, Paul pointed out the way God builds you up: he uses other believers. As you pray for strength to be faithful to God, you should expect his answer to come through those believers who worship every Sunday with you. Likewise, you should earnestly pray that God might use you to strengthen other believers. ❖

PRAYER

O God, help my love to grow and overflow to other believers ...

february16

THE REQUEST OF ABRAHAM'S SERVANT

Then he prayed, "LORD, God of my master Abraham, make me successful today, and show kindness to my master Abraham. See, I am standing beside this spring, and the daughters of the townspeople are coming out to draw water. May it be that when I say to a young woman, 'Please let down your jar that I may have a drink,' and she says, 'Drink, and I'll water your camels too'—let her be the one you have chosen for your servant Isaac. By this I will know that you have shown kindness to my master."

Before he had finished praying, Rebekah came out with her jar on her shoulder.

GENESIS 24:12–15

When believers face momentous decisions, they long to be aligned with God's will and purposes. Abraham had asked his servant to find the right bride for his son, Isaac. Abraham's servant realized the great weight of responsibility he carried, and he submitted the matter directly to God. He didn't depend primarily on his own wisdom or discernment. Instead he asked God for a sign—one that would set one woman apart from the others. Certainly most women would offer Abraham's servant water; but the one hospitable enough to water his camels for him also would be the one God had chosen to be Isaac's wife. God answered the servant's prayer instantaneously. Before he finished praying, Rebekah arrived and offered to give him water for both himself and his camels. What a remarkable answer to prayer!

God wants to direct our lives in similar ways as well. Do we have the courage to seek out God's direction and ask for his guidance as Abraham's servant did? ✤

PRAYER

Dear Lord, help me to accomplish your purpose . . .

february**17**

PAUL'S INTERCESSION FOR THE EPHESIANS

I pray that out of his glorious riches he may strengthen you with power through his Spirit in your inner being, so that Christ may dwell in your hearts through faith. And I pray that you, being rooted and established in love, may have power, together with all the Lord's holy people, to grasp how wide and long and high and deep is the love of Christ, and to know this love that surpasses knowledge—that you may be filled to the measure of all the fullness of God.

EPHESIANS 3:16–19

To love and to be loved are among the most fulfilling of human experiences. But precisely because so many people want love, many counterfeits are offered. The word *love* has become increasingly cheap, sentimental, and commercialized. The apostle Paul proved, by the way he lived his life, that he truly and unselfishly loved his converts. When he prayed for them, his greatest desire was that they would understand and experience the love of God—the real thing, not artificial substitutes. He understood that the lives of his converts had to be rooted in something that would last—God's eternal love; otherwise, they would spiritually wither away and die.

As we intercede in prayer for those we love most, we can ask nothing better than that they would establish their lives on God's everlasting love. ✣

PRAYER

Lord God, I pray that the ones I love might experience the love of Christ . . .

february18

PRAISE TO THE GOD WHO SATISFIES

I have seen you in the sanctuary
and beheld your power and your glory.
Because your love is better than life,
my lips will glorify you.
I will praise you as long as I live,
and in your name I will lift up my hands.
I will be fully satisfied as with the richest of foods;
with singing lips my mouth will praise you.

PSALM 63:2−5

Many of us put a great deal of time and effort into the pursuit of a rather elusive goal: fulfillment. We seek fulfillment in our work, in our relationships with friends and family, and in how much we possess. But our search for fulfillment in these areas turns up empty. We are consistently disappointed. David, however, described in his prayer to God a different type of search that leads to ultimate fulfillment. Having "beheld" God's power and glory, he had found a purpose and meaning for his life. God's love was better than life itself! That's why David stayed up at night meditating on God and honoring and praising him.

May our prayers reflect our excitement to come into the Lord's presence and experience his satisfying love. ✤

PRAYER

O God, your unfailing love is better to me than life itself . . .

A PRAYER TO OVERFLOW WITH LOVE

And this is my prayer: that your love may abound more and more in knowledge and depth of insight, so that you may be able to discern what is best and may be pure and blameless for the day of Christ, filled with the fruit of righteousness that comes through Jesus Christ — to the glory and praise of God.

PHILIPPIANS 1:9–11

The trademark of the Christian is love. Like fruit on a tree, it is produced by the life of God coursing within us. Jesus said as much when he said, "By this everyone will know that you are my disciples, if you love one another" (John 13:35). The apostle Paul prayed fervently for the new believers in Philippi, and he communicated the content of those prayers in his letter to them. In this way, they would know what his holy aspirations for their lives were. He wanted them to *abound* with love for each other — not with the gooey, sentimental sort of love, but with a real, God-inspired love, a pure love that was increasingly informed by an understanding of spiritual matters. Paul knew that their loving actions towards each other would be the best testimony of Christ's work within them.

Reflect for a few moments on how your life would look today if you were overflowing with God's love. ✤

PRAYER

Dear Lord, may my love for others overflow more and more . . .

CALLING ON GOD

> *As for me, I call to God,*
> *and the LORD saves me.*
> *Evening, morning and noon*
> *I cry out in distress,*
> *and he hears my voice.*
> *He rescues me unharmed*
> *from the battle waged against me,*
> *even though many oppose me.*
> *God, who is enthroned from of old,*
> *who does not change —*
> *he will hear them and humble them,*
> *because they have no fear of God.*

PSALM 55:16–19

"Help!" Should you hear such a cry, wherever you are, you know that immediate and decisive action is required. The person in distress must be at the end of his resources, completely lost without the intervention of another. Believers know that, whatever difficulty we encounter, the one to whom we must cry is God himself. He always hears. He is the one powerful enough to save. This was David's experience with God. So in trying circumstances, David reminded himself that the Lord "hears my voice" and that the Lord will rescue him. He was not timid with God: he admitted to God that he felt "distress" and cried out to God "evening, morning and noon."

The more desperate your situation, the more it makes sense to express your anguish to God, even aloud. Like David, you will find him responsive to your plea. ✤

PRAYER

I will call on you, God, in my distress ...

DELIGHT IN GOD'S PRESENCE

Oh, that you would rend the heavens and come down,
that the mountains would tremble before you!
As when fire sets twigs ablaze
and causes water to boil,
come down to make your name known to your enemies
and cause the nations to quake before you!
For when you did awesome things that we did not expect,
you came down, and the mountains trembled before you.
Since ancient times no one has heard,
no ear has perceived,
no eye has seen any God besides you,
who acts on behalf of those who wait for him.
You come to the help of those who gladly do right,
who remember your ways.

ISAIAH 64:1–5

Have you ever wished that God would reveal himself in frightening majesty? Apparently Isaiah, in his lonely and often unpopular role as prophet, sometimes longed for such a revelation to reinforce his message to the Israelites that they should renew their love toward God. As Isaiah reflected on what it would be like for God to burst forth from the heavens, he renewed his commitment to serve the Almighty no matter what the cost. He recalled how God had intervened on behalf of faithful believers in the past; and he affirmed that God certainly "acts on behalf of those who wait for him."

Take time today to calm your soul before the Lord. Commit your worries and problems to him, and wait on him to answer. ✤

PRAYER

Holy God, you work on behalf of those who wait for you ...

A PLEA FOR SAFETY

In you, LORD, I have taken refuge;
let me never be put to shame.
In your righteousness, rescue me and deliver me;
turn your ear to me and save me.
Be my rock of refuge,
to which I can always go;
give the command to save me,
for you are my rock and my fortress.

PSALM 71:1–3

Life if full of uncertainty, turmoil, and danger. Sometimes, these trials are more psychological or spiritual in nature than physical, but the threat is real nonetheless. Where can we turn to find a safe haven? The psalmist knew that God was his refuge. In fact, the Lord had been his only source of hope ever since he was a child. He knew that God was a just and compassionate God. The Lord wanted to protect his people. If God would only give the order, the psalmist knew he would be saved; so it was only natural for him to ask for help.

Consider what sorts of "enemies" confront you today. With the psalmist, turn to your rock and fortress. The Lord is always willing to save. ✤

PRAYER

O Lord, you are my rock of refuge. Rescue me from ...

A PRAYER TO WALK WITH GOD

> Yet I am always with you;
>> you hold me by my right hand.
> You guide me with your counsel,
>> and afterward you will take me into glory.
> Whom have I in heaven but you?
>> And earth has nothing I desire besides you.
> My flesh and my heart may fail,
>> but God is the strength of my heart
>> and my portion forever....
> But as for me, it is good to be near God.
>> I have made the Sovereign LORD my refuge;
>> I will tell of all your deeds.

PSALM 73:23–26, 28

Sometimes people are so "in love" that they would readily proclaim they need nothing else as long as they have one another. How much more do those in an intimate relationship with God have everything they need? In this prayer, Asaph considered the blessings that were his because he walked with God. God was guiding him and leading him to a glorious destiny. Asaph was so sure of the Lord's guidance that he felt as if the Lord was holding his right hand. To Asaph, the Lord was like a prized possession — more to be desired than anything or anyone on earth, outlasting even the breath of life itself.

Take a few moments in God's presence to reflect on the priceless gift of your relationship with him. Tell him how and why you love him. Ask him to keep you always close by his side. ❖

PRAYER

O God, I desire you more than anything on earth ...

BOASTING IN THE LORD

> *I will extol the LORD at all times;*
> > *his praise will always be on my lips.*
> *I will glory in the LORD;*
> > *let the afflicted hear and rejoice.*
> *Glorify the LORD with me;*
> > *let us exalt his name together.*
> *I sought the LORD, and he answered me;*
> > *he delivered me from all my fears.*
> *Those who look to him are radiant;*
> > *their faces are never covered with shame.*

PSALM 34:1–5

Sometimes people who are the most fearful come across with the most bravado. Their boasts mask a dark reality of discouragement and foreboding about the future. But there's another type of boasting grounded in reality: boasting in the Lord. In God, there's plenty to boast about. The Almighty has the power to save us; and he wants to save those who put their trust in him. In this prayer, David was rejoicing and boasting in God because he had narrowly escaped from his enemy. King Saul had wanted to murder him, so David had fled the country. David had nowhere to go, so he went to Israel's enemies, the Philistines. Instead of seeing David as a valuable defector, the Philistines wanted to kill David because he was a skilled Israelite warrior. Shrewdly, David feigned insanity and was set free. But in this prayer, David gave all the credit to God. He viewed his deliverance as an answer to prayer.

From what near-disaster has God delivered you recently? With David, direct your thanks and praise to God. ✤

PRAYER

I prayed to you, Lord; and you answered me . . .

A PETITION FOR MERCY

> Do not hold against us the sins of past generations;
> > may your mercy come quickly to meet us,
> > for we are in desperate need.
> Help us, God our Savior,
> > for the glory of your name;
> deliver us and forgive our sins
> > for your name's sake....
> Then we your people, the sheep of your pasture,
> > will praise you forever;
> from generation to generation
> > we will proclaim your praise.

PSALM 79:8–9, 13

A plea to God for mercy presumes that the petitioner is guilty. It is the cry of someone brought low, dishonored and in need of forgiveness. When God shows a sinner mercy, he isn't forgiving that person because of who that person is or what she has done. No, the Lord forgives because he is kind and compassionate to those who repent of their sins and ask for forgiveness. It is only because of God's goodness that sinners are forgiven. That is why only God's name should be honored when the Lord shows mercy to sinners. Asaph, the writer of this psalm, understood that it wasn't his worthiness but the Lord's greatness that prompted the Lord to rescue him. In light of this truth, Asaph dedicated this prayer to praising God for being so merciful.

Are you in need of God's mercy? His love and goodness are the source of your hope. Cast yourself on his mercy and let your lips overflow with grateful praise. ✤

PRAYER

O Lord, do not hold me guilty for my sins ...

february26

HEALING THROUGH CONFESSION

Have you rejected Judah completely?
Do you despise Zion?
Why have you afflicted us
so that we cannot be healed?
We hoped for peace
but no good has come,
for a time of healing
but there is only terror.
We acknowledge our wickedness, LORD,
and the guilt of our ancestors;
we have indeed sinned against you.
For the sake of your name do not despise us;
do not dishonor your glorious throne.
Remember your covenant with us
and do not break it.

JEREMIAH 14:19–21

When Jeremiah prayed for the spiritual healing of the nation of Judah, he confessed the sins of his people first. Sin—either our own or the sins of others—is the cause of all our pain and suffering. Often when Jesus healed a physical illness or infirmity, he addressed the sick person's sin first. When friends lowered a paralyzed man into a crowd before Jesus, he said: "Friend, your sins are forgiven" (Luke 5:20). Jeremiah understood that sin was the root cause of evil, so he confessed the sins of his people with an attitude of utter helplessness and dependence on God, his Savior. No other false god, no force of nature, only God himself was his hope, so Jeremiah was determined to wait on the Lord to act.

If you find yourself in need of forgiveness or healing, follow Jeremiah's lead and cast yourself on the Lord. Wait on him. ✤

PRAYER

For the sake of your own name, Lord, do not abandon me . . .

february27

PRAISE FOR GOD'S KNOWLEDGE OF US

You hem me in behind and before,
and you lay your hand upon me.
Such knowledge is too wonderful for me,
too lofty for me to attain....
If I say, "Surely the darkness will hide me
and the light become night around me,"
even the darkness will not be dark to you;
the night will shine like the day,
for darkness is as light to you.

PSALM 139:5 – 6, 11 – 12

God is everywhere. He see all things and knows all things. His presence can be either a source of comfort or a source of dread. Since we have all sinned, we may try to hide from God. Just as Adam and Eve hid after they had eaten the forbidden fruit, we often hide our sins before our holy and all-seeing Creator (Genesis 3:10). Yet at the same time, it can be comforting to know that the darkness — symbolic of danger and hopelessness — is "as light" to God. No sin, neither our own nor others, can cut us off irrevocably from the God who loved us and gave his own Son's life for us. Through Christ's resurrection, darkness was forever shattered. Such knowledge is too wonderful for us.

As you approach God today, take courage. Remind yourself of God's intimate knowledge of you and his commitment to guide you through the darkness into his eternal light. ✤

PRAYER

Dear Lord, even in darkness I cannot hide from you ...

february**28**

PRAISE TO MY SAVIOR

Teach me your way, LORD,
that I may rely on your faithfulness;
give me an undivided heart,
that I may fear your name.
I will praise you, Lord my God, with all my heart;
I will glorify your name forever.
For great is your love toward me;
you have delivered me from the depths,
from the realm of the dead.

PSALM 86:11–13

As we grasp the enormity of what God has done for us, we look for ways to declare our love for God. David proclaimed, "You have delivered me from the depths, from the realm of the dead." Because the Lord had saved David from death, David expressed his deep love for God and his exuberant gratitude. David was uninhibited in expressing praise and adoration: "With all my heart I will praise you." As he approached God in prayer, David realized how much his life didn't measure up to God's standards. He felt unworthy, but he still wanted to honor God with his life, so he prayed that God may grant him a pure heart. He wanted to remain in unbroken fellowship with God, so he asked God to teach him *his* ways.

When we pray, we need to remind ourselves of what a privilege it is to approach the Lord. We were in the depths of sin, but the Lord has elevated us so that we can stand in his presence. Ask the Lord today to teach you how you should live according to his ways. ✤

PRAYER

O Lord, teach me your ways ...

FILLED WITH AWE

A prayer of Habakkuk the prophet. On shigionoth.

> LORD, I have heard of your fame;
>   I stand in awe of your deeds, LORD.
> Repeat them in our day,
>   in our time make them known;
>   in wrath remember mercy.

HABAKKUK 3:1 – 2

Habakkuk was a prophet of God in a time when God's people were suffering disgrace and evil seemed to be winning the day. But Habakkuk didn't let the prominent events of his day discourage him. He reminded himself who God was and encouraged himself with memories of the "amazing things" God had accomplished in the past. He acknowledged that God's anger towards his people was justified. He knew, however, that God could save his generation as well as any other, for the Lord was merciful. So he laced his pleas for mercy and salvation with expressions of awe and praise.

In your time of need, let your prayers begin and end with praise for the God who is worthy of all glory and honor. ❖

PRAYER

O God, I am filled with awe by the amazing things you have done . . .

march**2**

A PLEA FOR COMPASSION

> LORD, *do not rebuke me in your anger*
> *or discipline me in your wrath.*
> *Have mercy on me, LORD, for I am faint;*
> *heal me, LORD, for my bones are in agony.*
> *My soul is in deep anguish.*
> *How long, LORD, how long?*
> *Turn, LORD, and deliver me;*
> *save me because of your unfailing love.*

PSALM 6:1–4

Like children, we sometimes get ourselves into situations from which we cannot extricate ourselves. We know that our plight is the result of sin, folly, or bad judgment. Anger certainly is a justifiable reaction on the part of our heavenly Father. In this psalm, David found himself in such a situation. He knew that God was the only one to whom he could appeal for compassion, so he prayed to God with unabashed candor. After all, God is both just and loving. He certainly disciplines; but he also forgives.

When you find yourself in a predicament, perhaps of your own making, don't hesitate to follow David's example and pour your heart out before God. ❖

PRAYER

Dear Lord, have compassion on me for I am weak ...

PRAISE FOR GOD'S DISCIPLINE

Blessed is the one you discipline, LORD,
the one you teach from your law;
you grant them relief from days of trouble,
till a pit is dug for the wicked.
For the LORD will not reject his people;
he will never forsake his inheritance.
Judgment will again be founded on righteousness,
and all the upright in heart will follow it.

PSALM 94:12–15

Does it ever seem as if those who try to live by God's laws are getting nowhere, while people with no thought of God seem to prosper? If so, you're not alone. The psalmist is one of many people in the Bible who pondered this problem in his prayers to the Lord. Yet, the psalmist walked with God long enough that he knew God's ways were just. The Lord had taught him, corrected him, and disciplined him so that the Lord's ways had become second nature to the psalmist. If we have that type of dynamic relationship with the Holy One, we are the ones who will ultimately prosper. The time will come when those who have ignored God's justice will face the tragic consequences of their evil actions.

Next time you become discouraged, join the psalmist in taking the long view. Remind yourself of the eternal benefits of following God. ✤

PRAYER

Happy are those whom you discipline, O Lord . . .

march4

MICAH'S PRAISE FOR GOD'S COMPASSION

Shepherd your people with your staff,
*   the flock of your inheritance,*
which lives by itself in a forest,
*   in fertile pasturelands.*
Let them feed in Bashan and Gilead
*   as in days long ago. . . .*
Who is a God like you,
*   who pardons sin and forgives the transgression*
*   of the remnant of his inheritance?*
You do not stay angry forever
*   but delight to show mercy.*
You will again have compassion on us;
*   you will tread our sins underfoot*
*   and hurl all our iniquities into the depths of the sea.*

MICAH 7:14, 18–19

In the course of his calling as a prophet to Judah, Micah often spoke *with* God as well as *for* God. He had a clear understanding of God's hatred of sin. This understanding enabled him to warn the people in no uncertain terms of God's coming judgment. But he also was intimately acquainted with God's compassionate nature. Though God might be justified in wiping out an entire nation, he consistently pardoned sinners who repented of their ways. Because he delighted in showing mercy, he could not remain angry forever. In a beautiful word picture, Micah described God throwing the sins of his people into the depths of the ocean. He prayed that God would show that type of mercy on his people soon and that he would grant his people peaceful prosperity.

Today, we can approach the same merciful God. He wants to forgive those who turn away from their sins. ✤

PRAYER

O God, who delights in showing mercy, restore me . . .

AN OPEN HEART BEFORE GOD

Search me, God, and know my heart;
test me and know my anxious thoughts.
See if there is any offensive way in me,
and lead me in the way everlasting.

PSALM 139:23–24

In Psalm 139, David celebrated God's intimate knowledge of him—for "your eyes saw my unformed body; all the days ordained for me were written in your book before one of them came to be" (139:16). David prayerfully realized that God knew everything he did and thought. His response was to ask God to purify him. He knew that his own perception of sin was limited. There might be something in his life that offended the Almighty, something he wasn't aware of. So David prayed, "See if there is any offensive way in me."

In the inescapable searchlight of God's knowledge, we too should confess our sins. After that we become dependent on him to show us other sins for one reason or another we can't see. Quiet your heart before the Lord today, and ask God to search your heart and point out anything that offends him. ✤

PRAYER

Holy Lord, point out anything in me that offends you ...

march**6**

A DESPERATE CONFESSION

Although our sins testify against us,
do something, LORD, for the sake of your name.
For we have often rebelled;
we have sinned against you.

JEREMIAH 14:7

When God brought a drought upon the people of Judah, they realized the extent of their sin. When their lives were threatened by a lack of water, they finally appealed to God. In essence, they had been "caught" in their sin. It was only when they could no longer escape the reality of their sin by simply denying it that they approached God in prayer. They prayed that the Lord might save them because of his own reputation. Surely, they thought, God would not want the world to see his people wiped out. Though God is indeed compassionate, we must not take him for granted nor make repentance a casual matter as the Judeans were doing.

Sometimes we, too, are so shaken by disastrous circumstances that we admit, belatedly, that "our sins testify against us." Let us not offer God half-hearted repentance. Pray that genuine sorrow may take root in your life so that God can work lasting change in your life. ✤

PRAYER

Dear Lord, my wickedness has caught up with me ...

ENTERING THE LORD'S PRESENCE

LORD, who may dwell in your sacred tent?
Who may live on your holy mountain?
The one whose walk is blameless,
who does what is righteous,
who speaks the truth from their heart;
whose tongue utters no slander,
who does no wrong to a neighbor,
and casts no slur on others;
who despises a vile person
but honors those who fear the LORD;
who keeps an oath even when it hurts,
and does not change their mind;
who lends money to the poor without interest;
who does not accept a bribe against the innocent.
Whoever does these things
will never be shaken.

PSALM 15:1–5

The people of Israel had a very tangible way to enter God's presence. Periodically, they "went up" to the Temple in Jerusalem for feasts. During these feasts, they celebrated God's saving acts on their behalf. In this prayer, David meditated on what characteristics he needed to enter God's presence without excessive fear. He had to be "blameless"—truthful, kind, generous, and loving.

Many church services include a time of confession in their worship services so that worshipers can prepare their hearts properly. As you enter God's presence for your own time of worship and prayer, be sure you have asked the Lord to cleanse your life. ✤

PRAYER

Dear Lord, I want to enter your presence on your holy hill ...

A PRAYER FOR STRENGTH

Return to us, God Almighty!
    Look down from heaven and see!
Watch over this vine,
        the root your right hand has planted,
        the son you have raised up for yourself....
Let your hand rest on the man at your right hand,
        the son of man you have raised up for yourself.
Then we will not turn away from you;
        revive us, and we will call on your name.
Restore us, LORD God Almighty;
        make your face shine on us,
        that we may be saved.

PSALM 80:14–15, 17–19

When we are exhausted—at the very end of our own strength—there is only one place to turn. God is our only hope for strength. Asaph, the psalmist, stated this truth in his prayer to God: "Make your face shine on us, that we may be saved." Why should God be willing to revive us again and again? God created us to be in relationship with him. He wants us to call on his name. We're his vine; and as such we're completely dependent on the one who has planted us—God himself. We can't grow unless he provides moist soil, pure water, and sunshine. Leaving or forsaking our Provider is ultimately suicidal. That's why, after being revived by the sunshine of God's love, Asaph proclaimed: "We will not turn away from you."

Dedicate some time today for praising and thanking God for his love for you. Thank him for reviving and strengthening you. ❖

PRAYER

O Lord God Almighty, make your face shine down upon us ...

march9

HEZEKIAH'S PRAYER FOR PURIFICATION

Although most of the many people who came from Ephraim, Manasseh, Issachar and Zebulun had not purified themselves, yet they ate the Passover, contrary to what was written. But Hezekiah prayed for them, saying, "May the LORD, who is good, pardon everyone who sets their heart on seeking God—the LORD, the God of their ancestors—even if they are not clean according to the rules of the sanctuary." And the LORD heard Hezekiah and healed the people.

2 CHRONICLES 30:18–20

King Hezekiah's prayer illustrates the timeless truth that ultimately we are made pure by God himself, not by our own works. The nations of Israel and Judah had been separate for many years, and many of their kings had been evil. But Hezekiah boldly defied the wicked traditions of Israel and invited everyone from Israel and Judah to renew their faithful observance of the Passover at the Temple in Jerusalem. Most of the Israelites spurned the invitation, but some from Israel "humbled themselves and went to Jerusalem" (30:11). Hezekiah's prayer for these impure Israelites was in keeping with God's nature. Hezekiah looked in the Israelites' hearts, not at their outward observance of the law, something their culture had long forgotten.

Although we must never take God's good will for granted, we can be assured that his primary concern is with the condition of our hearts. If we approach him humbly, knowing that we are incapable of justifying ourselves, he will purify us. ✤

PRAYER

May the Lord, who is good, pardon us who decide to follow the Lord . . .

march**10**

PRAISE FOR GOD'S MERCY

> *Praise be to the LORD,*
> *for he has heard my cry for mercy.*
> *The LORD is my strength and my shield;*
> *my heart trusts in him, and he helps me.*
> *My heart leaps for joy,*
> *and with my song I praise him.*

PSALM 28:6–7

God is merciful! How many times, like David, have we felt that our backs were up against the wall, our situation hopeless, unless God would see fit to intervene? David had such experiences with the Lord many times, so he expressed his gratitude with this type of prayer of praise again and again: God had heard his cry! The Lord had shielded him from every danger! "My heart trusts in him," David joyfully concluded.

When we ask for God's mercy, we must never neglect to sing his praise, for he is our only hope, our strength, and our shield. Even as we wait for a solution to our current dilemma, we can praise him for his faithfulness to us in the past. This will encourage our faith and nurture our trust in the God of Mercy. ✤

PRAYER

I praise you, Lord, for you have heard my cry for mercy . . .

THE TAX COLLECTOR'S HUMBLE PRAYER

The Pharisee stood by himself and prayed: "God, I thank you that I am not like other people—robbers, evildoers, adulterers—or even like this tax collector. I fast twice a week and give a tenth of all I get."

But the tax collector stood at a distance. He would not even look up to heaven, but beat his breast and said, "God, have mercy on me, a sinner."

LUKE 18:11–13

The prayer of the Pharisee and the prayer of the tax collector stand in sharp contrast to one another. The first one illustrates the way we often tend to pray. The Pharisee barely acknowledged God at all. He used his time in the Temple as an opportunity to justify himself. In the guise of thanking God, he cut down others and congratulated himself. There was no humility in him. The tax collector, on the other hand, was rightfully aware that he was in the presence of the most holy God. By his body language and heartfelt actions, he acknowledged the Holy One. He made no claims for himself. He didn't try to justify his action. He only admitted he was a sinner. Jesus declared that it was the tax collector, not the Pharisee, whom God was willing to justify.

May God give us the courage to admit our true condition before him. If we would only take time to meditate on God's holiness, we would give up the hopeless task of justifying ourselves. Rather in humility, we would cast ourselves on the Lord's mercy. ✤

PRAYER

O God, be merciful to me, for I am a sinner...

A PRAYER FROM THE DISCOURAGED

I am laid low in the dust;
    preserve my life according to your word.
I gave an account of my ways and you answered me;
    teach me your decrees.
Cause me to understand the way of your precepts,
    that I may meditate on your wonderful deeds.
My soul is weary with sorrow;
    strengthen me according to your word.
Keep me from deceitful ways;
    be gracious to me and teach me your law.

PSALM 119:25–29

When you're completely discouraged, where should you turn? The psalmist found the antidote in God's laws and commandments. They revived him, even though circumstances had left him laying in the dust. That made him want to know more about God and truly *understand* God's ways. When he was in the depths of despair, he forced himself to meditate on God's amazing miracles. He reminded himself that it was a privilege to know God and his laws. After all, God's law kept him from lying to himself. It liberated him from the quicksand of self-deceit and placed him firmly on the solid ground of God's law.

In the secular and self-absorbed climate of our times, despair is common. Yet few seek the solution in God's truth, justice, and mighty works. However, God's strength is still available today. Even in your deepest discouragement, ask God to help you to see things his way. ✤

PRAYER

Lord, I weep with grief. Encourage me by your word . . .

march**13**

STEPHEN'S PRAYER FOR FORGIVENESS

While they were stoning him, Stephen prayed, "Lord Jesus, receive my spirit." Then he fell on his knees and cried out, "Lord, do not hold this sin against them." When he had said this, he fell asleep.

ACTS 7:59–60

Stephen, a deacon of the early church, courageously proclaimed to the Jews the true identity of Jesus and the purpose of his death and resurrection. For his forceful and persuasive proclamation of the Good News, the Jews stoned him to death. As he was being pelted with stones, Stephen started praying. First, he committed himself to the Lord. He was completely at peace that he was going to die and that God had promised to receive him into the Lord's kingdom. Even more surprisingly, Stephen's last words before he died were a spoken prayer for his killers. He responded to their bloodthirsty wrath, by asking God to forgive them.

Many times in life we will experience mistreatment at the hands of others. Sometimes we will even have the privilege of being persecuted because we have taken a stand for the Lord. May God so infuse us with his love and mercy that we, like Stephen, may pray for those who persecute us. ✤

PRAYER

Dear Lord, don't charge ... with this sin, but have mercy ...

ASKING GOD TO FORGET OUR SINS

You come to the help of those who gladly do right,
who remember your ways.
But when we continued to sin against them,
you were angry.
How then can we be saved?
All of us have become like one who is unclean,
and all our righteous acts are like filthy rags;
we all shrivel up like a leaf,
and like the wind our sins sweep us away.
No one calls on your name
or strives to lay hold of you;
for you have hidden your face from us
and have given us over to our sins.
Yet you, LORD, are our Father.
We are the clay, you are the potter;
we are all the work of your hand.

ISAIAH 64:5 – 8

There are times when incidents in the world, within our churches, or within our families overwhelm us with the harsh reality of our sin. Isaiah found himself and the people of God in such a place. In no uncertain terms, he proclaimed, "we continued to sin." In the bright light of God's purity, all of the Israelites' "righteous deeds" were no better than filthy rags. Their sin had so weakened them that they were like autumn leaves, which are swept away by the winter winds. Even so, the Israelites were so stubborn that they refused to call upon God. Isaiah announced that the Lord would be justified in turning away from the Israelites. Yet, the prophet was bold enough to remind God that they were his creation, his chosen people. He pleaded with God not to destroy them.

Like Isaiah, we need to realize how thoroughly saturated we are by sin. But lest we start despairing, we need to remind ourselves that God can remake us into something new and holy. Like a potter, he can start over with the lump of clay. ❖

PRAYER

Dear Lord, you are the potter, and I am the clay . . .

A CRY TO HURRY

> Hasten, O God, to save me;
> come quickly, LORD, to help me....
> But may all who seek you
> rejoice and be glad in you;
> may those who long for your saving help always say,
> "The LORD is great!"
> But as for me, I am poor and needy;
> come quickly to me, O God.
> You are my help and my deliverer;
> LORD, do not delay.

PSALM 70:1, 4–5

Sometimes we're so desperately in need of God's help that we feel we cannot last much longer. Have you ever, like David, asked God to hurry? In this prayer, David asked God to defend him against his enemies. He asked that he might be given the opportunity once again to praise the Lord for his deliverance. Then his desperation becomes entirely clear when he prayed, "But as for me, I am poor and needy; come quickly to me, O God."

There will be times that you begin praying by asking for help. You might start by reminding yourself of God's faithfulness to you. And then, you'll panic! Even at those times, remember that you aren't alone. Faithful people of God have felt that kind of desperation in the past. God won't turn a deaf ear to you. He will hurry to your rescue. ✤

PRAYER

Dear Lord, you are my helper and my savior. O Lord, do not delay ...

SOLOMON'S PRAYER THAT GOD MAY FORGIVE

When they sin against you—for there is no one who does not sin—and you become angry with them and give them over to the enemy, who takes them captive to a land far away or near; and if they have a change of heart in the land where they are held captive, and repent and plead with you in the land of their captivity and say, "We have sinned, we have done wrong and acted wickedly"; and if they turn back to you with all their heart and soul in the land of their captivity where they were taken, and pray toward the land you gave their ancestors, toward the city you have chosen and toward the temple I have built for your Name; then from heaven, your dwelling place, hear their prayer and their pleas, and uphold their cause. And forgive your people, who have sinned against you.

2 CHRONICLES 6:36–39

King Solomon had been given the great honor of constructing the Temple for the worship of the Almighty. His prayer to God at the dedication of the Temple showed his wisdom and farsightedness. He foresaw the day when God would have to discipline his people because of their persistent sin. He also realized that the suffering of being captives in a foreign land might bring them to their senses. In that case, he asked God to hear their prayers and forgive them. For Solomon, it was not a matter of *if* God's people would anger the Lord—only *when*.

If we are honest with ourselves, we will realize that, despite our best intentions, we will disobey our Lord. We will inevitably stand in need of his discipline and correction. We shouldn't pray that God would withhold his correction. Instead we should pray, as Solomon did, that we may repent and turn back to God and that God may forgive. ✤

PRAYER

Dear Lord, if I sin against you—and who has never sinned?—please forgive . . .

PRAISE FOR THE GOD WHO HEARS

> *Come and hear, all you who fear God;*
>   *let me tell you what he has done for me.*
> *I cried out to him with my mouth;*
>   *his praise was on my tongue.*
> *If I had cherished sin in my heart,*
>   *the Lord would not have listened;*
> *but God has surely listened*
>   *and has heard my prayer.*
> *Praise be to God,*
>   *who has not rejected my prayer*
>   *or withheld his love from me!*

PSALM 66:16–20

Our prayers of petition are the ones that come most readily. We are all very much aware of our own needs. Like the psalmist, we often ask God for help. The prayer in Psalm 66, however, is a good model for us. First of all, the psalmist remembered to praise God for who he is. Of course, God is always worthy: our praise doesn't change who God is. But we need to remind ourselves of who the Lord is, how holy and powerful he is. Next, and more importantly, the psalmist confessed his sin. He went so far as to say that if he had not confessed his sin, God would *not* have responded to his prayer!

Confession should be the prelude to any request we want to make to God. It aligns our hearts with God's truth. It reminds us of our own unworthiness and the Lord's holiness. Before you make any requests of God today, take time to humbly confess your sins. Then, await God's answer, for he certainly hears you. ✤

PRAYER

Praise God, who did not ignore my prayer . . .

march18

PRAISING THE ONE WHO SATISFIES

Let them give thanks to the LORD for his unfailing love
and his wonderful deeds for mankind,
for he satisfies the thirsty
and fills the hungry with good things.

PSALM 107:8–9

Those who returned from their excruciating exile in Babylon spoke of God's "unfailing love" from experience. These words were originally recited at one of Israel's religious festivals by those who knew what it was like to thirst. This prayer praising God for his satisfaction of the soul was written for a people who truly knew what it was like to hunger. When do our prayers reflect a real hunger and thirst for God? Isn't it when we are going through difficult trials or are yearning for God's deliverance?

Many of us can relate to the feelings of these exiles. Our lives are often filled with great need—whether physical, spiritual, emotional, or financial. Whatever needs you have now, express it to him. When talking with God, ask for the deep satisfaction that he alone can bring to each of your longings. ✤

PRAYER

Dear Lord, I depend on you for my needs . . .

HEZEKIAH'S PRAYER FOR HEALTH

Hezekiah turned his face to the wall and prayed to the LORD, "Remember, LORD, how I have walked before you faithfully and with wholehearted devotion and have done what is good in your eyes." And Hezekiah wept bitterly.

Before Isaiah had left the middle court, the word of the LORD came to him: "Go back and tell Hezekiah, the ruler of my people, 'This is what the LORD, the God of your father David, says: I have heard your prayer and seen your tears; I will heal you. On the third day from now you will go up to the temple of the LORD.'"

2 KINGS 20:2–5

Hezekiah was on his deathbed. But he knew of God's power over disease and his compassion. That is why Hezekiah reminded God of his faithful love to his people and prayed that the Lord might heal him. When God answered Hezekiah's prayer, he did so in a dramatic way. Within three days, the king was able to go to the Temple.

God doesn't always respond to our prayers for healing in such a dramatic fashion. However, it's important to believe that he *can* and, furthermore, that he sometimes *will* act dramatically and suddenly. In sickness and in health, God's wisdom is far beyond our own. Though we may never understand "why" in this life, we should still meditate on God's attributes—his love, faithfulness, power, and justice. Then when our circumstances don't seem to make sense, we will be inclined to trust him—whatever his answer to our earnest pleas. ✤

PRAYER

Remember, O Lord, how I have always tried to be faithful to you . . .

march**20**

SORROW FOR SIN

> LORD, *do not rebuke me in your anger*
>   *or discipline me in your wrath.*
> *Your arrows have pierced me,*
>   *and your hand has come down on me.*
> *Because of your wrath there is no health in my body;*
>   *there is no soundness in my bones because of my sin.*
> *My guilt has overwhelmed me*
>   *like a burden too heavy to bear....*
> *I confess my iniquity;*
>   *I am troubled by my sin.*

PSALM 38:1−4, 18

Sometimes the gravity of our sin can overwhelm us. The physical and mental suffering can feel like God's heavy hand of judgment. This was David's situation as he prayed the words of Psalm 38. He stated his plea for mercy in dramatic terms. He spoke of God's anger and rage, of the Lord's arrows striking deep, and God's blows crushing him. Whether or not it was God's direct action, David realized that his own guilt was the cause of his suffering; and he knew where to turn for mercy and relief. He confessed his sin before God and expected to receive forgiveness.

Sometimes, when we are suffering, we are tempted to become bitter and let that experience turn us away from God. Let us learn to emulate David, who turned immediately to God, whether he was elated or devastated. Confession, acknowledgment of our own guilt, is the way to stop the spiral of sin that sends us reeling away from God. ❖

PRAYER

Lord, I confess my sins; I am deeply sorry for what I have done ...

PRAISE FOR THE GOD WHO IS NEAR

> *The LORD is near to all who call on him,*
>> *to all who call on him in truth.*
> *He fulfills the desires of those who fear him;*
>> *he hears their cry and saves them.*
> *The LORD watches over all who love him,*
>> *but all the wicked he will destroy.*
> *My mouth will speak in praise of the LORD.*
>> *Let every creature praise his holy name*
>> *for ever and ever.*

PSALM 145:18–21

Does God ever seem far away? In this prayer, David reminded himself that God is *close* to all who call on him sincerely. He went on to praise the Lord for consistently answering the prayers of his people and fulfilling the desires of those who fear God.

Sometimes, like David, we may need to remind ourselves of God's great kindness, of his history of fulfilling the desires of those who fear him. If we allow our minds to dwell on the fact that God hears the cries of his people and rescues them, we will be more likely to call upon God in faith. Though we may have our doubts about it sometimes, it is indeed true that God is in the business of protecting all those who love him.

Let us call upon God today and remind ourselves that he is certainly near to those who call out his name. ✣

PRAYER

O Lord, you are close to all who call on you . . .

march**22**

SEARCHING AFTER GOD

The path of the righteous is level;
*   you, the Upright One, make the way of the righteous smooth.*
Yes, LORD, walking in the way of your laws,
*   we wait for you;*
your name and renown
*   are the desire of our hearts.*
My soul yearns for you in the night;
*   in the morning my spirit longs for you.*
When your judgments come upon the earth,
*   the people of the world learn righteousness.*

ISAIAH 26:7–9

In every situation, the Lord God is the one we need. Isaiah knew this truth intimately. Isaiah wanted God to smooth out the road ahead for him. The path may have appeared steep and rough; but it wasn't impassable for those aligned with the Holy One. Isaiah's attitude was one of obedience and praise: "Your name and renown are the desire of our hearts." The world around the prophet seemed to be going from bad to worse; but Isaiah cultivated an attitude of waiting for God. He knew the power to face every situation resided in God alone. Likewise, the writer of Revelation ended the record of his visions of coming apostasy and wrath with the same heartfelt cry: "Amen. Come, Lord Jesus" (Revelation 22:20).

We, too, should nurture a longing for God to rescue us definitively from the sin within and around us. He is our ultimate hope. ✤

PRAYER

O Lord, all night long I search for you. Earnestly I seek you . . .

RESPONDING TO ANSWERED PRAYER

Praise awaits you, our God, in Zion;
to you our vows will be fulfilled.
You who answer prayer,
to you all people will come.
When we were overwhelmed by sins,
you forgave our transgressions.
Blessed are those you choose
and bring near to live in your courts!
We are filled with the good things of your house,
of your holy temple.
You answer us with awesome and righteous deeds,
God our Savior,
the hope of all the ends of the earth
and of the farthest seas.

PSALM 65:1–5

God is worthy of our praise. He does answer our prayers. Moreover, he forgives our sins. David dedicated this prayer to rejoicing in God and committing himself to fulfilling everything he had promised to God. He ecstatically exclaimed, "We are filled with the good things of your house, of your holy temple." For David, entering God's presence was the greatest joy he could imagine. He made sure that the Lord knew of his joy and showered praises on the one who deserved it the most—God Almighty.

On countless occasions, God has forgiven our sins and answered our prayers. With the same fervency that we pray for his help, let us remember to sing his praises. Let us follow through on our promises to the Lord, for he is the one who has answered our prayers. ✤

PRAYER

Dear Lord, I will fulfill my vows to you, for you answer my prayers ...

A PLEA FOR FORGIVENESS

Now, our God, hear the prayers and petitions of your servant. For your sake, Lord, look with favor on your desolate sanctuary. Give ear, our God, and hear; open your eyes and see the desolation of the city that bears your Name. We do not make requests of you because we are righteous, but because of your great mercy. Lord, listen! Lord, forgive! Lord, hear and act! For your sake, my God, do not delay, because your city and your people bear your Name."
DANIEL 9:17–19

Most of us can think of one or two "inherited consequences" in our lives. Others may have made bad decisions, but we seem to be suffering the results. Our nation may be bent on ignoring God, but all of us may experience the consequences. Daniel knew he was exiled in Babylon because his nation Israel was being punished for generations of sinfulness. He understood that many events in his life were not his fault directly, but connected to the actions of his ancestors in the past. So he prayed for his people—God's people. From the land of punishment, he begged the Lord for forgiveness. His plea for mercy was based solely on God's compassionate character.

Unlike Daniel's day, one nation doesn't comprise God's people. Instead the church is God's people; and as such, the Lord will discipline believers if we refuse to walk in his holy ways. Have you seen the results of sin in your church community? Spend some time today praying for the Lord's forgiveness and asking him to guide the church into his ways. ✤

PRAYER

Dear Lord, for your own sake, smile again on your desolate sanctuary . . .

WAITING PATIENTLY ON GOD

Teach me your way, LORD;
lead me in a straight path
because of my oppressors....
I remain confident of this:
I will see the goodness of the LORD
in the land of the living.
Wait for the LORD;
be strong and take heart
and wait for the LORD.

PSALM 27:11, 13–14

David knew what it meant to be under pressure. He knew what it was like to be surrounded by a vast army of enemies, seeking his downfall. But even in those desperate times, David understood God's ways. When he appealed to God for assistance, he used language that prepared his own soul for God's pace. Although David certainly had his own ideas on how God could fix his hopeless situation, he submitted himself to God's way. He asked the Lord to teach and lead him. Although he might be tempted to frantic action, he quieted his heart and decided to wait on the Lord, for everything would work out according to God's good plan anyway.

All too often we expect instant answers from the Lord. God isn't in a hurry to fulfill our every whim. Often he uses the impossible situations in our lives to forge character. Like David, we can be confident we will "see the goodness of the LORD." But God will ultimately control the timing of his answers. ❖

PRAYER

O Lord, teach me how to live and help me to wait patiently on you ...

march**26**

TRUE CONFESSION

> *Is it not from the mouth of the Most High*
> *that both calamities and good things come?*
> *Why should the living complain*
> *when punished for their sins?*
> *Let us examine our ways and test them,*
> *and let us return to the LORD.*
> *Let us lift up our hearts and our hands*
> *to God in heaven, and say:*
> *"We have sinned and rebelled*
> *and you have not forgiven."*

Lamentations 3:38–42

Jeremiah knew the highs and lows of faith. He felt and wrote about the exhilaration of hope in God's faithfulness, as well as the depths of despair over sin. If we can read Lamentations without having our pride pierced, we may have hardened our hearts towards God. In this prayer, Jeremiah attacked our tendency to call God to account for his actions. All too often, we presume to examine God's ways, so we can avoid examining our own sinful ways. The weeping prophet points out the cost: we miss God's forgiveness. The problem isn't God's willingness to forgive, but our willingness to repent.

Today, confess the ways you have tried to examine and test God in the past. In prayer, submit your own heart to the Lord's scrutiny. ✣

PRAYER

Dear Lord, let me examine and test my ways. I have sinned and rebelled . . .

ABRAHAM'S PRAYER FOR MERCY

Then Abraham approached him and said: "Will you sweep away the righteous with the wicked? What if there are fifty righteous people in the city? Will you really sweep it away and not spare the place for the sake of the fifty righteous people in it? Far be it from you to do such a thing—to kill the righteous with the wicked, treating the righteous and the wicked alike. Far be it from you! Will not the Judge of all the earth do right?"

GENESIS 18:23–25

In the days before their fiery judgment, the citizens of Sodom and Gomorrah probably had no idea that their neighbor Abraham was agonizing with God over their fate. Abraham saw the need for justice; but he also begged God to show them his mercy. In the case of the wildly sinful cities, Abraham wondered how many innocent citizens would have to be present to keep God from punishing everyone: fifty? forty? ten? God answered that a mere ten righteous people would save the cities from destruction. Even with less than ten righteous people, God sent his angels to protect Lot's innocent family and get them out of harm's way. In this way God demonstrated how far he would go to shower mercy on sinful people. But as Sodom and Gomorrah's destruction illustrates, there's a limit to his mercy for the God of justice can't let sin go unpunished forever.

Just as he listened to righteous Abraham long ago, God will listen to your cries for justice and your pleas for mercy. In the end, God will do what is right. ✤

PRAYER

Dear Lord, I know that you are the Judge of all the earth and will do what is right. Show mercy on sinners and save the innocent ...

march**28**

A PRAYER FOR GOD'S POWER

Arrogant foes are attacking me, O God;
ruthless people are trying to kill me —
they have no regard for you.
But you, Lord, are a compassionate and gracious God,
slow to anger, abounding in love and faithfulness.
Turn to me and have mercy on me;
show your strength in behalf of your servant;
save me, because I serve you
just as my mother did.

PSALM 86:14–16

What situations have revealed your weakness and vulnerability the most? When have you most needed God's power? In this prayer, David described to God the predicament he found himself in. Arrogant people were opposing him, and some wanted to murder him. The odds against him were overwhelming, and he frankly admitted that to God. Yet David used a simple word to turn his prayer around — the word *but*. He used the word *but* to move his thoughts from his sizable problems to his infinite and almighty God.

Once you have listed and lifted your troubles to God, follow David's example and acknowledge that no matter how daunting your situation may be, God is greater. He is the source of power — now and always. ✤

PRAYER

Dear Almighty, give me strength. Save me, for I am your servant . . .

DEDICATION OF THE TEMPLE

But will God really dwell on earth? The heavens, even the highest heaven, cannot contain you. How much less this temple I have built! Yet give attention to your servant's prayer and his plea for mercy, LORD my God. Hear the cry and the prayer that your servant is praying in your presence this day. May your eyes be open toward this temple night and day, this place of which you said, "My Name shall be there," so that you will hear the prayer your servant prays toward this place. Hear the supplication of your servant and of your people Israel when they pray toward this place. Hear from heaven, your dwelling place, and when you hear, forgive.

1 KINGS 8:27–30

Standing before the magnificent Temple in Jerusalem, Solomon considered the folly of limiting God to a building made of wood and stone. Solomon knew his Temple was only a small tribute to the God who cannot be contained in the entire universe. But Solomon also realized that setting apart a place for prayer and worship doesn't necessarily mean that we believe God is confined there. Holy places serve as reminders and markers of our dependence on God. Church buildings can't offer forgiveness or provide us with a relationship with God, but the God who we consciously and purposefully meet there certainly does.

What places serve as reminders of God's presence in your life? How do they make you accountable before your Holy Lord? ✤

PRAYER

Dear Lord, the highest heaven cannot contain you. But hear my prayer; and when you hear, forgive...

march**30**

SILENT BEFORE GOD

The LORD said to Job:

> *"Will the one who contends with the Almighty correct him?*
> *Let him who accuses God answer him!"*

Then Job answered the LORD:

> *"I am unworthy—how can I reply to you?*
> *I put my hand over my mouth.*
> *I spoke once, but I have no answer—*
> *twice, but I will say no more."*

JOB 40:1–5

Job lost everything: his children, his possessions, his health, and the loyalty of his wife. He was left with friends who tried to explain away his awful circumstances and tried to find out who was to blame. Job and his friends tried to understand all that transpired, and Job asked some penetrating questions. But in the end, they overlooked God's infinite wisdom and absolute sovereignty. As Job learned, the Almighty doesn't have to answer to anyone. His knowledge and his power far surpass our own. While we're on this earth, we'll never completely understand his ways. But God has revealed more than enough of his loving character that we can fully trust him.

It's okay to ask God those difficult questions that continue to confound you. God is big enough to handle them all. But be careful not to use those questions as an excuse to accuse God or abandon him. Remind yourself that God is righteous and fair, that his ways are above your ways, his thoughts are above your thoughts. Then, sit in humble silence before the Almighty. ✤

PRAYER

Dear Almighty, I have questions, but I don't have answers. You have the answers; and I will put my hand over my mouth in silence . . .

march31

MEDITATING ON GOD'S WORD

Teach me, LORD, the way of your decrees,
that I may follow it to the end.
Give me understanding, so that I may keep your law
and obey it with all my heart.
Direct me in the path of your commands,
for there I find delight.
Turn my heart toward your statutes
and not toward selfish gain.
Turn my eyes away from worthless things;
preserve my life according to your word.

PSALM 119:33–37

Psalm 119 is one long, poetic prayer that praises God's law. What a privilege to know with certainty what God expects! What a privilege to be able to walk on the path that leads to eternal life! The poet who penned this prayer wasn't so arrogant that he believed he could always follow God's law. He knew he needed help. He needed someone to teach him God's law and help him understand the Lord's decrees. But more importantly, he needed a heart that eagerly sought out the Lord's will instead of his own will. He had experienced the tenacious lure of money and possessions. Intellectually, he knew that these things were worthless in the light of eternity; but their attraction was still strong. So the psalmist prayed to God, asking for the eagerness to follow God's ways.

One of the discipline of the spiritual life is reading and studying God's Word. It's through Scripture that we can meet God when we pray. Ask the Lord today to increase your hunger for his Word and to strengthen your determination to obey his commands. ✤

PRAYER

Dear Lord, make me walk along the path of your commands, for that is where happiness is found . . .

april1

PRAISING GOD FOR REMAINING THE SAME

You, LORD, reign forever;
your throne endures from generation to generation.
Why do you always forget us?
Why do you forsake us so long?
Restore us to yourself, LORD, that we may return;
renew our days as of old

LAMENTATIONS 5:19–21

Jeremiah possessed one unshakable conviction: God doesn't change. Our faithfulness and our feelings are as fleeting as a breeze, but God remains the same. We wander away; God brings us back. We surrender our joy; God renews it. Though the ancient prophet was praying for his lost and threatened people, his words formed a prayer that can also put our own lives into perspective: The Lord will remain the same forever: He will sit on his heavenly throne forever. He is in complete control and will remain in complete control forever and forever. In his prayer, Jeremiah conveyed a profound sense of his lowly position before the mighty King of kings. How appropriate for a creature who was approaching his infinite Creator!

Acknowledging our complete dependence upon God in our prayers should be one of the first steps we take in prayer, for it's on that basis that we keep coming to him with our humble requests. God remains forever the same; we are the ones who have wandered from him. Today, take time to praise the Lord for his unchanging character. ❖

PRAYER

O Lord, you remain the same forever! Bring me back to you again ...

april2

PRAISE AT THE TRIUMPHAL ENTRY

A very large crowd spread their cloaks on the road, while others cut branches from the trees and spread them on the road. The crowds that went ahead of him and those that followed shouted,

"Hosanna to the Son of David!"
"Blessed is he who comes in the name of the Lord!"
"Hosanna in the highest heaven!"

MATTHEW 21:8–9

The starting point of our prayers should be praise for our wonderful Savior. The Jews, who gathered for the annual Passover celebration, knew what it meant to praise their Savior. Every year, they assembled at the Temple in Jerusalem to celebrate the God who had miraculously delivered their ancestors from slavery in Egypt. Their celebration wasn't limited to a commemorative Passover meal. Before and during the Passover feast, the people prayed and sang hymns of praise to God, their Deliverer. Psalms 113–118 records the five prayers the Israelites sang to the Lord during this feast. So it was natural for the crowd of Passover pilgrims to greet Jesus with the words from Psalm 118:26: "Blessed is he who comes in the name of the LORD." Why wouldn't they enthusiastically welcome Jesus—the teacher and miracle-worker who had obviously come in God's name—to their grand celebration?

Let your prayer time be a celebration of God and his Son, Jesus. Today, use the words of the people of Israel to celebrate Jesus. ❖

PRAYER

Dear Lord, I praise you for sending the Son of David . . .

april3

AWE FOR THE CREATOR

By the word of the LORD the heavens were made,
their starry host by the breath of his mouth.
He gathers the waters of the sea into jars;
he puts the deep into storehouses.
Let all the earth fear the LORD;
let all the people of the world revere him.
For he spoke, and it came to be;
he commanded, and it stood firm.

PSALM 33:6–9

When was the last time you took time to admire God's handiwork in the night sky? The brilliant stars hanging in the sky and the oceans crashing against the coastline give us reasons to stand in awe of God, the Creator of it all. God merely spoke; and these wonders came into being. How we should marvel in the presence of such unimaginable power! God's creation—the vast universe populated by innumerable stars—make us all feel so small and insignificant. How much more should we bow before the infinite God who can command the cosmos into existence, or wipe it out in a moment!

Focus on some aspect of nature that is meaningful to you. Is it a sparkling river? A peaceful lake? A spectacular skyline? Then, offer your praises to its great Creator. ♣

PRAYER

Dear Lord, you merely spoke, and the heavens were created ...

april4

HEAVENLY PRAISE FOR THE LAMB

After this I looked, and there before me was a great multitude that no one could count, from every nation, tribe, people and language, standing before the throne and before the Lamb. They were wearing white robes and were holding palm branches in their hands. And they cried out in a loud voice:

> *"Salvation belongs to our God,*
> *who sits on the throne,*
> *and to the Lamb."*

REVELATION 7:9–10

Many times our prayers tend to focus on this world—on the difficulties, the trials, and the evil we encounter in our lives. God understands and accepts these prayers. Our earthly limitations are often God-given reminders of our desperate need for God. We might begin our prayers by presenting our troubling situations to God, but we must also direct our thoughts and prayers to the victory we will share with Christ. In Revelation, God gives us a splendid portrayal of that final victory. In a vision, the apostle John sees a magnificent scene—a vast multitude celebrating the triumph of the Lamb of God. Waving palm branches, the traditional symbol of victory, people from all over the world extol God for the salvation he has provided through his Son.

As followers of Christ, we today are privileged to be part of this multitude—the communion of believers. Because Jesus has overcome death, a new life of wholeness and peace through him has opened up to us. This is worth shouting about—praising God with all that is in us! ✤

PRAYER

Dear Lord, I join your praying people through the ages to shout about that salvation which comes from you . . .

RECALLING GOD'S WONDERFUL DEEDS

I will remember the deeds of the LORD;
yes, I will remember your miracles of long ago.
I will consider all your works
and meditate on all your mighty deeds."
Your ways, God, are holy.
What god is as great as our God?
You are the God who performs miracles;
you display your power among the peoples.
With your mighty arm you redeemed your people,
the descendants of Jacob and Joseph.

PSALM 77:11 – 15

How pleasurable it is to recall with our friends and loved ones those amusing and fun experiences we've shared together! Psalm 77 helps us remember God's wonderful works and praise him for them. Spending time recalling how God has intervened in our lives can and should be an enjoyable experience. But the writer of this psalm wasn't simply remembering God's deeds for fun. It was a necessity for him. Asaph was in trouble and desperately needed God's help. Recalling the ways God had miraculously and powerfully intervened in the lives of the Israelites in the past helped to reassure him that God would act in his distressing situation as well. By focusing on our Savior instead of our situation we can regain our composure and truly believe that God will guide us through our problems.

Remind yourself of what God did for his people long ago. Then, look back on your life and find the ways God has worked in your life. ✤

PRAYER

I recall all you have done, O Lord . . .

GLORY TO GOD'S NAME ALONE

"Now my soul is troubled, and what shall I say? 'Father, save me from this hour'? No, it was for this very reason I came to this hour. Father, glorify your name!"

Then a voice came from heaven, "I have glorified it, and will glorify it again."

JOHN 12:27–28

Our normal tendency, when faced with a difficult situation, is to pray that our troubles will go away. Certainly, God is our Deliverer from all evil; and it is appropriate to pray in this manner. Jesus, too, asked his Father to spare him from the agony of suffering a cruel death on a cross (Luke 22:42). But Jesus knew that enduring such suffering would bring greater glory to the God the Father. Because of Jesus' death on the cross, God could offer salvation to all who believed in Jesus. So in the end, Christ's prayer was simply that God's name would be glorified in his life.

When we are apprehensive about events that loom in the future, we may certainly ask our Father to keep us from harm. But, following our Savior's example, we may also pray that, whatever will come our way, God's name might be honored in our lives. ✤

PRAYER

Dear Father, bring glory to your name, whatever I must pass through in the days to come ...

GRATITUDE FOR GOD'S MERCY

The LORD is compassionate and gracious,
*   slow to anger, abounding in love.*
He will not always accuse,
*   nor will he harbor his anger forever;*
he does not treat us as our sins deserve
*   or repay us according to our iniquities.*
For as high as the heavens are above the earth,
*   so great is his love for those who fear him;*
as far as the east is from the west,
*   so far has he removed our transgressions from us.*

PSALM 103:8–12

We often pray for other friends, family members, loved ones, missionaries, and those in need, but some of our prayers should be all about God. This was the case with David's prayer in Psalm 103. He described God as compassionate, gracious, slow to anger, and "abounding in love." "Praise the LORD," David intoned, because the Lord doesn't remain angry forever nor does he punish us to the extent we deserve. The greatness of God's love is as high as the heavens are above the earth. He has removed our sins from us as far as the east is from the west! With these beautiful and intriguing metaphors, David expressed his gratitude and awe for God's immeasurable greatness.

In the next few moments, see if you can express the extent of your gratitude to God. Then, offer these as a praise-gift to your Lord. ❖

PRAYER

Dear Lord, you are merciful and gracious. You are slow to get angry and full of unfailing love . . .

april8

A PRAYER FOR GOD'S WILL

Going a little farther, he fell with his face to the ground and prayed, "My Father, if it is possible, may this cup be taken from me. Yet not as I will, but as you will."

MATTHEW 26:39

Submitting to God's will for our lives can be a formidable challenge. At times, our dreams and aspirations conflict with God's will for our lives. Jesus wrestled with this issue in prayer in the Garden of Gethsemane. At stake, for Jesus, was the way God wanted to accomplish the salvation of his people. God's way included suffering and finally death on a cross. Jesus saw the difficult road ahead and spent a night agonizing in prayer over it. The strength and courage he found in prayer that night helped him withstand the terrible suffering he faced the next day.

The choices we must make are less momentous than Jesus' choices, but they may still be agonizing ones which drive us to our knees before the Father. As his will becomes clearer—through the commands of God's Word, through the insights of godly friends, and through the unfolding of circumstances—may God give us the ability to yield to his will, as Jesus did. ✤

PRAYER

Dear Lord, I want your will to be done, and not mine own will, in this matter which lies before me ...

april9

REVERING THE LORD

The works of his hands are faithful and just;
all his precepts are trustworthy.
They are established for ever and ever,
enacted in faithfulness and uprightness.
He provided redemption for his people;
he ordained his covenant forever —
holy and awesome is his name.
The fear of the LORD is the beginning of wisdom;
all who follow his precepts have good understanding.
To him belongs eternal praise.

PSALM 111:7–10

Much of society today no longer values reverence. Instead, our culture tends to uphold the irreverent — those people who don't hold anything or anyone sacred. But this doesn't mean God is less worthy of reverence than when the psalmist penned these words. God should be honored because all he does is just and good. All his commandments are to be trusted because they are, and always will be, true. We shouldn't approach God with a flippant or demanding attitude. We should approach him with the respect, honor, and reverence he deserves. True wisdom is knowing to whom we owe our very existence. And there are tangible rewards for those who align their life with this truth.

Revisit the foundation of your faith and the fount of all wisdom today. Bow before the Lord and give him the reverence he deserves. ✤

PRAYER

Dear Lord, all you do is just and good. I honor, worship, and revere you . . .

JESUS' PRAYER FOR GLORY

After Jesus said this, he looked toward heaven and prayed:

"Father, the hour has come. Glorify your Son, that your Son may glorify you. For you granted him authority over all people that he might give eternal life to all those you have given him. Now this is eternal life: that they know you, the only true God, and Jesus Christ, whom you have sent. I have brought you glory on earth by finishing the work you gave me to do. And now, Father, glorify me in your presence with the glory I had with you before the world began."

JOHN 17:1–5

At the Last Supper, the night before his betrayal, Jesus prayed this prayer. Precisely at the time when Jesus was preparing himself and his disciples for the suffering he would endure in the days ahead, Jesus prayed that God would be glorified in his life. We often think the road to glory is lined with success. Yet, Jesus' road to glory was lined with suffering and defeat: a horrible death on the cross. How could this "defeat" bring God glory? Jesus explained in his prayer that his own obedience to God's plan was bringing glory to God. Rarely do we view our suffering and defeats as giving glory to God. But we also rarely have God's view of our circumstances. God has a plan, in which he is working all things out for the good of his people and for the glory of his name. While we may look forward to the glory we will share with God in heaven, perhaps the greater wonder of the Christian life is that God's glory is reflected in our acts of obedience, love, and faithfulness in this life.

Follow Christ's example today, by praying that God might be glorified in your life. ✤

PRAYER

Dear Father, let me bring glory to you here on earth by doing everything you have told me to do ...

april11

PLACING OUR HOPE IN GOD

Sing to the LORD with grateful praise;
make music to our God on the harp.
He covers the sky with clouds;
he supplies the earth with rain
and makes grass grow on the hills.
He provides food for the cattle
and for the young ravens when they call.
His pleasure is not in the strength of the horse,
nor his delight in the legs of the warrior;
the LORD delights in those who fear him,
who put their hope in his unfailing love.

PSALM 147:7–11

God isn't impressed by the things that impress most people. People tend to value the trappings of wealth, power, beautiful children, and prestige, while God looks for those who depend on him and honor him. Psalm 147 was written after a group of Judeans had returned from exile in Babylon. These people had learned the "hard way" that their purpose on earth was to honor God and submit to him. The psalmist in this prayer pointed out that the created world is a perfect illustration of life in harmony with God. No part of it is self-sufficient. God is the one who provides the rain. He allows the grass to grow. God himself gives food to the wild animals and to the birds that soar above. Later, Jesus would echo the psalmist's sentiment, "If that is how God clothes the grass of the field, which is here today, and tomorrow is thrown into the fire, how much more will he clothe you" (Luke 12:28).

In your prayer today, acknowledge your dependence on God and thank him for providing for you. ✤

PRAYER

O Lord, you cover the heavens with clouds and provide rain for the earth . . .

JESUS' MERCIFUL PRAYER

Jesus said, "Father, forgive them, for they do not know what they are doing." And they divided up his clothes by casting lots.

LUKE 23:34

It is hard enough to forgive those who offend and injure us; but it is even more difficult to forgive those who mock and taunt us when we're suffering. The torment Jesus had to endure on the cross was made even more unbearable by the taunts of the angry crowd and the mockery of the Roman soldiers. The Bible says that all this suffering and shame was part of the Father's plan to reconcile a rebellious humanity to himself. Not realizing that Jesus was the Lord of glory, his unwitting opponents fulfilled the prophecies in the Scriptures by putting Jesus to death. Yet Jesus' grace—his willingness to forgive—is evident even at the time when he was suffering the worst insults. It is a well-known fact that suffering reveals someone's character: It can bring out the best and the worst in people. Here, on the cross, we can see most clearly who Jesus is. His prayer, "Father, forgive them," shows us divine love like nothing else can.

As followers of Christ, we are called to pray the same prayer for our own enemies. ✤

PRAYER

May I, like you Lord Christ, forgive those who wrong me . . .

SINGING PRAISES TO OUR GOD

Sing for joy to God our strength;
shout aloud to the God of Jacob!
Begin the music, strike the timbrel,
play the melodious harp and lyre.

PSALM 81:1–2

Any celebration—whether it's an orchestrated wedding or a small gathering of friends—involves music. There's almost always some type of music being played in the background. Music and song can express the emotions of the human heart like nothing else can. That's why when believers gather to worship God, they sing. Together in song, they remind themselves of how majestic God is and express in harmonious melodies how happy they are to be his people. Psalm 81 calls God's people to worshipful prayer by directing them to sing their praises to God. What a wonderful and exhilarating way to begin one's own prayer time!

As you pray to God today, praise him for his strength. If you have access to hymnals, praise books, or worshipful songs on tapes or compact discs, use these to help you wholeheartedly express your gratitude to God. ✤

PRAYER

O sing praises to God, our strength . . .

JESUS' CRY TO HIS FATHER

About three in the afternoon Jesus cried out in a loud voice, "Eli, Eli, lema sabachthani?"
(which means "My God, my God, why have you forsaken me?").

MATTHEW 27:46

From the earliest centuries of the church, Christians have pondered the import of Jesus' cry from the cross. Was Jesus really abandoned by God the Father to bear in isolated torment the sin of all people for all time? The best way to approach this unusual prayer is to place it in its biblical context. In Jesus' day, teachers would identify a Scripture passage by quoting its opening words. Jesus' prayer is a quote from the first verse of Psalm 22—a psalm which ends not in abandonment by God but in God's deliverance. Perhaps, Jesus recited the entire psalm, up to its concluding thoughts: "For he has not despised or scorned the suffering of the afflicted one; he has not hidden his face from him but has listened to his cry for help" (Psalm 22:24). Certainly, Jesus knew that his suffering on the cross wasn't God's ultimate abandonment of him; as the writer of Hebrews says, "For the joy set before him he endured the cross, scorning its shame, and sat down at the right hand of the throne of God" (Hebrews 12:2).

Although we won't suffer as much as our remarkable Savior; nevertheless, we must look beyond our trials to our triumph with God. ❖

PRAYER

When I feel you have forsaken me, my God, help me see your victory . . .

WORTHY IS THE LAMB

In a loud voice they were saying:

> *"Worthy is the Lamb, who was slain,*
> *to receive power and wealth and wisdom and strength*
> *and honor and glory and praise!"*

Then I heard every creature in heaven and on earth and under the earth and on the sea, and all that is in them, saying:

> *"To him who sits on the throne and to the Lamb*
> *be praise and honor and glory and power,*
> *for ever and ever!"*

REVELATION 5:12–13

Scripture encourages Christians to offer prayers of praise and thanksgiving to their God continually (1 Thessalonians 5:17–18). But, as important as our personal worship of God may be, a vital dimension is missing until we join our prayers of praise with that of others. To be caught up in adoration of the Lord together with his people is the fulfillment of our calling to be his priests and worshipers, for it is to a people — gathered from all places and all eras — that the Lord will come to receive the homage he richly deserves. His people will respond to his coming with a unified hymn of blessing exalting the Lord God and the Lamb. May we ever be found in the fellowship of that praising, prayerful people! ✤

PRAYER

Blessing and honor, glory and power to you, Lord God, upon your throne, and to the Lamb . . .

april**16**

A PRAYER FOR COURAGE

*When they heard this, they raised their voices together in prayer to God. "Sovereign Lord,"
they said, "you made the heavens and the earth and the sea, and everything in them....*

*"Indeed Herod and Pontius Pilate met together with the Gentiles and the people of Israel
in this city to conspire against your holy servant Jesus, whom you anointed. They did what
your power and will had decided beforehand should happen. Now, Lord, consider their
threats and enable your servants to speak your word with great boldness. Stretch out your
hand to heal and perform signs and wonders through the name of your holy servant Jesus."*
ACTS 4:24, 27–30

Before his ascension into heaven, Jesus had told his followers: "You will receive power
when the Holy Spirit comes on you; and you will be my witnesses in Jerusalem, and
in all Judea and Samaria, and to the ends of the earth" (Acts 1:8). On the day of
Pentecost, they did receive that power; but the Spirit's power didn't inoculate them
against opposition. It was after the Jewish council firmly threatened Peter and John
for preaching the Good News that the believers met together to pray. Their prayer
is instructive. They didn't ask God to destroy the Jewish opposition. Instead they
prayed for boldness—for God to demonstrate his power through them. They not
only reported to God the threats they had received, they also reminded themselves
of the way religious leaders had opposed Jesus, their Savior. They didn't pray that
God will make their lives easier. Instead, they prayed that they might have the
power to spread the Good News as he had commanded them to do.

Today, ask Jesus to give you the courage and power to proclaim the Good News
to your unsaved friends and family members. ✤

PRAYER

Dear Lord, grant me boldness in my witness for you ...

april**17**

ENTERING GOD'S PRESENCE

> *Therefore my heart is glad and my tongue rejoices;*
> *my body also will rest secure,*
> *because you will not abandon me to the realm of the dead,*
> *nor will you let your faithful one see decay.*
> *You make known to me the path of life;*
> *you will fill me with joy in your presence,*
> *with eternal pleasures at your right hand.*

PSALM 16:9–11

Often the fears and difficulties of this life fill our prayers with all kinds of concerns that center on ourselves. In this prayer, David described what it meant for him to enter God's presence. No longer did he have to be concerned about protecting and defending himself, for his loving God was his Protector. Entering the Lord's presence released him from self-absorption to a joyful celebration of the King. For in prayer, David encountered one who was so awesome, yet comforting, that his prayer was directed away from himself to his Creator. The joy of God's presence should bring our lives into perspective and supply the power to continue serving the Lord in this life.

As you enter into God's presence in prayer today, ask God to fill your life with his presence. ✤

PRAYER

Grant me, Lord, the joy of your presence . . .

A PRAYER FOR POWER

Now may the God of peace, who through the blood of the eternal covenant brought back from the dead our Lord Jesus, that great Shepherd of the sheep, equip you with everything good for doing his will, and may he work in us what is pleasing to him, through Jesus Christ, to whom be glory for ever and ever. Amen.

HEBREWS 13:20–21

Many Bible prayers draw images from agriculture—especially, from shepherding. God's people are continually compared to a flock of sheep, which is wholly dependent upon the Shepherd's leadership for food and protection. Although most of us now live and work in urban settings, where individual achievement is prized, we should never imagine that we can be all the Lord wants us to be all by ourselves. In serving him, we are part of a "flock." We belong to a people who have been brought into a covenant relationship with the Lord, and with one another, through the blood of Jesus. It is the Lord, our Shepherd, who equips us to do together what he wants us to do. That is why the author of Hebrews wrote down his prayer for believers. He wanted all believers to join him in praying for the resources to do God's work together.

Pray that God might equip you and the believers in your church community to accomplish God's work. ✢

PRAYER

Dear Shepherd, equip me with all that I need to do your will . . .

THANKS FOR GOD'S FORGIVENESS

You, LORD, showed favor to your land;
*   you restored the fortunes of Jacob.*
You forgave the iniquity of your people
*   and covered all their sins.*
You set aside all your wrath
*   and turned from your fierce anger.*
Restore us again, God our Savior,
*   and put away your displeasure toward us.*

PSALM 85:1–4

However much our culture denies the reality and effect of guilt, there are many today who live under its burden. Our culture may be cast adrift from its moral moorings, but many people still have the sense that their lives are not what they ought to be. A sense of guilt may actually be a gift from God that helps redirect us to God's way—the pathway that leads to a productive and happy life in conformity with the Lord's principles. But God's greater gift to us is his mercy, which awakens within us the incentive to start anew on the path of right living. In this prayer to God, the psalmist thanks the Lord for forgiving his people and restoring his land. He had learned from his experience that when people ask God for forgiveness, he doesn't turn them away. He forgives. The psalmist wrote this prayer of thanksgiving to celebrate his wonderfully, merciful Lord.

Remind yourself of the ways the Lord has forgiven you and renewed your life. Then, offer your praises to your Savior. ✤

PRAYER

Thank you, Lord, that you have forgiven my guilt and covered all my sin …

GRATITUDE FOR GOD'S REIGN

> *We give thanks to you, Lord God Almighty,*
> *the One who is and who was,*
> *because you have taken your great power*
> *and have begun to reign.*
> *The nations were angry,*
> *and your wrath has come.*
> *The time has come for judging the dead,*
> *and for rewarding your servants the prophets*
> *and your people who revere your name,*
> *both great and small—*
> *and for destroying those who destroy the earth.*

REVELATION 11:17–18

When oppressors of innocent children go unpunished, when murderers don't pay for their crimes, we might be tempted to despair of ever obtaining justice. When opposition to God's ways are rewarded in society, we might even question why we're serving the Lord. The Scriptures, however, encourage us to take the long-range view of history and culture. The twenty-four elders, who sit in God's throne room, paint this long-range view for us in their prayer of praise to the Almighty. They thank the "One who is and who was" for controlling all of history. They praise him for administering his perfect justice at the appropriate time. Reminding ourselves of this long-range view can give us confidence that God's justice will ultimately prevail—that God's servants will ultimately be vindicated.

Take a moment to envision yourself before God's throne room at the end of time. What prayer of praise will you offer the Lord? ✤

PRAYER

Dear Lord, I give thanks that you will one day reward all who fear your name . . .

THANKS FOR GOD'S BENEFITS

Praise the LORD, my soul;
*   all my inmost being, praise his holy name.*
Praise the LORD, my soul,
*   and forget not all his benefits—*
who forgives all your sins
*   and heals all your diseases,*
who redeems your life from the pit
*   and crowns you with love and compassion,*
who satisfies your desires with good things
*   so that your youth is renewed like the eagle's.*

PSALM 103:1–5

Every firm with a sizable workforce gives a benefits package to its workers. A benefits package usually includes health-care, life, and disability insurance. Our Lord, too, provides benefits to us—he "satisfies your desires with good things." In this prayer, David listed God's benefits package. First of all, David's very life and health was directly from God's hand. But God's benefits package didn't end there. The Lord filled David's life with all kinds of good things and gave David the youthful strength and disposition to enjoy these benefits. But in this prayer, David recognized that the key benefit God gave to him was forgiveness—God's grace which broke down the barrier of sin between God and him. David knew that his abilities, his hard work, and his determination wasn't the reason he was enjoying all these things. Instead, he freely acknowledged that his life was thoroughly dependent on the merciful Life-giver.

During your prayer time, list God's benefits to you on a piece of paper. Then, use that list to remind you to thank the Lord throughout the day. ✤

PRAYER

Dear Lord, I will never forget the good things you do for me ...

PRAISE FOR GOD'S SALVATION

In that day you will say:

> *"I will praise you, LORD.*
> *Although you were angry with me,*
> *your anger has turned away*
> *and you have comforted me.*
> *Surely God is my salvation;*
> *I will trust and not be afraid.*
> *The LORD, the LORD himself, is my strength and my defense;*
> *he has become my salvation."*

ISAIAH 12:1–2

These verses contain the collective prayer that will issue from the lips of God's people when Christ reigns over the earth forever. God's people will greet Christ with a short prayer of praise that aptly describes their marvelous relationship with him. The Lord is worthy of their enthusiastic praise because, though once angry at their sin, he now comforts them. He won't come to judge, but to save. What a joy it is to know that, though we deserve judgment, we don't have to live in fear of God — our Savior. Moses praised God for this when he was delivered from the Egyptian army: "The LORD is my strength and my defense; he has become my salvation" (Exodus 15:2); and on that last day, God's people will echo Moses' prayer.

Today, our prayers of praise are linked with all believers who have gone before us and all who will follow us until the end of time. It is the powerful and rapturous cry of the redeemed — those who realize that God was willing to sacrifice his own Son in order to heal and save them. Join your voice in this prayer today. ✣

PRAYER

Dear Lord, you are my strength and my song; you have become my salvation ...

PRAISE FOR GOD'S ANSWERS

> *To you, LORD, I called;*
> *to the Lord I cried for mercy:*
> *"What is gained if I am silenced,*
> *if I go down to the pit?*
> *Will the dust praise you?*
> *Will it proclaim your faithfulness?*
> *Hear, LORD, and be merciful to me;*
> *LORD, be my help."*
> *You turned my wailing into dancing;*
> *you removed my sackcloth and clothed me with joy,*
> *that my heart may sing your praises and not be silent.*
> *LORD my God, I will praise you forever.*

PSALM 30:8–12

Why does God answer prayers? God certainly knows what is best for us before we voice our requests. Why does the all-knowing, all-powerful God work out his plan through our simple requests? David possessed some insight into this question. He realized that it was through answered prayers, more than anything else, that God could demonstrate his love and mercy most clearly to this world. Too often, we don't recognize God's work in our lives. In contrast, an answered prayer is a clear sign to us of God at work. The Lord wants those who have experienced answered prayer to tell others about it. God treasures the heartfelt gratitude and the joyful praise of those who recognize his loving hand in their lives.

When we receive answers to prayer, may we, like David, never take that miracle for granted. ❖

PRAYER

Dear Lord, I will give you thanks forever!...

april24

SINGING OF GOD'S GLORIOUS DEEDS

Sing to the LORD, all the earth;
proclaim his salvation day after day.
Declare his glory among the nations,
his marvelous deeds among all peoples.
For great is the LORD and most worthy of praise;
he is to be feared above all gods.

1 CHRONICLES 16:23–25

Sometimes on beautiful spring days, with the glory of renewal evident all around us, we long to blend our expressions of praise with something much larger than ourselves. In David's prayer of praise, which he wrote to music and taught to the musicians in the court of the Lord, captured this sentiment: "Sing to the LORD, all the earth." For David, every day was an occasion to proclaim the good news of salvation, to announce to everyone the glorious and amazing deeds that God has done and continues to do. But this prayer was written for a special celebration, when David brought the ark of God into the tent of meeting he had prepared for it. Especially on such occasions when the community met together to praise and thank God, it was appropriate to declare God's greatness with great enthusiasm. Imagine for a moment that a whole gathering of believers plus all of nature for miles around united in a prayer of praise to God. What would it sound like? What words would you use to praise your Lord? ❖

PRAYER

Let the whole earth sing to the Lord . . .

DELIGHT IN GOD'S LOVE

Your love, LORD, reaches to the heavens,
your faithfulness to the skies.
Your righteousness is like the highest mountains,
your justice like the great deep.
You, LORD, preserve both people and animals.
How priceless is your unfailing love, O God!
People take refuge in the shadow of your wings.
They feast on the abundance of your house;
you give them drink from your river of delights....
Continue your love to those who know you,
your righteousness to the upright in heart.

PSALM 36:5–8, 10

In this prayer, David uses what he can see—the sky, the mountains, and the oceans—to illustrate how great God is. The Lord's unfailing love is as vast as the sky; his faithfulness to his people exceeds the height of the clouds that float above him; his righteousness is more secure than the greatest mountain; his commitment to justice exceeds the depths of the deepest ocean. The fact that God daily feeds all of his creation—both people and animals alike—clearly demonstrates the depths of his love for all that he has made. In fact, God loves to allow his people to experience the "river of delights."

Take some time today to see the world around you and the simple elements of your daily life from David's vantage point. Our God is very great; and his signature is everywhere. Let us bow before him in worship and awe. ✤

PRAYER

How precious is your unfailing love, O God!...

REMEMBERING GOD'S MERCY

Because of the LORD's great love we are not consumed,
 for his compassions never fail.
They are new every morning;
 great is your faithfulness.
I say to myself, "The LORD is my portion;
 therefore I will wait for him."
The LORD is good to those whose hope is in him,
 to the one who seeks him;
it is good to wait quietly
 for the salvation of the LORD.

LAMENTATIONS 3:22 – 26

In the book of Lamentations, the prophet Jeremiah expressed his anguish over the fall of Jerusalem — the culmination of God's judgment which Jeremiah had foretold over a period of years. Yet even through his tears over his destitute people, Jeremiah had an occasion to praise God. He dared to hope in God's undying love for his people. He recalled God's faithfulness and mercy. God himself was the reason the nation of Israel had been rescued from slavery and established in a prosperous land. God himself was the reason that Israel and Judah were not completely destroyed.

Hope is born from this kind of remembering of what God has done. And once our hope is revived, we find ourselves able, even eager, to wait quietly for his salvation, which surely will come. Even in difficult circumstances, we too can praise our merciful God and wait for his salvation. ✤

PRAYER

Dear Lord, you are wonderfully good to those who wait for you and seek you . . .

april27

ADMIRING GOD'S HANDIWORK

When I consider your heavens,
the work of your fingers,
the moon and the stars,
which you have set in place,
what is mankind that you are mindful of them,
human beings that you care for them?
You have made them a little lower than the angels
and crowned them with glory and honor....
LORD, our Lord,
how majestic is your name in all the earth!

PSALM 8:3–5, 9

After pondering the beauty and immensity of just one aspect of God's creation—the stars in the heavens, David was moved to say: "What is mankind that you are mindful of them?" We are mere specks in the vast universe in which we live. Yet the marvel is that God made us only a little lower than himself! He granted us great honor—by first creating us as the pinnacle of all other life on this earth and later, when we had sinned, sending his own Son to save us.

When we are moved by the majesty or intricacy of something God has created in the physical world, we should remind ourselves that the God who created this amazing world has showered his infinite love on us. In prayer, express your wonder and gratitude to God today. ✢

PRAYER

O Father, you made us only a little lower than yourself, and you crowned us with glory and honor ...

THANKS FOR CHRIST'S VICTORY

But thanks be to God, who always leads us as captives in Christ's triumphal procession and uses us to spread the aroma of the knowledge of him everywhere.

2 CORINTHIANS 2:14

Ancient Roman generals, returning to Rome from a victory in a distant land, would parade down the main streets of Rome with the spoils of battle—including a throng of captives from the conquered territory. These dejected captives were solid evidence to the Roman public of the great victory the general was celebrating. In this prayer of thanksgiving, Paul uses this image of a triumphal procession to thank Christ for defeating the evil forces of this world. Interestingly enough in this prayer, Paul identifies believers as Christ's captives. We were once part of Satan's army; but Jesus has taken us captive. As such, our transformed lives clearly proclaim Christ's great victory. But unlike the captives of Roman conquerors, we aren't destined to be sold into demeaning servitude. Instead, Christ has freed us from our old evil master to become his adopted children. So our captivity is really a release into the joy of Christ's service. Liberated by Christ, we become a multimedia testimony to his power: a witness, Paul suggests, of sound, sight, and savor!

Thank God, today, that you're included in Christ's victory parade. ✤

PRAYER

Thanks be to you, my God, who made me your captive in Christ's triumphal procession . . .

CALLING ON CREATION TO PRAISE GOD

Let the heavens rejoice, let the earth be glad;
  let the sea resound, and all that is in it.
Let the fields be jubilant, and everything in them;
  let all the trees of the forest sing for joy.
Let all creation rejoice before the LORD, for he comes,
  he comes to judge the earth.
He will judge the world in righteousness
  and the peoples in his faithfulness.

PSALM 96:11–13

At times, our own voices seem so inadequate for praising God, the one who created the vast universe. Sometimes our hearts are slow to comprehend what a privilege it is to approach the infinite God in prayer. Too often, we rush into God's presence with a hasty word of thanks. In contrast, the author of Psalm 96 took the time to contemplate to whom he was praying. The psalmist was so overwhelmed with God's greatness that he called upon the heavens and the earth to extol the King of the universe. The entire earth was a magnificent instrument designed to sing the Lord's praises. The wheat and barley, ripe for the harvest, were bursting with joy before the Lord, while the wind was playing a beautiful melody of praise on the leaves and branches of the forest.

In prayer today, take a moment to appreciate the world God has created for you and rejoice in it. ✤

PRAYER

Let the heavens be glad, and let the earth rejoice in God!...

april**30**

PAUL'S PRAYER FOR THE GALATIANS

Grace and peace to you from God our Father and the Lord Jesus Christ, who gave himself for our sins to rescue us from the present evil age, according to the will of our God and Father.

GALATIANS 1:3–4

The Christians in Galatia were confused about Christian doctrine and practice. Under the influence of false teachers, the Galatians were letting go of their hold on the truth. Confusion and dissension were setting in, weakening their ability to withstand the temptations of the evil world around them. Paul knew these believers were in a precarious position, so he not only wrote them but prayed for them. He prayed that the Galatians might truly possess the grace and peace Christ has offered all believers. As believers, our peace was won when Jesus Christ came to earth and died for our sins. This is how God rescues us from the evil that would otherwise destroy us.

The confusion of the Galatians may be echoed in your life or the life of someone close to you. Begin, as Paul did, by praying for God's grace and peace to rescue you. Thank God for delivering you through Christ's death on the cross. ✤

PRAYER

May grace and peace be ours from God our Father and from the Lord Jesus Christ …

may 1

HOPING IN GOD ALONE

> *We wait in hope for the LORD;*
>   *he is our help and our shield.*
> *In him our hearts rejoice,*
>   *for we trust in his holy name.*
> *May your unfailing love be with us, LORD,*
>   *even as we put our hope in you.*

PSALM 33:20–22

We all crave security. Most of us seek to build up a network of friends and family around us to assure that we will come through even in the most trying of circumstances. There are, however, no ultimate guarantees in this life. This prayer reminds us that not even the best-equipped army or the strongest warhorse can assure a victory. Only Almighty God can ultimately rescue and protect us. It is good to acknowledge our dependence on the Lord when we approach him in prayer. Remember that he is our shield. As we concentrate on this marvelous truth, our fear can turn to rejoicing.

Stop for a few moments to consider the ways you seek security—in small matters and in large matters. Then, before God, acknowledge that ultimately you depend on him *alone*. ✤

PRAYER

Let your unfailing love surround us, O Lord, for our hope is in you alone . . .

SEARCHING FOR THE LORD

> *Give praise to the LORD, proclaim his name;*
> *make known among the nations what he has done.*
> *Sing to him, sing praise to him;*
> *tell of all his wonderful acts.*
> *Glory in his holy name;*
> *let the hearts of those who seek the LORD rejoice.*
> *Look to the LORD and his strength;*
> *seek his face always.*
> *Remember the wonders he has done,*
> *his miracles, and the judgments he pronounced.*

PSALM 105:1–5

Small crises can set us on a frantic search. Losing a ring or a key can set us on a search that leaves no sofa cushion unturned. The quest for a missing child can make the evening news and tie up an entire police department. But the psalmist speaks of a search that won't make the evening news: the search for the living God. In this prayer, the psalmist led God's people in thanking and praising the Lord for the wonderful things he had done for them. He encouraged God's people to search out the ways God was working in their lives and thank him for it.

What a marvelous search! Before you move ahead in the promise of this new spring month, search your life for the delightful blessings God has given you. ♣

PRAYER

Dear Lord, as I think of the wonderful works you have done . . .

A SPIRITUAL BLESSING

Praise be to the God and Father of our Lord Jesus Christ, who has blessed us in the heavenly realms with every spiritual blessing in Christ. For he chose us in him before the creation of the world to be holy and blameless in his sight.

EPHESIANS 1:3–4

Although penned in prison, Paul's letter to the Ephesians is one of encouragement. Ephesus was one of the more prominent and strong churches that Paul established on an earlier missionary journeys. Paul encouraged this church to praise God for the abundance of blessings they were enjoying. Just in case some of the Ephesians started searching their lives for material blessing, Paul lifted their eyes beyond this world toward heaven for the treasures stored for them there. "Spiritual blessings," he called them.

In like manner, we, too, should praise God for all the spiritual blessings he has give us—our salvation, our inheritance in heaven, our promised new bodies. As you begin to pray today, thank God for blessings you can't see—joy, inner peace, and hope. Meditate on your eternal reward that money cannot buy, yet remains valuable beyond compare. Praise God for his kindness from which our spiritual blessings spring. ✤

PRAYER

Dear Lord, I praise you for the spiritual blessings in my life such as ...

may4

GRATEFULNESS FOR JUSTICE

I will give thanks to you, LORD, with all my heart;
*   I will tell of all your wonderful deeds.*
I will be glad and rejoice in you;
*   I will sing the praises of your name, O Most High....*
For you have upheld my right and my cause,
*   sitting enthroned as the righteous judge.*

PSALM 9:1‒2, 4

"It's not fair." How often that phrase comes to our minds when we feel we are mistreated! Yet, in this prayer, David resisted the all too human temptation to complain about injustice. Instead, he reaffirmed his faith in God's justice, even though he had personally suffered and even faced death at the hands of his enemies. Such mistreatment could have defeated David's hope in God. But he refused to dwell on his cruel enemies or on the injustices that he was suffering. Instead, he concentrated on his just and all-powerful God.

Instead of praying for God's ultimate revenge on your enemies, pray that God's justice will be carried out. Whatever God chooses to do in each situation will be right; and we can, in prayer, entrust our problems with others to him. ✤

PRAYER

Dear Lord, I praise you for being a God of justice . . .

DAVID'S PRAYER FOR A CLEAN HEART

Create in me a pure heart, O God,
  and renew a steadfast spirit within me.
Do not cast me from your presence
  or take your Holy Spirit from me.
Restore to me the joy of your salvation
  and grant me a willing spirit, to sustain me.
Then I will teach transgressors your ways,
  so that sinners will turn back to you.

PSALM 51:10–13

A web of selfishness, adultery, betrayal, lies, and murder in David's life had just been exposed. His friend Nathan had turned the searing light of truth on David's secret sin. In that moment of crushing self-examination, David saw how sinful he was. Instead of withdrawing into a cocoon of self-pity, he prayed to the Lord. At this point in his prayer, David had turned the corner from ruthless self-examination to hopeful meditation. His sins were on his mind, but so was God's mercy. He knew that the remedy for his guilt wasn't self-sacrifice or a determination to make it right. No, David knew God was the only one who could save him from his sins and clean his filthy life. So David asked God to heal him. He asked for a renewed joy and revived willingness to obey.

Perhaps like David you are due for a heart exam by God. Whatever the condition of your heart, God is the only physician with an unfailing cure. ✤

PRAYER

Dear Lord, create in me a clean heart . . .

may**6**

A PRAYER FOR SPIRITUAL WISDOM

I have not stopped giving thanks for you, remembering you in my prayers. I keep asking that the God of our Lord Jesus Christ, the glorious Father, may give you the Spirit of wisdom and revelation, so that you may know him better.

EPHESIANS 1:16–17

During his stay in Rome, Paul's chains reminded him of his limitations. Although his new converts in Ephesus needed more spiritual guidance, he couldn't be there to guide them. They were miles away, while he sat chained to a Roman guard. During that time when he could do the least, Paul utilized the power of prayer. He began his letter to the Ephesians by revealing to them the pages of his prayer journal. His prayers had one theme: that the Ephesians might gain spiritual wisdom from God. Like good news in a family, a copy of his prayers was circulated among the churches in and around Ephesus.

Are there loved ones who need you to pray they'll have God's wisdom in making life's choices? Better yet, do they need to know that you pray for them on a regular basis? May Paul's heartfelt prayer lead you to pray for those you love. ❖

PRAYER

Dear Lord, I pray for wisdom for ...

may7

LOVE FOR GOD'S SANCTUARY

I wash my hands in innocence,
*   and go about your altar, LORD,*
proclaiming aloud your praise
*   and telling of all your wonderful deeds.*
LORD, I love the house where you live,
*   the place where your glory dwells.*

PSALM 26:6–8

Communion with God in our prayer will nurture a love and respect for God's people—the community of worshiping believers. David expressed such a desire in this prayer. He yearned to join God's people to worship and celebrate the Lord of the universe, who had made his home in the throne room or Most Holy Place inside the tabernacle. David could think of no better place to be than standing in God's presence, among his people, praising the Lord who cared so much for him.

Do you love his people more as a result of quiet times of prayer with God? Let David's prayer inspire you to renew your commitment to God and his church. ✤

PRAYER

Dear Lord, I love to worship you in your church . . .

may8

ASKING FORGIVENESS FOR PAST SINS

Do not remember the sins of my youth
*   and my rebellious ways;*
according to your love remember me,
*   for you, LORD, are good.*
Good and upright is the LORD;
*   therefore he instructs sinners in his ways.*
He guides the humble in what is right
*   and teaches them his way.*
All the ways of the LORD are loving and faithful
*   toward those who keep the demands of his covenant.*

PSALM 25:7–10

We all have something we've done or said in the past that we deeply regret—whether it's a caustic, unloving remark or some selfish action. Often we allow such youthful transgressions to impede our prayers, today. We dare not ask God for too much for we know we have deeply offended him. Even David had such thoughts. But instead of letting his past determine his future, David prayed for the Lord's help to overcome his past failures. He prayed that the Lord would forget the sins of his youth and asked God to teach him how to live in an upright way.

What sins still pester you? Today, ask the Lord to forgive and forget your past failures. But don't end your prayer there. Ask the Lord to teach you how to live differently. ✤

PRAYER

Dear Lord, show me the right way to deal with my problems today . . .

may9

HONORING THE GOD WHO GIVES REST

Praise be to the LORD, who has given rest to his people Israel just as he promised. Not one word has failed of all the good promises he gave through his servant Moses. May the LORD our God be with us as he was with our ancestors; may he never leave us nor forsake us.

1 KINGS 8:56–57

As King Solomon surveyed the magnificent Temple God had allowed him to build in Jerusalem, he reflected on how much the Lord had blessed his people. His ancestors had wandered the deserts as nomads for decades, but now the Israelites owned their own land. In earlier generations, they had endured several invasions, but now they enjoyed peace. Solomon wisely recognized that this was from the Lord's hand. He praised God for not only given them land, food, and shelter, but also a time of rest from their enemies. What a marvelous God! Not one of God's promises had failed—through all those generations!

Pause now to review your life. How has God blessed you? How has he provided you with food and shelter? In what ways has he given you rest? List God's blessings to your family. Remind yourself of God's promise to give believers an eternal rest from the sufferings of this world. Then, offer your praise to the God who is faithful. ❖

PRAYER

Praise God, not one word has failed of all his wonderful promises. May God never forsake my family . . .

FINDING SECURITY IN GOD'S PRESENCE

So I said:

> *"Do not take me away, my God, in the midst of my days;*
> *your years go on through all generations.*
> *In the beginning you laid the foundations of the earth,*
> *and the heavens are the work of your hands.*
> *They will perish, but you remain;*
> *they will all wear out like a garment.*
> *Like clothing you will change them*
> *and they will be discarded.*
> *But you remain the same,*
> *and your years will never end.*
> *The children of your servants will live in your presence;*
> *their descendants will be established before you."*

PSALM 102:24–28

This prayer reflects the lament of someone in great distress—no name or story attached. The words could be a journal entry of almost anyone whose problems are overwhelming. And yet, this troubled soul, after pouring out his problems before the Lord, sees a ray of hope in his desperate situation: He remembers he is a child of God, whose Protector is the eternal Lord. God transcends not only our problems, but also all of space and time. God's plan is to rescue us from the evils of this world to live eternally in God's secure presence.

If today you see the temporary treasures, relationships and circumstances of this life fading fast, take this prayer as your own. Voice your concerns to God and, then, thank him for providing stability in your ever-changing world. ❖

PRAYER

Dear Lord, I thank you for being the security in my life . . .

may11

PLACING ONE'S HOPE IN GOD

For you have been my hope, Sovereign LORD,
my confidence since my youth.
From birth I have relied on you;
you brought me forth from my mother's womb.
I will ever praise you.
I have become a sign to many;
you are my strong refuge.
My mouth is filled with your praise,
declaring your splendor all day long.

Psalm 71:5 – 8

This prayer may be from the aging King David, who looked back over his life and praised God for being ever present throughout his life. He thanked God for comforting and protecting him in his youth when almost everyone had abandoned him, as well as upholding him in his old age. The essence of David's experience with God was hope. God gave him hope when everything else was going wrong.

How would you describe God's role in your life thus far? Savior? Strength? Comfort? Through prayer, we can daily communicate our hope in God and reaffirm our love for him. Do you have your word in mind now? Whisper it in prayer as a quiet affirmation of his role in your life. ✣

PRAYER

Dear Lord, you alone are my hope. I trust in you . . .

HANNAH'S PRAISE FOR GOD

"The LORD brings death and makes alive;
he brings down to the grave and raises up.
The LORD sends poverty and wealth;
he humbles and he exalts.
He raises the poor from the dust
and lifts the needy from the ash heap;
he seats them with princes
and has them inherit a throne of honor.
"For the foundations of the earth are the LORD's;
on them he has set the world."

1 SAMUEL 2:6–8

How easy it would have been for Hannah to use the birth of her son Samuel as an occasion for pride. She could have easily felt vengeful and triumphant over her rival, Peninnah. Hannah had not only a son, but also the love of the husband they shared. Plagued for years by Peninnah, Hannah could have found solace in spewing back sharp words. Instead of doing this, she offered her praise and thanks to God for answering her prayer for a son, for lifting her up out of her despair.

When faced with a troubling or difficult situation, do you find yourself embittered? Or are you inclined to prayer? Are you tempted to speak your mind? Remember Hannah's prayer and example before you do. Speak to God instead. ✤

PRAYER

Dear Lord, I praise you for honoring and lifting me up ...

may13

PRAISING GOD FOR STRENGTH

Let them praise the name of the LORD,
for his name alone is exalted;
his splendor is above the earth and the heavens.
And he has raised up for his people a horn,
the praise of all his faithful servants,
of Israel, the people close to his heart.
Praise the LORD.

PSALM 148:13–14

This prayer summons all creation to praise the power and glory of our God. Although we as mere humans live with our weaknesses and limitations, this prayer reminds us of God's supernatural strength. Where else would we find comparable power? Nowhere. Therefore, all creation praises God for his name alone is "exalted." Our possessions, prestige, even our friends and family can't save us from our troubles. God is bigger than our earthly problems and provides strength to endure hardships and overcome temptations. No prayer is powerless, for prayer connects us with the ultimate power of the universe.

So, as you approach God in prayer today, repeat the words of this psalm as a testament to his strength. ✤

PRAYER

Dear Lord, I praise you for making me strong ...

AN APPEAL FOR HELP

Surely God is my help;
the Lord is the one who sustains me.
Let evil recoil on those who slander me;
in your faithfulness destroy them.
I will sacrifice a freewill offering to you;
I will praise your name, LORD, for it is good.
You have delivered me from all my troubles,
and my eyes have looked in triumph on my foes.

PSALM 54:4, 6–7

David prayed these words when he was on the run. He was fleeing from the murderous grasp of King Saul because the people living in the Desert of Ziph had revealed David's location. Because of their betrayal, Saul's men were hot on David's trail. It is a story fit for a movie—a desperate man fleeing for his life because of the betrayal of his so-called friends. Such a person doesn't hold back when asking for help. He throws himself in the arms of his rescuers.

When you face a serious problem, feel entirely alone, or are betrayed by someone you trusted, calm your soul by appealing to God for help. When you face a crisis, turn to your Helper in prayer, asking him to rescue you. ✤

PRAYER

Dear Lord, I need you to come to my rescue today . . .

CELEBRATING FULFILLED PROMISES

> "You, LORD, are my lamp;
>> the LORD turns my darkness into light.
> With your help I can advance against a troop;
>> with my God I can scale a wall.
> "As for God, his way is perfect:
>> The LORD's word is flawless;
>> he shields all who take refuge in him.
> For who is God besides the LORD?
>> And who is the Rock except our God?
> It is God who arms me with strength
>> and keeps my way secure.
> He makes my feet like the feet of a deer;
>> he causes me to stand on the heights."

2 SAMUEL 22:29–34

Do you keep your word? Although we strive to follow through on our promises, we all fall short at one time or another. Not so with our God! Toward the end of his reign, King David praised God, proclaiming, "The LORD's word is flawless." Then, he used a series of wonderful images to illustrate how dependable God was to him. God's love is as solid as a rock. God is like a protective shield for those who look to him for protection. With wisdom, he leads his people along the mountain heights like a surefooted deer. These images imply danger and difficult circumstances. God does not insulate us from all trouble, but he enables us to stay faithful to him. Among all the false objects of worship that people may venerate—wealth, security, power, or fame, only the Lord is truly God. The others are impostors, incapable of keeping their word.

Today, whether your circumstances put you in bright sunshine or dark shadow, consider the trustworthiness of your God and offer him your worship in prayer. ❖

PRAYER

Lord God, all of your promises prove true …

GIVING THANKS MORNING AND NIGHT

> *It is good to praise the LORD*
> *and make music to your name, O Most High,*
> *proclaiming your love in the morning*
> *and your faithfulness at night,*
> *to the music of the ten-stringed lyre*
> *and the melody of the harp.*
> *For you make me glad by your deeds, LORD;*
> *I sing for joy at what your hands have done.*

PSALM 92:1–4

What a way to start the day! This psalm was one of the first prayers on the priests' lips on the Sabbath day: "You make me glad by your deeds, LORD."

What if before you read your morning paper, before you head out the door, before you start the countless tasks you have to do for each day, you determine that you're going to start your day with praise for how God has made you glad? Right now, you have the chance to start afresh. A new spring day is before you. Why not start things off right with a regimen of praise instead of the old routine? In prayer today, proclaim his "love in the morning" and tonight, before going to bed, praise him again for his faithfulness. A perfect start and a perfect ending to a day that, with prayer, takes on new significance. ✤

PRAYER

Dear Lord, I praise you for your unfailing love in the morning . . .

may**17**

DAVID'S PRAYER FOR CLEANSING

Have mercy on me, O God,
according to your unfailing love;
according to your great compassion
blot out my transgressions.
Wash away all my iniquity
and cleanse me from my sin.
For I know my transgressions,
and my sin is always before me.
Against you, you only, have I sinned
and done what is evil in your sight;
so you are right in your verdict
and justified when you judge.

PSALM 51:1−4

Sometimes a prayer for simple forgiveness seems inadequate. Our sins feel like an indelible stain. When the prophet Nathan confronted King David with his sin of adultery with Bathsheba and his murder of her husband, David was convicted. He didn't have to be persuaded of the justice of God's case against him. Despite the harm he had done to specific people and to the honor of the nation, his greatest concern was for the damage he had caused to his relationship with the Lord.

When you feel the Holy Spirit convicting you of sin, make sure your first concern is the disruption of your relationship with God. Like David, concur wholeheartedly with God's judgment and cast yourself upon his compassion. He alone is the one who can cleanse and purify you. ✤

PRAYER

Dear God, wash me clean from my guilt. Purify me from my sin, for I recognize my shameful deeds ...

JOYFUL PRAISES TO GOD

> *Shout for joy to God, all the earth!*
> *Sing the glory of his name;*
> *make his praise glorious.*
> *Say to God, "How awesome are your deeds!*
> *So great is your power*
> *that your enemies cringe before you.*
> *All the earth bows down to you;*
> *they sing praise to you,*
> *they sing the praises of your name."*

PSALM 66:1 – 4

God answers prayer! And when he does, we should shout out his praises and give him thanks. Psalm 66 was written after a great victory in battle. Perhaps, like many of Israel's victories, it had been won against all odds. Clearly, in these circumstances, God's people saw his miraculous intervention on their behalf. They wanted to tell one another, tell the world, and tell God himself how great he was. What joy to be aligned with God, who makes his enemies cringe!

Often, our prayers are heartfelt and fervent when we are petitioning God about some pressing need. But may our gratitude overflow with equal zeal when we see answers to those prayers. ✤

PRAYER

Shout joyful praises to God, all the earth! ...

may**19**

JESUS' PRAISE FOR GOD'S WAYS

At that time Jesus said, "I praise you, Father, Lord of heaven and earth, because you have hidden these things from the wise and learned, and revealed them to little children. Yes, Father, for this is what you were pleased to do."

MATTHEW 11:25–26

When Jesus walked this earth, he prayed within the hearing of his disciples. We might well assume that he did this for their instruction. In this prayer, Jesus thanked God for his marvelous ways. Indeed, God's ways are inscrutable to many people, especially those who think they are self-sufficient and already know enough. Often those who are wise in the ways of this world or have achieved power, don't have enough time for God. The Lord, however, chooses to ignore the powerful of this world. Instead, he reveals his truth to those who are humble and willing to listen to him. God prizes a heart that is humbled before him and eager to learn his ways.

Praise God that he reveals his truth to anyone who comes to him to learn. May God give us tender and receptive hearts to approach the Lord in humility and trust. May we learn to seek wisdom and knowledge in God. ❖

PRAYER

Dear God, thank you for hiding the truth from those who think themselves so wise and clever and for revealing it to the childlike ...

PRAISE FOR THE GOD WHO ANSWERS

> *I love the LORD, for he heard my voice;*
> *he heard my cry for mercy.*
> *Because he turned his ear to me,*
> *I will call on him as long as I live.*
>
> Psalm 116:1–2

Children easily discern which adults are going to pay attention to them and who will likely tune them out. This prayer pictures God as one who "turned his ear to me." Like a caring father, he comes down to our level to let us know that we are heard, cared about, and valued. Like that discerning child, we can continue to come to God in prayer because he has proven to be trustworthy. He hears; but not only that, he answers too. If we are not receiving an answer to our petitions, we can gain perspective, patience, and faith by reminding ourselves of all the times he *has* answered.

How the Lord deserves our adoration and trust! May God grant us eyes to see the trustworthiness of his character. ❖

PRAYER

I love the Lord because he hears and answers my prayers . . .

RECOGNIZING GOD'S MIRACLES

> *How great are your works, LORD,*
> *how profound your thoughts!*
> *Senseless people do not know,*
> *fools do not understand,*
> *that though the wicked spring up like grass*
> *and all evildoers flourish,*
> *they will be destroyed forever.*
> *But you, LORD, are forever exalted.*

PSALM 92:5 – 8

Eternity provides us with an excellent measuring against the present. When we consider God's unlimited power and glory, the problems of this earthly life are cut down to size. "Though the wicked spring up like grass and all evildoers flourish, they will be destroyed forever." The story never ends with the wicked enjoying success. We know that in every case God will triumph over his enemies. His kingdom and authority are forever, while the success of the wicked quickly vanishes. Every other power on earth, no matter how formidable it may seem, won't last in its rebellion against the Lord of all creation.

Our God is a rock that cannot be moved. He will last forever. Let us join our voices in exalting his name. ✤

PRAYER

Dear Lord, you are exalted in the heavens. You continue forever . . .

PRAYING FOR EYES TO OPEN

And Elisha prayed, "Open his eyes, LORD, so that he may see." Then the LORD opened the servant's eyes, and he looked and saw the hills full of horses and chariots of fire all around Elisha.

As the enemy came down toward him, Elisha prayed to the LORD, "Strike this army with blindness." So he struck them with blindness, as Elisha had asked.

2 KINGS 6:17 – 18

Elisha the prophet had a price on his head. The king of Aram was tired of the prophet warning the king of Israel every time he tried to set an ambush for the Israelites. So this king decided to go after Elisha. Elisha's servant went out and saw all of the enemy troops amassed against his master and began to despair. But Elisha prayed simply that the servant's eyes would be opened. In answer, God allowed this servant's eyes to see the awesome forces of God surrounding them and protecting them. Then Elisha, whose own faith must have been very great, asked God to blind the enemy. Again, God answered immediately and powerfully.

If you ever find yourself overwhelmed by the forces gathered against you, as Elisha's servant was, pray for your own eyes to be opened. Ask God to show you how his power is protecting you. ✤

PRAYER

O Lord, open my eyes and let me see ...

may23

COMMITTING OURSELVES TO GOD'S WORD

Your word is a lamp for my feet,
*   a light on my path.*
I have taken an oath and confirmed it,
*   that I will follow your righteous laws.*
I have suffered much;
*   preserve my life, LORD, according to your word.*
Accept, LORD, the willing praise of my mouth,
*   and teach me your laws.*
Though I constantly take my life in my hands,
*   I will not forget your law.*

PSALM 119:105 – 109

In this psalm, a lamp symbolizes the guidance, wisdom, and knowledge that come from God's Word. Just as a lamp helps a traveler in the darkness, "Your word is a lamp for my feet, a light on my path." In this life, we walk through a dark forest of evil. But the Bible can be our light to show us the way, so we don't stumble as we walk. The psalmist prayed that God might give him more light—more understanding of God's Word—to keep him on the path of life.

Ask God to reveal the false values and philosophies that you hold, to show you wrong choices you have made, and to guide you through circumstances that may trip up your spiritual life. Recommit yourself to God's Word as the psalmist did: "Though I constantly take my life in my hands, I will not forget your law." ♣

PRAYER

Dear Lord, your word is a lamp for my feet and a light for my path ...

FLEEING TO GOD IN THE DAY OF DISTRESS

> *But I will sing of your strength,*
> *in the morning I will sing of your love;*
> *for you are my fortress,*
> *my refuge in times of trouble.*
> *You are my strength, I sing praise to you;*
> *you, God, are my fortress,*
> *my God on whom I can rely.*

PSALM 59:16–17

Human love is equally a source of great joy as well as great pain. Sometimes we bring pain upon ourselves because our love is fickle and fallible. God's love, in contrast, is *unfailing*! David wrote one of his great songs for worship on this theme. He sang the praises of God's power as well as his love. Because of who he is, he is a safe haven for us in the "day of distress." The day of distress for David was the day when King Saul sent men to wait outside his home to kill him. On that day, David called out to God. He learned that God was his "strength," and he praised the Lord for a love that never failed him.

What was your own day of distress like? In your personal "day of distress," find your strength and your hiding place in the God who loves you unfailingly. ✤

PRAYER

You, O God, are my fortress. You are the one on whom I can rely . . .

A PRAYER FOR THE WHOLE EARTH

May God be gracious to us and bless us
and make his face shine on us —
so that your ways may be known on earth,
your salvation among all nations.
May the peoples praise you, God;
may all the peoples praise you.

PSALM 67:1 – 3

God's salvation was meant not only for his chosen people, Israel, but also for all the peoples of the earth. This prayer first asks God to show his favor to Israel. Such a prayer is understandable. It resembles how we pray for ourselves and those we love. But the psalmist goes on to ask that God's ways and his saving power would be made known "among all nations." The cry of his heart was that God would receive the praises due him from all nations — not just Israel. Some of these nations were, at the time, Israel's enemies. But the psalmist didn't pray that God's power and glory would overwhelm them; he prayed that they would know God's salvation. The birth, death, and resurrection of his Son answered this prayer. When Jesus ascended into heaven, he told his friends, "Repentance for the forgiveness of sins will be preached in his name to all nations, beginning at Jerusalem" (Luke 24:47).

May God grant us the understanding of his will so that we, too, will pray for the salvation of all nations. ✤

PRAYER

May your ways be known throughout the earth, your saving power among people everywhere . . .

may**26**

MOSES' PRAYER OF PRAISE

The LORD is a warrior;
the LORD is his name.
Pharaoh's chariots and his army
he has hurled into the sea.
The best of Pharaoh's officers
are drowned in the Red Sea.
The deep waters have covered them;
they sank to the depths like a stone.
Your right hand, LORD,
was majestic in power.
Your right hand, LORD,
shattered the enemy.

EXODUS 15:3–6

The Israelites had been slaves for generations—totally at the mercy of their Egyptian masters. Only after God struck the Egyptians with a series of plagues did Pharaoh agreed to let them go. But after the Israelites set off into the desert, Pharaoh changed his mind again and pursued them with chariots and horsemen. How terrified they must have been! Yet, God miraculously pushed back the Red Sea; and when the Israelites had all made it to the other side, he closed it back on the Egyptians. Suddenly, their military might didn't matter at all. God had shown himself to be the Ruler of all nations and the Deliverer of Israel. This miracle inspired awe in the hearts of the Israelites, and so they praised him for it.

Today, this miracle stands as a symbol of our own deliverance from sin. He is the God of the helpless. He is undaunted by the strength of the proud; and for this, he deserves our heartfelt praise. ✤

PRAYER

Your right hand, O Lord, is glorious in power . . .

MAY EVERYONE PRAISE THE LORD

Praise the LORD.
  Praise the LORD, you his servants;
  praise the name of the LORD.
Let the name of the LORD be praised,
  both now and forevermore.
From the rising of the sun to the place where it sets,
  the name of the LORD is to be praised.
The LORD is exalted over all the nations,
  his glory above the heavens.

PSALM 113:1−4

The God we worship reigns over all nations. He is the God of the poor and rich alike, for people of all races and nationalities. Our God is also the Lord of all time—from the time of Abraham's day to our own. This prayer calls on people everywhere and in every age to bless the name of the Lord. Why is he worthy of our continual praise? Because he is "exalted over all the nations" and "his glory is above the heavens."

When you approach God in prayer today, first praise him for being Lord in all times and all places. Then, your prayers, rather than being small and selfish, will be better aligned with God's character and his purposes for the whole earth. Praise him forever and ever. ❖

PRAYER

Dear Lord, you are high above the nations; your glory is far greater than the heavens …

AWE FOR THE ALL-POWERFUL KING

Ascribe to the LORD, all you families of nations,
ascribe to the LORD glory and strength.
Ascribe to the LORD the glory due his name;
bring an offering and come into his courts.
Worship the LORD in the splendor of his holiness;
tremble before him, all the earth.
Say among the nations, "The LORD reigns."
The world is firmly established, it cannot be moved;
he will judge the peoples with equity.

PSALM 96:7 – 10

In the presence of powerful people, the typical reaction is awe. How much more should we experience reverence and fear before the all-powerful Lord of the universe! Throughout Scripture, people who have caught a glimpse of God's glory have fallen facedown before him. Abraham, Moses, Aaron, Joshua, King David, and even the disciples Peter, James, and John reacted this way to an encounter with the Almighty. But our response should never stop there. Psalm 96 encourages us to "ascribe to the LORD the glory due his name." We do so by bringing offerings to him, worshiping him in public gatherings, and telling others the good news. "Tell all the nations that the Lord is king," declares the writer. His glory and power is revealed in all of creation and in the way he controls all the nations: "The world is firmly established, it cannot be moved." God "will judge the peoples with equity."

Use your personal prayer time to worship God and express your awe at his greatness. ♣

PRAYER

Dear Lord, I will worship the Lord in all his holy splendor. Let all the earth tremble before him ...

HEZEKIAH'S PRAYER FOR DELIVERANCE

And Hezekiah prayed to the LORD: "LORD, the God of Israel, enthroned between the cherubim, you alone are God over all the kingdoms of the earth. You have made heaven and earth. Give ear, LORD, and hear; open your eyes, LORD, and see; listen to the words Sennacherib has sent to ridicule the living God....

"Now, LORD our God, deliver us from his hand, so that all the kingdoms of the earth may know that you alone, LORD, are God."

2 KINGS 19:15 – 16, 19

When King Hezekiah ruled in Jerusalem, the Assyrians were the scourge of the peoples around them. Their king, Sennacherib, scoffed at Judah's faith in God. He taunted them with arrogant claims that their God would as powerless against the advancing Assyrian army as had been the gods of every other nation the Assyrians had conquered. When Hezekiah went to ask for God's help, he appealed, in a sense, to God's reputation. He asked God to clear his own name and to prove Sennacherib wrong in his predictions. Hezekiah understood that his nation was weak in comparison with these conquerors. But he also knew that God was capable of defending his own name.

There may be instances when, with all humility and holy fear, we can ask God to intervene on our behalf in order to defend the holiness of *his* name. At those times, don't be afraid to ask God to defend his reputation by saving you. ✤

PRAYER

Now, O God, deliver me from ...

CELEBRATING GOD'S POWER

All your works praise you, LORD;
your faithful people extol you.
They tell of the glory of your kingdom
and speak of your might,
so that all people may know of your mighty acts
and the glorious splendor of your kingdom.
Your kingdom is an everlasting kingdom,
and your dominion endures through all generations.
The LORD is trustworthy in all he promises
and faithful in all he does.

PSALM 145:10–13

David couldn't stop praising the extraordinary reign of the Lord over all of creation. God's power was so awesome to David that he couldn't imagine only people praising God's goodness. In this prayer, David described all of creation as praising the Lord: "All your works praise you, LORD." He portrayed God's people and all of God's creation excitedly celebrating instances of God's power, and telling others of the wonderful deeds the Lord had done.

Look around you today. Imagine all of creation—including the wild flowers of the fields—expressing in their own non-verbal ways their thanks to God. Join in that chorus with your own expression of thanks to your Creator. ✤

PRAYER

All of your works will thank you, Lord, and your faithful followers will bless you . . .

PRAYING FOR GOD'S CORRECTION

LORD, I know that people's lives are not their own;
it is not for them to direct their steps.
Discipline me, LORD, but only in due measure—
not in your anger,
or you will reduce me to nothing.

JEREMIAH 10:23–24

When we get impatient for God to show us what he wants us to do, it's so easy to move ahead with our own plans. When that happens, we lose perspective, and we need someone to correct us. We need someone to tell us we're off course and need to change directions. It's not always easy to accept that correction, but it's necessary. Jeremiah must have sensed that he was making his own plans and following his own way. "Discipline me, LORD, but only in due measure," he prayed. "Not in your anger, or you will reduce me to nothing."

The Lord has a plan for us, a course he wants us to follow. When we get "off course," we would do well to pray as Jeremiah did and ask the Lord to make the necessary correction in our life. ♣

PRAYER

Heavenly Father, somehow I've gotten off course. Correct me, Lord. Get me back on the right path . . .

DECLARING GOD'S AWESOME POWER

> *To him who rides across the highest heavens, the ancient heavens,*
> *who thunders with mighty voice.*
> *Proclaim the power of God,*
> *whose majesty is over Israel,*
> *whose power is in the heavens.*
> *You, God, are awesome in your sanctuary;*
> *the God of Israel gives power and strength to his people.*
> *Praise be to God!*

PSALM 68:33–35

In this prayer, David attempted to find images that would adequately describe God's power and might. His desire was that the whole assembly of God's people would raise their voices as one to praise the God of Israel. So he used the sun and thunder as illustrations of God's power—"to him who rides across the highest heavens, the ancient heavens" and "who thunders with mighty voice." God embodies the power that gives brilliance to the sun and the terrifying noise of thunderclaps of a stormy day. And remarkably, he gives power and strength to his people. Surely the Almighty is worthy of praise.

We, too, can receive God's power and strength just as David did. Take time today to meditate on his power. Find an image that communicates power and strength in an awesome way to you personally—whether it be the sturdiness of a rocky mountain cliff or the power of the deep ocean currents. Then, use that image to praise the Almighty. ✤

PRAYER

O God of Israel, you give power and strength to your people . . .

june2

DEBORAH'S PRAISE FOR GOD'S VICTORY

Hear this, you kings! Listen, you rulers!
I, even I, will sing to the LORD;
I will praise the LORD, the God of Israel, in song.
When you, LORD, went out from Seir,
when you marched from the land of Edom,
the earth shook, the heavens poured,
the clouds poured down water.
The mountains quaked before the LORD, the One of Sinai,
before the LORD, the God of Israel.

JUDGES 5:3 – 5

Deborah wasn't the type of woman to wait for someone else to do God's work. When God told her that the Israelites should attack Sisera's army, she immediately gave Balak the news. And when Balak hesitated, she encouraged him by marching into battle with him. Her courage and trust in God inspired Israel to win the battle. Another woman, Jael, killed the enemy, Sisera, when she had the chance. At the victory celebration, Deborah took the lead again. She didn't take all the glory for herself. Neither did she praise Balak or Jael for their courage. She praised the Almighty for the victory. In the presence of God, the mountains quake; and he makes that same power available to his people.

Where has God given you a victory in your life? Where has he shown his power? Praise the Lord for working in your life and tell others how great he is. ✤

PRAYER

Dear Lord, the mountains quake at your coming . . .

TRUSTING IN GOD'S JUSTICE

> *My shield is God Most High,*
> *who saves the upright in heart.*
> *God is a righteous judge,*
> *a God who displays his wrath every day....*
> *I will give thanks to the LORD because of his righteousness;*
> *I will sing the praises of the name of the LORD Most High.*

> PSALM 7:10–11, 17

Often we turn to God in prayer when we are facing a complicated and difficult circumstance. David was facing such a situation. A man named Cush from the tribe of Benjamin had accused him of wrongdoing. The members of the tribe of Benjamin had never been willing subjects of David, for David had overthrown the dynasty of Saul—a Benjamite. Apparently Cush, a life-long enemy of David, had found an opportunity to accuse him. David didn't respond to Cush's accusations with counteraccusations. Instead, he brought his case before God, the perfect Judge. David's prayer demonstrated a complete reliance on God. He trusted God's ability to judge this situation correctly and defend his cause. He was confident that no matter what the current circumstances were, God would have the final word.

When have you felt unjustly accused? Are there people in your life who seem out to get you? Commit these situations and people to the God who promises to bring justice to this earth. ✤

PRAYER

Dear Lord, I thank you for being just. I place my life in your hands, trusting in your justice and mercy...

june4

PRAISE FOR ANSWERED PRAYER

I will praise you, LORD, with all my heart;
before the "gods" I will sing your praise.
I will bow down toward your holy temple
and will praise your name
for your unfailing love and your faithfulness,
for you have so exalted your solemn decree
that it surpasses your fame.
When I called, you answered me;
you greatly emboldened me.

PSALM 138:1–3

God answers prayers. He is faithful. But all too often, we don't look for the ways God is working in our lives. We abandon our prayers, don't look for answers, and forget to thank him. It's clear from this psalm that David kept track of what he prayed for and how God had answered him. The long list of answered prayers in David's life inspired him to thank the Lord. Here, David thanked God with all his being for answering his prayers. He didn't simply offer a quick "thank you" sandwiched between a long list of needs. He sang his thanks to God, bowed before God in reverence, and offered an animal sacrifice as a thank offering. His thanksgiving included gestures and symbols, incense and music.

This week, express your thanks to God in an unique way. Use what you love to do—whether it's gardening, woodworking, cooking, or playing an instrument—to express your thanks to the Lord. ✤

PRAYER

Dear Lord, I give you thanks with all my heart ...

june5

TO GOD BE THE GLORY

> Not to us, LORD, not to us
>> but to your name be the glory,
>> because of your love and faithfulness.
> Why do the nations say,
>> "Where is their God?"
> Our God is in heaven;
>> he does whatever pleases him.

PSALM 115:1 – 3

In the cycle of the growing seasons, June is often the waiting time. The crops have been planted, the spring rains have fallen, and fall's bounty is now in God's hands. The waiting time can bring questions. Will the crops grow? Will God provide for us? On a global scale, as history trudges on and we await Christ's return, we may hear people ask, "Where is their God?" How quickly people forget that God will not be held accountable to them nor will he be rushed into accomplishing his plans. God has given people abundant reasons to trust him. Only arrogance would demand God continue to prove himself again and again.

When we're tempted to question God, perhaps we can instead respond "Your will be done, on earth as it is in heaven" (Matthew 6:10). ❖

PRAYER

Dear Lord, you are in the heavens, and you do as you wish. May you receive the glory . . .

june6

MANOAH'S PRAYER FOR INSTRUCTION

Then Manoah prayed to the LORD: "Pardon your servant, Lord. I beg you to let the man of God you sent to us come again to teach us how to bring up the boy who is to be born."

God heard Manoah, and the angel of God came again to the woman while she was out in the field; but her husband Manoah was not with her.

JUDGES 13:8-9

Manoah and his wife were surprised by the news that they would be the parents of a special son. For this infertile couple, the possibility of pregnancy was unexpected enough. Yet, God had even greater plans. Manoah wisely recognized that he needed more instruction on how to handle the responsibilities for raising this special boy. So Manoah simply prayed, "Teach us how to bring up the boy," and God answered by sending an angel.

Unexpected developments often reveal our inadequacies. When they do, our spiritual maturity will be measured by our willingness to ask God for help. "If any of you lacks wisdom, you should ask God, who gives generously to all without finding fault, and it will be given to you" (James 1:5). ♣

PRAYER

Dear Lord, teach me more about ...

june7

WAITING ON THE LORD

Truly my soul finds rest in God;
*   my salvation comes from him.*
Truly he is my rock and my salvation;
*   he is my fortress, I will never be shaken.*
How long will you assault me?
Would all of you throw me down—
*   this leaning wall, this tottering fence?...*
Yes, my soul, find rest in God;
*   my hope comes from him.*

PSALM 62:1–3, 5

Surrounded by enemies, David felt like a broken-down wall, ready to collapse at any time. Just as a tottering fence can't withstand the battering of a persistent bull, David knew he couldn't withstand the attacks of his enemies. David didn't bemoan his circumstances. He didn't frantically try to counter every assault and every lie. Instead, he quietly waited on the Lord—the only one who could deliver him.

When you feel surrounded by your enemies and feel broken, express your feelings and concerns to God. But also resolve to trust the Lord to deliver you no matter what situation comes your way today. ✤

PRAYER

Dear Lord, I wait quietly before you, for my hope is in you ...

PRAISE FOR THE GOD BEYOND COMPARISON

Who is like the LORD our God,
the One who sits enthroned on high,
who stoops down to look
on the heavens and the earth?
He raises the poor from the dust
and lifts the needy from the ash heap;
he seats them with princes,
with the princes of his people.
He settles the childless woman in her home
as a happy mother of children.
Praise the LORD.

PSALM 113:5–9

Who can be compared to God? Comparisons only work between things in the same category. It's foolish to compare the speed of a runner with the speed of an ice skater. The two are participating in entirely different types of races. We run into the same problem when it comes to God. There is no one in God's category! Who is strong enough for us to be able to compare that person to the Almighty? The only way we can describe our Infinite God is to recount what he has done for his people. He has lifted up the poor out of poverty. He has given children to the barren. Who else could do such things?

Remind yourself of how great God is. Recount the ways God has worked in your life and the life of others. Then, praise the Lord for his love and concern for you. ♣

PRAYER

Dear Lord, who can I compare you to? You are so powerful and great . . .

REJOICING IN GOD'S WORK

At that time Jesus, full of joy through the Holy Spirit, said, "I praise you, Father, Lord of heaven and earth, because you have hidden these things from the wise and learned, and revealed them to little children. Yes, Father, for this is what you were pleased to do.

"All things have been committed to me by my Father. No one knows who the Son is except the Father, and no one knows who the Father is except the Son and those to whom the Son chooses to reveal him."

LUKE 10:21–22

When we experience success — whether it's completing a long project, toilet training a child, gaining a new position — it's natural to celebrate. But sometimes when others experience success, we reluctantly congratulate them. We harbor a little envy in our hearts. Jesus didn't act this way. When his seventy-two disciples came back from teaching and performing miracles in the countryside of Israel, he rejoiced with them over what God had empowered them to do. During this celebration, Jesus prayed. He directed the thoughts of his disciples to the one who deserved all the glory for their success: God. It wasn't the disciples' wisdom or cleverness that made them useful in God's work. No, it was simply God's marvelous and wonderful plan.

List some ways God has used believers in churches in your area to advance God's work. Thank God for using these people; and take some time this week to jot a note of encouragement to one person in particular. ✤

PRAYER

Dear Lord, thank you for revealing your truth to the childlike. Thank you for using...

IN AWE OF GOD

The heavens praise your wonders, LORD,
*   your faithfulness too, in the assembly of the holy ones.*
For who in the skies above can compare with the LORD?
*   Who is like the LORD among the heavenly beings?*
In the council of the holy ones God is greatly feared;
*   he is more awesome than all who surround him.*
Who is like you, LORD God Almighty?
*   You, LORD, are mighty, and your faithfulness surrounds you.*

PSALM 89:5–8

People have always been fascinated by angels. The thought of compassionate spirit beings watching over us comforts many. But when Scripture describes people meeting angels, it uniformly depicts the person in shock and awe. The glory and power of these beings are beyond our imaginations. Yet angelic glory is only a reflection of the glory of their Creator. Angels, as awesome as they may be, owe reverence and praise to the even mightier Lord of the heavens. In this prayer, the psalmist exalted and honored God by contemplating heaven's throne room, where the greatest angelic powers bow in awe before the Lord.

God alone is worthy of our worship. Reflect on what it will be like to join the myriads of angels in exalting and praising God. Offer your praise to God today. ✤

PRAYER

Dear Lord, I want to join my voice and heart to those of the myriad of angels who praise you ...

PONDERING GOD'S PRECIOUS THOUGHTS

How precious to me are your thoughts, God!
How vast is the sum of them!
Were I to count them,
they would outnumber the grains of sand—
when I awake, I am still with you.

PSALM 139:17–18

When a couple falls in love, they fondly think about each other many times throughout the day. Can you relate? They look forward to the time when they can be together again, when they can read the joy in each other's faces, when they can enjoy each other's presence again. During the times when they are apart, they try to imagine what each other is doing; and they make note of experiences they would like to share with each other later. If thoughts of lovers are so consumed with each other, how much more are God's thoughts focused on us—the ones he loves with eternal love! God's thoughts about *you*, an individual he has created, are "precious" and "vast," outnumbering "the grains of sand."

Take some time to ponder and marvel at the immensity of God's love for you. Thank him for caring about you. ✤

PRAYER

How precious are your thoughts about me, O God...

june**12**

REJOICING IN GOD'S LAWS

I have hidden your word in my heart
that I might not sin against you.
Praise be to you, LORD;
teach me your decrees.
With my lips I recount
all the laws that come from your mouth.
I rejoice in following your statutes
as one rejoices in great riches.
I meditate on your precepts
and consider your ways.

PSALM 119:11–15

Psalm 119 is a long prayer that celebrates God's law. Why would anyone rejoice over laws? Most of us find laws restricting. They tell us what we can't do. But the psalmist praised God's laws. He even committed himself to a form of "studying" that few of us have ever done. He memorized them and recited them aloud. Why was he so eager to learn God's ways? Because he had discovered that in these laws there is *life!* Sin separates us from God and from the fullness of life God offers. Those who reject God's law are on a path that leads to self-destruction and death. Knowing what God's law says can keep us from sinning against him.

As you approach God in prayer today, ask him to teach you his law. Ask him to show you how you should apply it to your life. ✤

PRAYER

Dear Lord, I want to hide your word in my heart so that I might not sin against you ...

MOSES' PRAYER TO ENTER THE LAND

At that time I pleaded with the LORD: "Sovereign LORD, you have begun to show to your servant your greatness and your strong hand. For what god is there in heaven or on earth who can do the deeds and mighty works you do? Let me go over and see the good land beyond the Jordan — that fine hill country and Lebanon."

DEUTERONOMY 3:23–25

One can detect wistfulness in Moses' desperate prayer. He wanted to enter the land God had promised his people so long ago. He wanted to see the land flowing with milk and honey. But God's answer was a resounding "no." Unfortunately, Moses had allowed his anger with the Israelites to affect how he obeyed God's directions (see Numbers 20:1–13). The cost for Moses' outburst: he would never stand in the land God had promised. Even though Moses faced a "no" to his prayer, he knew God had a good plan for his life and submitted himself to it. When God says "no"; there's a reason. His "no" is always a loving "no" — a "no" that has our best interests at heart.

It's never wrong to ask God for our desires. As you approach God in prayer today, submit your longings to him. Then, ask him to prepare you for his good plan for your life. ✤

PRAYER

Dear Sovereign Lord, I too am your servant. Help me accept your good plan for me ...

EXALTING THE KING

I will exalt you, my God the King;
  I will praise your name for ever and ever.
Every day I will praise you
  and extol your name for ever and ever.
Great is the LORD and most worthy of praise;
  his greatness no one can fathom.

PSALM 145:1–3

There are many reasons to praise the Lord. Not only has he made us and given us life, but he has provided for our needs in the abundance of his creation and given us the capacity to understand his ways. He has set us into a community of believers, through which we can grow into the person he wants us to be. Above all, he has reconciled us to himself through Jesus Christ. But David here celebrated none of the above. Instead, he praised God for simply being his great King. God's position alone makes him worthy of praise! What is more, David not only praised God but *blessed him!* What an incredible thought! God receives some blessing, or benefit, as we turn to him in worship and prayer. We, who cannot add one iota of splendor to God, nevertheless bring God deep satisfaction when we praise him!

For a few moments, meditate on how God reigns not only over our earth but also over the entire cosmos. In prayer, praise and bless the great King of kings. ✤

PRAYER

I will praise you every day, O Lord, for you are most worthy of praise . . .

CONQUERING FEAR THROUGH PRAYER

The LORD is my light and my salvation—
whom shall I fear?
The LORD is the stronghold of my life—
of whom shall I be afraid?
When the wicked advance against me
to devour me,
it is my enemies and my foes
who will stumble and fall.
Though an army besiege me,
my heart will not fear;
though war break out against me,
even then I will be confident.

PSALM 27:1–3

In his first inaugural address in 1933, President Franklin D. Roosevelt tried to assure a worried nation going through the depression that "the only thing we have to fear is fear itself." Fear can be paralyzing. Fear of an uncertain future can rob us of our peace and joy; and fear of failure can keep us from stepping out on faith and doing something God wants us to do. In this prayer, David declared that even if a mighty army were to surround and attack him, he would remain confident and his heart would know no fear. David could say that because the Lord was his "light" and his "salvation." He knew the Lord would protect him from danger.

If fear threatens to paralyze you and rob you of your joy, take courage that the Lord will protect you. In prayer, place your trust in God, your Savior. ✤

PRAYER

Dear Lord, you are my light and my salvation. Take away the fear in my heart and help me to trust you more . . .

june16

BOWING LOW BEFORE THE KING

The LORD reigns,
let the nations tremble;
he sits enthroned between the cherubim,
let the earth shake.
Great is the LORD in Zion;
he is exalted over all the nations.
Let them praise your great and awesome name—
he is holy.
The King is mighty, he loves justice—
you have established equity;
in Jacob you have done
what is just and right.
Exalt the LORD our God
and worship at his footstool;
he is holy.

PSALM 99:1 – 5

"The King is mighty." The Psalms are filled with such declarations of God's reign—his just and righteous reign. The Israelites certainly knew what it was like to live under less than perfect kings—weak kings, unjust kings, and evil kings. When the rule of law breaks down in a country, injustice, fear, and terror reign. So when the psalmist proclaimed God as King in his prayer, he was acknowledging that God was ultimately in charge of the anarchy and evil he often experienced under the rule of earthly kings. He was acknowledging that his ultimate allegiance was to God—not to any worldly power.

To be a glad servant of the great King of kings should be the joy and delight of every worshiper. But too often, we want to put ourselves on the throne and have our own way. Join the psalmist in casting your crown before the King of kings in prayer. ❖

PRAYER

I exalt you, O Lord, my God. I bow before you, for you alone are King . . .

FIXING OUR THOUGHTS ON GOD

> *In that day this song will be sung in the land of Judah:*
> > *We have a strong city;*
> > *God makes salvation*
> > *its walls and ramparts.*
> *Open the gates*
> > *that the righteous nation may enter,*
> > *the nation that keeps faith.*
> *You will keep in perfect peace*
> > *those whose minds are steadfast,*
> > *because they trust in you.*
> *Trust in the LORD forever,*
> > *for the LORD, the LORD himself, is the Rock eternal.*

> ISAIAH 26:1–4

We all want to be secure — to feel safe from the attacks of strangers and enemies. In Israel, security meant living in a city with strong walls to keep out invaders. In this prayer of praise, believers proclaim that their security is in the Lord. While a stone wall may one day fall to the ground, God will be the Protector and the Savior of the righteous forever. Who or what should believers fear? They have eternal security — a security that gives them peace of mind.

How is it possible to have such peace of mind in the face of life's problems, difficulties, and pain? Fix your thoughts on your Almighty God, as this prayer instructs all of us to do. Reaffirm your trust in God today. ✤

PRAYER

Dear Lord, my thoughts are fixed on you. May I trust in you always, for you are my eternal Rock ...

june18

REJOICING IN OUR MAKER

Praise the LORD.

> *Sing to the LORD a new song,*
>   *his praise in the assembly of his faithful people.*
> *Let Israel rejoice in their Maker;*
>   *let the people of Zion be glad in their King.*
> *Let them praise his name with dancing*
>   *and make music to him with timbrel and harp.*
> *For the LORD takes delight in his people;*
>   *he crowns the humble with victory.*
> *Let his faithful people rejoice in this honor*
>   *and sing for joy on their beds.*
> *May the praise of God be in their mouths*
>   *and a double-edged sword in their hands.*

PSALM 149:1–6

Psalm 149 is the prayer of a joyful group of believers. Together in this prayer, they rejoice over one another because God is their King. Yet he isn't King over individuals; he's King over a community of faithful people. It is appropriate, then, for these believers to express their joy and lift their praises to God together, utilizing the expressive gifts God has given—dancing, singing, and playing various instruments. The message is that God takes delight in his people and saves those who humble themselves before God. Being included in this celebration has nothing to do with anyone deserving anything. It has everything to do with God's goodness.

Rejoice over the goodness of God; and reaffirm your commitment to worship the Lord in your church with the talents God has given you. ❖

PRAYER

Dear Lord, I rejoice in you, my Maker. I will sing your praises in the assembly of the faithful . . .

june19

A CRY FOR GOD'S PROTECTION

LORD, how many are my foes!
How many rise up against me!
Many are saying of me,
"God will not deliver him."
But you, LORD, are a shield around me,
my glory, the One who lifts my head high.
I call out to the LORD,
and he answers me from his holy mountain.
I lie down and sleep;
I wake again, because the LORD sustains me.

PSALM 3:1 – 5

Because David had sinned by murdering Uriah and taking his wife, Bathsheba, God had told him his own family would turn against him. In time, David's son Absalom rebelled, tried to kill David, and take over his throne. David fled for his life, hiding from his son and his powerful army. Some of his enemies were saying, "God will not deliver him." In the midst of those problems, David was able to lie down and sleep. He was unafraid because he knew God was his shield. God was watching over him.

It may seem that your enemies have risen up against you. Some may even be saying to your face, "God will not deliver you." Do what David did. Cry out to God, your shield, for his deliverance and protection. Then, lie down and sleep in peace, for God is your shield. ✤

PRAYER

Dear Lord, you know my situation. I know you are watching over me. Be my shield . . .

june20

MEDITATING ON GOD'S SPLENDOR

One generation commends your works to another;
they tell of your mighty acts.
They speak of the glorious splendor of your majesty—
and I will meditate on your wonderful works.
They tell of the power of your awesome works—
and I will proclaim your great deeds.
They celebrate your abundant goodness
and joyfully sing of your righteousness.

PSALM 145:4–7

In just these few verses of prayerful meditation, David mentioned many of God's attributes which make the Lord worthy of our praise and worship: his "majesty," his "glorious splendor," his "wonderful works," his "great deeds," "abundant goodness," and righteousness. In this same prayer, David went on to praise God for his kindness, love, mercy, and compassion. No wonder David's prayer was full of praise and adoration. No wonder he encouraged each generation to tell others of God's mighty acts. No wonder he foresaw the day when God's awe-inspiring deeds would be on every tongue.

Take few moments to mediate on God's splendor—how perfect he is, how powerful he is, how marvelous the gifts he has given you are. Focus your thoughts on how great God is, and let David's prayer of praise lead you in meditating on the Almighty. Then, tell someone else this week about what God has done for you. ✣

PRAYER

Dear God, I will meditate on your majestic splendor. Help me to share the story of your wonderful goodness with . . .

PROCLAIMING HOW PERFECT GOD IS

> *I will proclaim the name of the LORD.*
> *Oh, praise the greatness of our God!*
> *He is the Rock, his works are perfect,*
> *and all his ways are just.*
> *A faithful God who does no wrong,*
> *upright and just is he.*

DEUTERONOMY 32:3–4

God is perfect! This was the theme of the song of praise that Moses taught to the people toward the end of his life. No matter how much we admire famous people and tell about their impressive deeds and qualities, neither we nor they would ever claim perfection. But God's very name testifies to his uncompromised glory. If, as the song of Moses proclaims, "all his ways are just," then we will sometimes need to adjust our perspective on life. From our own limited vantage point, we cannot always fit the things that happen with our ideas of justice and fairness. But God does no wrong, or he would not be our perfect God! He is faithful, just, and upright. When we confess our sin or our unbelief, we confirm again that he has the answers, he alone is holy and mighty.

Join your voice with that of Moses and all believers through the centuries. Praise our holy and perfect God! ✤

PRAYER

Dear God, your work is perfect. Everything you do is just and fair ...

june**22**

REJOICING OVER OUR INHERITANCE

I say to the LORD, "You are my Lord;
  apart from you I have no good thing."
I say of the holy people who are in the land,
  "They are the noble ones in whom is all my delight."
Those who run after other gods will suffer more and more.
  I will not pour out libations of blood to such gods
  or take up their names on my lips.
LORD, you alone are my portion and my cup;
  you make my lot secure.
The boundary lines have fallen for me in pleasant places;
  surely I have a delightful inheritance.

PSALM 16:2, 5−6

We've all heard of families who are divided forever because they disagreed over an inheritance. Brothers and sisters who once loved each other spend the rest of their lives greedily fighting to protect their share of their parents' inheritance, while others go to their grave hating and resenting their siblings who got a bigger share than they did. How refreshing to hear David—with all the riches that were his as a king—say to the Lord, "The boundary lines have fallen for me in pleasant places; surely I have a delightful inheritance."

Are we satisfied with what the Lord has given us, no matter how great or small? Can we say—and really mean it—" You are my Lord; apart from you I have no good thing"? List in your mind all God has given to you. Then, rejoice over your inheritance, over all the good things God has given you. ✤

PRAYER

Dear Lord, you alone are my inheritance. All the good things I have are from you . . .

AN APPEAL FOR GOD TO LISTEN

Hear my voice when I call, LORD;
*   be merciful to me and answer me.*
My heart says of you, "Seek his face!"
*   Your face, LORD, I will seek.*
Do not hide your face from me,
*   do not turn your servant away in anger;*
*   you have been my helper.*
Do not reject me or forsake me,
*   God my Savior.*
Though my father and mother forsake me,
*   the LORD will receive me.*

PSALM 27:7–10

David went through times when he felt God had abandoned him and he was alone. In this psalm, David pleads for God to hear his prayer and answer him. We, too, will go through dark nights of the soul—when it seems there's a wall between us and God—when it feels like he is far away. We, too, will cry out with a heart of anguish, "Lord, you've told me to come and talk with you. Here I am, trying to talk to you! Are you listening? Lord, please listen to my pleading and answer me!" Even before David received an answer, as he struggled in this storm of doubt, he prayed, "Though my father and mother forsake me, the LORD will receive me." He reassured his troubled soul that God was close—no matter how he felt.

During those times when God seems so distant, we must remind ourselves that God is near to those who call out to him. ♣

PRAYER

Dear Lord, listen to my pleading. I know that even if my father and mother forsake me, you will receive me . . .

SEARCHING FOR A REFUGE

I look to you for help, O Sovereign Lord.
*   You are my refuge; don't let them kill me.*
Keep me out of the traps they have set for me,
*   out of the snares of those who do evil.*
Let the wicked fall into their own snares,
*   but let me escape.*
But my eyes are fixed on you, Sovereign LORD;
*   in you I take refuge — do not give me over to death.*
Keep me safe from the traps set by evildoers,
*   from the snares they have laid for me.*
Let the wicked fall into their own nets,
*   while I pass by in safety.*

PSALM 141:8 – 10

A newspaper story told of a lost hiker who wandered in a blinding snowstorm for hours without seeing any sign of life. Finally, exhausted, hungry, numb from the cold, and ready to give up, he saw a log cabin through the trees. While not luxurious, the abandoned cabin provided warmth and shelter until rescuers found the young man. What a welcome sight that rustic cabin must have been to that lost hiker! It was his refuge — a place of safety. That warm cabin literally saved his life. In this psalm, David described the Lord as that kind of protection — a refuge from his enemies.

It's comforting to know that when our enemies surround us, we can turn to the Lord. Today, commit your troubles to God in prayer. ✣

PRAYER

Dear Lord, I look to you for help. You are my refuge . . .

LOOKING TO GOD FOR OUR NEEDS

Your kingdom is an everlasting kingdom,
  and your dominion endures through all generations.
The LORD is trustworthy in all he promises
  and faithful in all he does.
The LORD upholds all who fall
  and lifts up all who are bowed down.
The eyes of all look to you,
  and you give them their food at the proper time.
You open your hand
  and satisfy the desires of every living thing.

PSALM 145:13–16

Life presents us with many competing demands—children ask for attention and new clothes, bosses ask for greater productivity, and spouses ask us to attend to the chores at home. While we are attending to all these responsibilities, we tend to feel as if we need more and more as well. We might even wonder if God can provide for all of our needs—whether they are spiritual, social, or material needs. But God, through his actions in the past, has demonstrated again and again that he can provide for our needs. He is in the habit of lifting the downcast from their heavy burdens—even those who have stumbled and fallen. God satisfies the hunger and thirst of "every living thing" at the proper time. What a comfort to know that the Lord will not abandon or forsake us!

Jesus said to not worry about what we need, for God will provide for our needs (Matthew 6:25–33). In prayer today, commit your worries to him and trust him to provide for you. ♣

PRAYER

Dear God, all eyes look to you for help. Open your hand and satisfy my needs ...

june**26**

PRAYING FOR STRENGTH FROM THE LORD

Then Samson prayed to the LORD, "Sovereign LORD, remember me. Please, God, strengthen me just once more, and let me with one blow get revenge on the Philistines for my two eyes." Then Samson reached toward the two central pillars on which the temple stood. Bracing himself against them, his right hand on the one and his left hand on the other, Samson said, "Let me die with the Philistines!" Then he pushed with all his might, and down came the temple on the rulers and all the people in it. Thus he killed many more when he died than while he lived.

JUDGES 16:28–30

Before Samson's birth, an angel of the Lord told his mother she would have a son. His hair was never to be cut. He was to be dedicated to God, and he was destined to rescue Israel from the Philistines. Samson was dedicated to God at birth; and he grew into a man of great strength. He served the Lord for years but later strayed away from God. Now, languishing in a Philistine prison, blind, weak, and far from God, he remembered the source of his strength. He prayed and asked God to strengthen him once again. The Lord answered his prayer, and Samson was able to win a great victory over the Philistines.

If you're not seeing any victories in your life, remember the source of your strength. Pray the God may strengthen you to win the battles you must fight. ✤

PRAYER

Dear God, I've been trying to do things in my own strength. Please remember me and strengthen me . . .

june27

LOOKING TO GOD FOR MERCY

I lift up my eyes to you,
to you who sit enthroned in heaven.
As the eyes of slaves look to the hand of their master,
as the eyes of a female slave look to the hand of her mistress,
so our eyes look to the LORD our God,
till he shows us his mercy.
Have mercy on us, LORD, have mercy on us,
for we have endured no end of contempt.

PSALM 123:1–3

One of the most difficult things to do in life is wait. Our desire is to have the finished product or get to our intended goal immediately! But the psalmist in this prayer knew that waiting on the Lord was best and would wait as long as it took to see God's mercy revealed in his life. God grants us mercy, not because we deserve it, but because he chooses to give it in his own timing. In this prayer, the psalmist described servants who keep their eyes on their master and a female slave who watches her mistress for the slightest signal. We too shall be attentive to God's leading. We should patiently wait on God for his help.

Like the servants described in this prayer, we should lift our eyes to God, looking to him for mercy. We can't earn it, and we don't deserve it. But the Lord grants us his mercy as he chooses. Remember to thank God for his kindness and mercy today. ✤

PRAYER

Dear Lord, I lift my eyes to you to find mercy …

june28

FINDING STRENGTH IN TIMES OF TROUBLE

LORD, be gracious to us;
we long for you.
Be our strength every morning,
our salvation in time of distress.
At the uproar of your army, the peoples flee;
when you rise up, the nations scatter.

ISAIAH 33:2–3

Right after this prayer for God to rescue Israel, the prophet Isaiah described Israel's desperate plight: The Assyrians had refused their petition for peace. All the land was in trouble. The roads were deserted; and no one dared to travel them anymore. Lebanon has been destroyed. The Plain of Sharon was a wilderness; and Bashan and Carmel had been plundered (Isaiah 33:7–9). Yet, Isaiah's trust in the Lord never wavered during this difficult time. Because he believed God's promise to protect and deliver his people, Isaiah could pray with confidence, "Be our strength every morning, our salvation in time of distress."

God's promises haven't changed. He is still our strength each day and our salvation in times of trouble. In our time of trouble, we can call upon him as Isaiah did. ❖

PRAYER

Dear Lord, even though I'm weak and in trouble, I believe your promise. Be my strength each day . . .

RECOGNIZING GOD'S GREATNESS

I know that the LORD is great,
that our Lord is greater than all gods.
The LORD does whatever pleases him,
in the heavens and on the earth,
in the seas and all their depths. . . .
Your name, LORD, endures forever,
your renown, LORD, through all generations.
For the LORD will vindicate his people
and have compassion on his servants.

PSALM 135:5–6, 13–14

What is greatness? The writer of Psalm 135 contrasted the greatness of the living God with the pagan gods that were worshiped at his time. Simply put, there is no comparison: "Our Lord is greater than all gods." While other gods were thought to exercise control over different parts of creation (for instance, there was a rain god, a god of the seas, and so on), "the Lord does whatever pleases him, in the heavens and on the earth." His power isn't limited. He can do anything he wants. But the greatest thing about God is the way he uses his power. He uses it to save his servants, to rescue them from trouble, and to provide them with all they need. He willingly answers those who call on him. What a loving and compassionate God!

Take some time today to meditate on the *greatness* of the Lord. ✤

PRAYER

Dear Lord, I know about your greatness. I know you will have compassion on me . . .

june30

INTERCEDING FOR THOSE WHO HURT US

When the cloud lifted from above the tent, Miriam's skin was leprous—it became as white as snow. Aaron turned toward her and saw that she had a defiling skin disease, and he said to Moses, "Please, my lord, I ask you not to hold against us the sin we have so foolishly committed. Do not let her be like a stillborn infant coming from its mother's womb with its flesh half eaten away."

So Moses cried out to the LORD, "Please, God, heal her!"

NUMBERS 12:10–13

As the Israelites camped in the wilderness near Hazeroth, Aaron and Miriam criticized Moses for marrying a Cushite woman. As punishment, God caused Miriam to be infected with a terrible skin disease. Aaron appealed to Moses to intercede on Miriam's behalf. Moses did. He earnestly prayed and begged the Lord to heal her. God answered Moses' prayer; Miriam was healed, though she was placed outside of the camp for seven days. Even though Miriam had criticized Moses, he was still willing to intercede in prayer for her.

One of our greatest responsibilities is to intercede in prayer for someone else. Are you willing, as Moses was, to be an intercessor, even for someone who has been unkind to you? Today, intercede before God for someone who has hurt you. ♣

PRAYER

Dear God, make me a willing intercessor for those who criticize me. Please heal . . .

AN APPEAL FOR ASSISTANCE

Rescue me from the mire,
do not let me sink;
deliver me from those who hate me,
from the deep waters.
Do not let the floodwaters engulf me
or the depths swallow me up
or the pit close its mouth over me.

PSALM 69:14–15

Earlier, David complained to God about the injustice of those who hated him, the maliciousness of those who attacked him with lies. He explained to God how he was being "scorned, disgraced and shamed" (69:19) by everyone. Even his own brothers were pretending not to know him. He moaned about being the favorite topic of town gossip. But even though everyone was against him, David didn't give up. He didn't let the flood of criticism overwhelm him. He didn't let his enemies pull him down. Instead, he cried out for God to rescue him—to pull him "from the mire."

At some time in our lives most of us have felt like David felt. When you're the object of ridicule, when you've been lied about, humiliated, and mocked, when you feel "the floodwaters engulf" you, react as David did. Don't give up. Take your shame to God in prayer. ✤

PRAYER

Dear Lord, you know what I'm going through. Please answer my prayer. Pull me out of the mud . . .

GIVING GOD THE GLORY HE DESERVES

Ascribe to the LORD the glory due his name;
bring an offering and come before him.
Worship the LORD in the splendor of his holiness.
Tremble before him, all the earth!
The world is firmly established; it cannot be moved.
Let the heavens rejoice, let the earth be glad;
let them say among the nations, "The LORD reigns!"
Let the sea resound, and all that is in it;
let the fields be jubilant, and everything in them!
Let the trees of the forest sing,
let them sing for joy before the LORD,
for he comes to judge the earth.

1 CHRONICLES 16:29–33

We talk about champions—whether they are basketball players or an accomplished chess player—glorying in their hard-won victories. After years of hard work and self-discipline, these victors soak up the praise and applause that fans naturally shower on them. How much more does God deserve our enthusiastic praise? God is the loving Creator of the entire earth. He created bright-blue summer days, stately green forests, and golden fields of grain. In this prayer which was sung as the Ark of God was brought into Jerusalem, David called on all of creation to join him in rejoicing over the Creator.

Plan to take a walk outside this week so you can appreciate everything God has created. Take some time to listen to nature. Give glory to God for what he has created and see how creation celebrates the Lord with you. ✣

PRAYER

Dear Lord, I give you all the glory you deserve. Let the heavens be glad in God; and let the earth rejoice ...

REMINDING OURSELVES OF GOD'S GREATNESS

Among the gods there is none like you, Lord;
*   no deeds can compare with yours.*
All the nations you have made
*   will come and worship before you, Lord;*
*   they will bring glory to your name.*
For you are great and do marvelous deeds;
*   you alone are God.*

PSALM 86:8–10

Sometimes our prayers can become so punctuated with the word, "help," so focused on the dangers and trials, that we overlook the one we are imploring. David avoided this error. He noticed the vast difference between the living God, who had demonstrated his miraculous power in countless ways, and the false gods of myth and superstition. He foresaw a day when all the nations, not just the Israelites, would acknowledge the sovereignty of God Almighty. He alone is God.

Let us lift our eyes from the problem at hand to our triumphant King. Place the difficulties that are bothering you today before your infinite, wonder-working God. ❖

PRAYER

O Lord, you are great and perform great miracles. You alone are God . . .

july4

WELCOMING THE KING OF GLORY

The earth is the LORD's, and everything in it,
the world, and all who live in it;
for he founded it on the seas
and established it on the waters. . . .
Lift up your heads, you gates;
lift them up, you ancient doors,
that the King of glory may come in.
Who is he, this King of glory?
The LORD Almighty —
he is the King of glory.

PSALM 24:1 – 2, 9 – 10

When a president of a nation travels, it is a major event. He's accompanied by his entourage — advisors, press secretaries, and armed secret service men. The long line of limousines can tie up traffic in a major city for hours. When a president's entourage reaches a gated home, the president *never* gets out of his limousine to identify himself to the guards. He *never* opens the gate himself. No, everything has been prearranged. The guard simply knows from the sirens of the approaching police motorcycles that the president is approaching. In David's day, a city's gates would be barred up in times of war in order to protect the city from invaders. But when its king came back from battle victorious, the gate would be flung open to welcome and celebrate the returning, triumphant king. David's prayer is that the conquering King of kings would be welcomed to Jerusalem in a similar way.

When the King of kings comes, no gate — even the gates that enclose our inner lives — can remain closed. All secrets will be revealed. Just as David welcomed God to Jerusalem so long ago, in prayer today welcome God and celebrate his presence in your life. ❖

PRAYER

Dear Lord, I know my gates are not ancient, but I want them always to be open to you . . .

189

MOSES' PRAYER OF PRAISE

Who among the gods
*   is like you, LORD?*
Who is like you —
*   majestic in holiness,*
awesome in glory,
*   working wonders?*
You stretch out your right hand,
*   and the earth swallows your enemies.*
In your unfailing love you will lead
*   the people you have redeemed.*
In your strength you will guide them
*   to your holy dwelling.*

EXODUS 15:11–13

Freedom at last! Precious freedom. After watching their Egyptian oppressors drown as the water of the Red Sea crashed in on them, the Israelites — former slaves in Egypt — felt an exhilarating sense of freedom. They were beyond the grasp of their former owners; and the Promised Land lay before them. At the site of the watery tomb of Pharaoh's army, Moses led the Israelites in celebrating their Victor. At this celebration of freedom, Moses reminded the Israelites why they were freed. They weren't freed to do whatever they wanted to do. They were freed to serve God as his holy people. Moses asked that God might "guide" them to that place.

Set aside some time to celebrate your freedom in Christ. Remember that you were freed to serve God as his child. ✤

PRAYER

Dear Lord, don't let me stray from your path. Guide me to where your holiness dwells . . .

july6

PLACING ONE'S CONFIDENCE IN GOD

My heart, O God, is steadfast,
    my heart is steadfast;
    I will sing and make music.
Awake, my soul!
    Awake, harp and lyre!
    I will awaken the dawn.
I will praise you, Lord, among the nations;
    I will sing of you among the peoples.
For great is your love, reaching to the heavens;
    your faithfulness reaches to the skies.
Be exalted, O God, above the heavens;
    let your glory be over all the earth.

PSALM 57:7–11

David prayed these words while fleeing for his life. We would expect a man running for his life to be focused on what his enemies were doing and how he could elude their traps. But David, after describing his predicament to the Lord, focused on how powerful his Helper was. His prayer for help quickly turned to praise: "My heart is steadfast; I will sing and make music." His praises were loud and heartfelt: "I will awaken the dawn.... I will sing of you among the peoples." Why was David moved to such gratitude when facing danger? Because he knew God's unfailing love was greater than his difficulty. David's prayer put his earthly trials in eternal perspective.

How could God's eternal perspective help you face the difficulties in your life? In prayer, place your confidence in your all-powerful God. ❖

PRAYER

Wake up my soul! Dear God, my heart is confident in you ...

PRAISE FOR ACCOMPLISHMENTS

> *LORD, you establish peace for us;*
>> *all that we have accomplished you have done for us.*
> *LORD our God, other lords besides you have ruled over us,*
>> *but your name alone do we honor.*
> *They are now dead, they live no more;*
>> *their spirits do not rise.*
> *You punished them and brought them to ruin;*
>> *you wiped out all memory of them.*
> *You have enlarged the nation, LORD;*
>> *you have enlarged the nation.*
> *You have gained glory for yourself;*
>> *you have extended all the borders of the land.*

ISAIAH 26:12−15

The object of any sporting event is to be the winner of the contest. Competitors do what's necessary to win, whether it involves hitting home runs, scoring touchdowns, or winning races. Some athletes take personal credit for their feats, declaring success came only from their diligence in the weight room and determination on the field. Today's prayer offers a different attitude about who gets the credit. Isaiah prophesied that one day the Judeans would be victorious—but only because of what God would do for them. The Judeans, instead of lauding their victory and touting their own accomplishments, praised God: "All that we have accomplished you have done for us."

What accomplishments have you experienced within the last year? Today, acknowledge that it was God who enabled you to achieve those goals. Worship him for what he has done. ✤

PRAYER

Dear Lord, all we have accomplished is really from you ...

HOW LONG?

How long will the enemy mock you, God?
  Will the foe revile your name forever?
Why do you hold back your hand, your right hand?
  Take it from the folds of your garment and destroy them!...
Rise up, O God, and defend your cause;
  remember how fools mock you all day long.
Do not ignore the clamor of your adversaries,
  the uproar of your enemies, which rises continually.

PSALM 74:10–11, 22–23

How often does God listen to our impatient prayers? Nothing reveals our lack of faith more than impatient "why" and "how long" prayers. Yet, God arranged that even these prayers were recorded in Scripture. Here, the psalmist cried out to the Lord to defend his holy name from those who "reviled" and "mocked" him. He wanted God to take revenge swiftly against those people. Although the Lord doesn't always tell us when he'll act, we can be confident that it will be at the proper time.

Express your urgent request to God. Pray against the enemies of faith with conviction. God wants us to express our feelings to him in prayer. But trust him for the future, since the final results will always remain in his hands. ❖

PRAYER

Dear Lord, why do you hold back your strong right hand? Rise up and defend your cause...

july9

A PLEA FOR PROTECTION

Have mercy on me, my God, have mercy on me,
for in you I take refuge.
I will take refuge in the shadow of your wings
until the disaster has passed.
I cry out to God Most High,
to God, who vindicates me.
He sends from heaven and saves me,
rebuking those who hotly pursue me—
God sends forth his love and his faithfulness.

PSALM 57:1–3

Ever feel the need to hide? David was in hiding. Saul's pursuit had driven him into a desert cave. But David knew that his hope didn't rest in how fast he could run or how creatively he could hide. Protection came from God. The darkness of a cave could not protect him as well as the shadow of God's wings. David placed his trust in God alone for his safety.

What have the violent storms of life taught you about God's faithfulness? Are you confident, as David was, that God protect and vindicate you? Rest in the protection God offers under his wings and trust his direction for your life. ✣

PRAYER

Dear Lord, I cry out to you for you to help me . . .

PRAISE FOR THE GOD OF COMFORT

Praise be to the God and Father of our Lord Jesus Christ, the Father of compassion and the God of all comfort, who comforts us in all our troubles, so that we can comfort those in any trouble with the comfort we ourselves receive from God. For just as we share abundantly in the sufferings of Christ, so also our comfort abounds through Christ.

2 CORINTHIANS 1:3 – 5

Without pain and suffering we might never know the pleasure of God's heavenly comfort. Unless we have learned the depths of despair in our own troubles, we can not authentically reach out to others. Paul praises the Lord in his letter to the Corinthian church that God "comforts us in all our troubles, so that we can comfort those in any trouble with the comfort we ourselves receive from God." How providential it is that soon after we receive comfort, we are led to someone facing a similar trouble to our own! It is God who leads us to these people, for the comfort we provide for them seems more credible because they know we have gone through the same situation.

In what ways has God comforted you in the trials you have had to go through? Pray that God may use you to comfort others. ✤

PRAYER

Dear Lord, thank you for comforting me. Use me to comfort others ...

A PRAYER FOR DISCERNMENT

Deal with your servant according to your love
and teach me your decrees.
I am your servant; give me discernment
that I may understand your statutes.
It is time for you to act, LORD;
your law is being broken.
Because I love your commands
more than gold, more than pure gold,
and because I consider all your precepts right,
I hate every wrong path.

PSALM 119:124–128

The struggles in our lives usually force us to turn somewhere for help. Too often, however, we anxiously seek out any listening ear when we're confronted with a troublesome situation. The psalmist knew to turn to the Lord first for wisdom and discernment. He asked God, "Teach me your decrees," and "give me discernment." He knew that living God's way would keep him from foolish actions and the path of destruction. That is why he committed himself to learning God's principles in the Scriptures and applying them to his life.

What situation in your life are you most in need of God's discernment? Pray that you might be able to apply God's wisdom to that situation. ✤

PRAYER

Dear Lord, as your servant I ask you to give discernment to me ...

july12

PRAISE FROM THE NATIONS

Praise the LORD, all you nations;
    extol him, all you peoples.
For great is his love toward us,
    and the faithfulness of the LORD endures forever.
Praise the LORD.

PSALM 117:1–2

God is worthy of our praise because he is the God of every nation. His followers come from every part of the world and lift their voices together to praise the Creator of the universe. Psalm 117, the shortest chapter in the Bible, is a simple prayer of praise encouraging people from the ends of the earth to proclaim God's greatness. We are inspired to praise him because his love and faithfulness are continually demonstrated through the lives of his followers. Imagine: one day in heaven people from every nation, every tribe, and every language group will bow before the Lord and sing his praises (Revelation 7:9–10)!

Today, join with God's people around the globe in offering praise to the risen King. ✤

PRAYER

Dear Lord, you have loved me with an unfailing love. That is why I join people from all nations to praise you . . .

A PRAYER FOR COMFORT AND STRENGTH

May our Lord Jesus Christ himself and God our Father, who loved us and by his grace gave us eternal encouragement and good hope, encourage your hearts and strengthen you in every good deed and word.

2 THESSALONIANS 2:16–17

As Paul was writing to the young church at Thessalonica, he was concerned about the persecution and false teachers that inevitably would come their way. Paul never sugarcoated true Christian discipleship. He wanted more than anything for Christians to be prepared to face trials for Christ's sake. This prayer reveals a fatherly concern—expressed urgently because he was unable to be at their side. Paul prayed that God himself would comfort them and give them strength whenever they stood up for right living and against false teaching.

God's "eternal encouragement and good hope" is for all believers. We, too, can approach God with confidence, asking for God's comfort and strength. He is faithful. ✤

PRAYER

Dear Lord Jesus Christ, comfort our hearts and give us the strength to do and say what is right . . .

july14

PRAYER AS INCENSE BEFORE THE LORD

I call to you, LORD, come quickly to me;
hear me when I call to you.
May my prayer be set before you like incense;
may the lifting up of my hands be like the evening sacrifice.
Set a guard over my mouth, LORD;
keep watch over the door of my lips.
Do not let my heart be drawn to what is evil
so that I take part in wicked deeds
along with those who are evildoers;
do not let me eat their delicacies.

PSALM 141:1−4

What image reminds you of prayer, of those times when you communicate with God? Is it the sun peeping through the clouds? Or is it hands clasped together? For David, the sight of sweet-smelling incense floating from the altar into the heavens reminded him of prayer. Such incense was usually offered in the tabernacle along with a burnt offering. David wanted his prayers to be like this incense, reaching up to God so that God would hear him and give David the determination to live according to his righteous ways.

Prayer helps us to raise our concerns and offer our life to God. Ask God that your life and your prayers may be pleasing to him. ✤

PRAYER

Dear Lord, accept my prayer as incense offered to you. Allow me to experience your pleasure as you help me resist evil . . .

A REQUEST FOR ACTION

> *O God, do not remain silent;*
> *do not turn a deaf ear,*
> *do not stand aloof, O God.*
> *See how your enemies growl,*
> *how your foes rear their heads....*
> *Cover their faces with shame, LORD,*
> *so that they will seek your name.*
> *May they ever be ashamed and dismayed;*
> *may they perish in disgrace.*
> *Let them know that you, whose name is the LORD—*
> *that you alone are the Most High over all the earth.*

PSALM 83:1–2, 16–18

The nation of Israel was under attack. At least ten nations were allied against Israel. The outlook seemed hopeless. But the Israelites had been in desperate situations before this. God had crushed their enemies in the past; surely he would do it again. So the psalmist prayed. He asked God not so much for Israel's survival as for the establishment of God's sovereign rule over all nations. The plans of Israel's enemies were, in effect, plans against God.

Much of the turmoil in the world comes from nations assuming the role of God by trying to establish their own sovereignty over others. Christians should pray for God's power to overrule these tyrants. May the time soon come when the world knows, by faith or by God's power, that God alone is rightfully called "the Lord." ✤

PRAYER

Dear Lord, don't sit idly by. Make them learn that you alone are the Most High ...

THE PRAYER OF A PERSECUTED SHEPHERD

I have not run away from being your shepherd;
*   you know I have not desired the day of despair.*
*   What passes my lips is open before you.*
Do not be a terror to me;
*   you are my refuge in the day of disaster.*
Let my persecutors be put to shame,
*   but keep me from shame;*
let them be terrified,
*   but keep me from terror.*
Bring on them the day of disaster;
*   destroy them with double destruction.*

JEREMIAH 17:16–18

God is always faithful to us, but we aren't always faithful to him. The prophet Jeremiah, however, knew that he had been faithful to God's call. He had consistently warned the people to repent—a message God's people didn't want to hear. They persecuted Jeremiah. The prophet could have defended himself, but he chose not to. He simply delivered God's message and waited for God to take whatever action he chose, trusting that God would protect him. As the Bible says, "'Do not repay anyone evil for evil.... 'It is mine to avenge; I will repay,' says the Lord" (Romans 12:17, 19).

Let us pray that we might be able to stand before God in good conscience and say that we have been faithful. And may we depend on him alone as our sure defense. ♣

PRAYER

Dear Lord, it is your message I have given them, not my own. Do not desert me now!...

ACCEPTANCE OF GOD'S PLAN

> *Though I walk in the midst of trouble,*
>> *you preserve my life.*
> *You stretch out your hand against the anger of my foes;*
>> *with your right hand you save me.*
> *The LORD will vindicate me;*
>> *your love, LORD, endures forever —*
>> *do not abandon the works of your hands.*

PSALM 138:7–8

Can we believe God controls our circumstances when we feel "in the midst of trouble"? This is a difficult challenge for people of faith. We have to cling by faith to what we know to be true about God, even when we don't see it in action. So David says, "You stretch out your hand against the anger of my foes." He pictures God clenching his fist against them, saving David by his power. Though we are tempted to plan out our entire life as well as its possibilities, we can assert with David that "the LORD will vindicate me." In a touching plea of the embattled soul, David cried, "Do not abandon the works of your hands."

Today in prayer, thank God that he has a good plan for you. Pray that you might withstand those dark moments when it seems as though he might have abandoned you. ❖

PRAYER

Though I am surrounded by troubles, Lord, you will act on my behalf . . .

july18

A PLEA FROM THE HUMILIATED

You know how I am scorned, disgraced and shamed;
*   all my enemies are before you.*
Scorn has broken my heart
*   and has left me helpless;*
I looked for sympathy, but there was none,
*   for comforters, but I found none....*
But as for me, afflicted and in pain—
*   may your salvation, God, protect me.*
I will praise God's name in song
*   and glorify him with thanksgiving.*

PSALM 69:19–20, 29–30

The old African American spiritual captures the feeling of this psalm so well: "Nobody knows the trouble I've seen, / Nobody knows but Jesus." This lament reflects David's sentiments. He felt that everyone had turned against him. He was being humiliated and insulted. It is clear that David was hurting inside. He wished for even one human being to show him pity and offer him comfort. But instead of reaching out for more human comfort, he continued to pray to God. He trusted that no matter how bad his suffering might get, God was still going to save him.

May you, in your moment of trial, be so full of God's love that you will wait for him and find your solace and rescue only in him. ❖

PRAYER

Dear God, I am suffering and in pain. Rescue me, O God, by your saving power ...

JEREMIAH'S COMPLAINT ABOUT THE WICKED

> *You are always righteous, LORD,*
>   *when I bring a case before you.*
> *Yet I would speak with you about your justice:*
>   *Why does the way of the wicked prosper?*
>   *Why do all the faithless live at ease?*
> *You have planted them, and they have taken root;*
>   *they grow and bear fruit.*
> *You are always on their lips*
>   *but far from their hearts.*
> *Yet you know me, LORD;*
>   *you see me and test my thoughts about you.*
> *Drag them off like sheep to be butchered!*
>   *Set them apart for the day of slaughter!*

JEREMIAH 12:1–3

Have you ever wondered why people who don't fear God—violent and sexually immoral people—are so well off in life? Have you questioned God about it? Jeremiah did. This prophet of the Lord had a hard time understanding why wicked people were prosperous and happy. After all, he had devoted his life to telling Israel that true happiness and security would come only through obedience to God. Indeed, Jeremiah boldly went to God. Can you be so honest and bold as Jeremiah? Though God may not "explain" it to us in a sudden revelation, he is the source of all wisdom and the only one who can satisfy our souls' quests. God sees through the false religiosity of the wicked. He remembers our faithfulness to him.

May you, with Jeremiah, ask him to know your heart and test your thoughts. May God work by his Spirit to cleanse *you* of all evil. Then, you can wait with confidence for him to deal with those who never repent. ♣

PRAYER

Dear Lord, why does the way of the wicked prosper? Why are evil people so happy?...

A PRAYER FOR RESTORATION

Then the king said to the man of God, "Intercede with the LORD your God and pray for me that my hand may be restored." So the man of God interceded with the LORD, and the king's hand was restored and became as it was before.

1 KINGS 13:6

Sometimes God does something dramatic to get our attention. This was certainly the case when a prophet confronted King Jeroboam over the wicked worship practices he had instituted at Bethel. Jeroboam was so brash that after a prophet finished condemning his actions, he dared to order his soldiers to arrest the prophet. However, the hand with which he gestured suddenly shriveled up. It was clear that Jeroboam was defying God himself. Jeroboam recognized his sin and asked the prophet he almost imprisoned to pray for him. The prophet prayed and the Lord answered, again making it clear that Jeroboam was wrong. How merciful is our God! He would have been justified in simply striking the king dead. And he certainly was not obligated to hear any prayer on behalf of this opportunistic blasphemer. But he heard and answered.

When you have strayed from God's ways, be encouraged to ask for restoration. Thank God for the ways he has restored you in the past. Pray for those who need God's restoration now. ❖

PRAYER

O Lord God, restore me again . . .

PRAISING THE LORD

Praise the LORD.

> *Praise God in his sanctuary;*
> > *praise him in his mighty heavens.*
> *Praise him for his acts of power;*
> > *praise him for his surpassing greatness.*
> *Praise him with the sounding of the trumpet,*
> > *praise him with the harp and lyre,*
> *praise him with timbrel and dancing,*
> > *praise him with the strings and pipe,*
> *praise him with the clash of cymbals,*
> > *praise him with resounding cymbals.*
> *Let everything that has breath praise the LORD.*

Praise the LORD.

PSALM 150:1–4, 6

When we call out, "Praise the Lord," it serves two purposes. It expresses our heartfelt adoration of our living Lord; yet, it also calls upon others to do the same. We praise our God first of all for who he is—"his surpassing greatness"—and what he does—"his acts of power." We search for ways to describe the Infinite: "Praise him in his mighty heaven!" We underscore our praise to God with music: the blowing of a trumpet, the strumming of a "harp and lyre," and "with the strings and pipe." Nothing but a chorus of all living things would be fit to render praise to our Creator.

Meditate today on the depth and enthusiasm of the praise expressed here, and find your own words to sing his praise. ❖

PRAYER

Let everything that lives sing praises to the Lord!...

july22

THANKSGIVING FOR GOD'S GOODNESS

Give thanks to the LORD, for he is good;
  his love endures forever.
Cry out, "Save us, God our Savior;
  gather us and deliver us from the nations,
that we may give thanks to your holy name,
  and glory in your praise."
Praise be to the LORD, the God of Israel,
  from everlasting to everlasting.

Then all the people said "Amen" and "Praise the LORD."

1 CHRONICLES 16:34–36

King David had just brought the Ark of God into the city of Jerusalem. The whole community had gathered to mark this milestone in Israel's history. God had established them in their land and defeated their enemies. The Ark was a reminder of God's presence with them. David gave this prayer of praise to the priests leading the worship. God's goodness and faithfulness are recurring themes in this prayer. David prayed, "Save us, God our Savior; gather us and deliver us from the nations *that we may give thanks to your holy name.*" As we consider the good things God has done for us thankfulness flows from our hearts. We thank God again and again for establishing us and graciously providing us with everything we need.

Recount the ways God has been good to you and your family. Thank and praise him for his goodness. ♣

PRAYER

Dear Lord, I give thanks to you for you are good! Your love endures forever . . .

PRAISE FOR GOD'S JUSTICE

> *To the faithful you show yourself faithful,*
> *to the blameless you show yourself blameless,*
> *to the pure you show yourself pure,*
> *but to the devious you show yourself shrewd.*
> *You save the humble*
> *but bring low those whose eyes are haughty.*

PSALM 18:25–27

David wrote this prayer after God had delivered him from his enemy, Saul. David had refused to take Saul's life on several occasions when he had the opportunity. Instead of taking justice into his own hands, David had let God enact justice in his own way and in his own time. For this, God honored him. In response, David sang his praises to God: "To the faithful you show yourself faithful.... but to the devious you show yourself shrewd." God is truly the Chief Justice. One day, he will make everything right. He will bring down the arrogant and the wicked, and he will lift up the righteous. Though this world may appear to be turned upside down, though the wicked may appear to be rewarded for their crimes, God will one day restore justice to this world. On that day, believers will rejoice, for their Defender has come.

Take this opportunity to praise your God for his justice as you have seen it played out in the world around you. ❖

PRAYER

O Lord, you rescue those who are humble, but you humiliate the proud ...

GREAT IS THE LORD!

Praise the LORD.

> *How good it is to sing praises to our God,*
> *how pleasant and fitting to praise him!*
> *The LORD builds up Jerusalem;*
> *he gathers the exiles of Israel.*
> *He heals the brokenhearted*
> *and binds up their wounds.*
> *He determines the number of the stars*
> *and calls them each by name.*
> *Great is our Lord and mighty in power;*
> *his understanding has no limit.*

PSALM 147:1–5

How great is our God? How can we measure or express the extent of his majesty? His greatness is revealed through his mercy. This prayer was written right after a remnant of God's people returned from exile in Babylon. The psalmist delighted in praising God because of the miracle that was taking place before his eyes: "The Lord builds up Jerusalem; he gathers the exiles of Israel." The God of mercy, who binds up the wounds of the brokenhearted, is the same almighty God who calls all the stars by name. God is wise and powerful. For all these reasons, the psalmist prayed, "How good it is to sing praises to our God."

Consider how great the Lord of the universe is. Express your feelings to him in prayer. ✤

PRAYER

O Lord, how good it is to sing praises to you!...

PRAISE FOR GOD'S PROTECTIVE ARMS

"There is no one like the God of Jeshurun,
who rides across the heavens to help you
and on the clouds in his majesty.
The eternal God is your refuge,
and underneath are the everlasting arms.
He will drive out your enemies before you,
saying, 'Destroy them!'
So Israel will live in safety;
Jacob will dwell secure
in a land of grain and new wine,
where the heavens drop dew.
Blessed are you, Israel!
Who is like you,
a people saved by the LORD?
He is your shield and helper
and your glorious sword.
Your enemies will cower before you,
and you will tread on their heights."

DEUTERONOMY 33:26–29

At the end of his life, after seeing God's miraculous interventions in the life of his people, Moses stood before the people. He reviewed their history with God, admonished them to be faithful, and pronounced a unique blessing on each tribe. After blessing all the tribes, he eloquently praised God, who had established such a wonderful relationship with Israel. So precious were the Israelites to God that he "rides across the heavens to help" them. In a marvelous image, Moses pictured God's everlasting arms beneath the Israelites, protecting them from harm. "Blessed are you, Israel! Who is like you, a people saved by the LORD?"

We need to ask ourselves the same question: "How has God uniquely blessed you?" Take some time to review your personal history for the ways God has upheld you and your family. ✤

PRAYER

Dear Lord, you are my refuge. I know your everlasting arms are under me . . .

THANKS FOR THE LORD BEING NEAR

We praise you, God,
> *we praise you, for your Name is near;*
> *people tell of your wonderful deeds.*
You say, "I choose the appointed time;
> *it is I who judge with equity.*
When the earth and all its people quake,
> *it is I who hold its pillars firm...."*
As for me, I will declare this forever;
> *I will sing praise to the God of Jacob,*
who says, "I will cut off the horns of all the wicked,
> *but the horns of the righteous will be lifted up."*

PSALM 75:1–3, 9–10

God is near. At times, he performs mighty miracles to remind us of his nearness. But there are many times when his power and justice are not readily apparent to us. This prayer addressed this situation head-on. When we find ourselves questioning God's ability to establish truth and justice on this earth, we should pray. First, we can remember to thank and praise God for his power. We can also remind ourselves of God's nearness and of every evidence of his power at work in our world. Only then will we gain a proper perspective on our own difficult circumstances. God has promised to bring justice to this earth in his own timing. As we wait for God to act, our proper posture is praise.

In whatever situation you find yourself on this summer day, acknowledge one good thing God has done for you this past year. Genuinely thank him for it, and praise him for being near. ✣

PRAYER

But as for me, O Lord, I will always proclaim what you have done and thank you for being near ...

SAMSON'S CRY FOR WATER

Because he was very thirsty, he cried out to the LORD, "You have given your servant this great victory. Must I now die of thirst and fall into the hands of the uncircumcised?" Then God opened up the hollow place in Lehi, and water came out of it. When Samson drank, his strength returned and he revived. So the spring was called En Hakkore, and it is still there in Lehi.

JUDGES 15:18–19

Out of fear, no one among the Israelites would stand up to their oppressors, the Philistines. Then, Samson came along. God accomplished mighty deeds through Samson. He wreaked havoc among the Philistines so that their primary goal became Samson's personal destruction. When Israel's leaders saw the Philistine troops coming to capture Samson, they quickly made plans to turn Samson in to stop further bloodshed. But Samson put the Philistines to flight, by killing a thousand of his would-be captors with the jawbone of a donkey! After accomplishing this amazing feat, he realized that he was *very* thirsty. Like a grouchy child, he asked God for water: "Must I now die of thirst?" God answered Samson's prayer by opening up a spring of water on the spot to care for Samson. But the Lord also reminded Samson, who had a tendency to congratulate himself, that he alone was God. Only he could supply Samson's needs in such a miraculous way.

When we pray for God to meet our needs, let us do so in humility, realizing that we are only vessels of his transcendent power. Commit one of your needs to God today. ✤

PRAYER

Dear God, you have accomplished a great victory by the strength of your servant. Must I now . . .

july28

APPLAUDING GOD'S GOODNESS

Praise the LORD.

> *Give thanks to the LORD, for he is good;*
> *his love endures forever.*
> *Who can proclaim the mighty acts of the LORD*
> *or fully declare his praise?*

PSALM 106:1–2

There are times, when we seek to offer praise and thanksgiving to God, but we find ourselves at a loss for words. The psalmist found himself in this situation: "Who can proclaim the mighty acts of the LORD or fully declare his praise?" In the light of God's holiness and goodness, the psalmist recounted in this psalm all the times Israel had proven unworthy of the Lord's love. The people were ungrateful and rebellious; and God grew angry with them and punished them. But because of his goodness, God never utterly destroyed them. In light of their history of unfaithfulness, how could they ever praise God enough for what he done for them?

As you ask God for mercy, remind yourself of one of the main reasons God saves us—so that we can join the chorus of people continually praising his name and thanking him. Can we ever offer enough praises to God? ✣

PRAYER

O God, who can ever praise you half enough?...

QUESTIONING GOD

But Abram said, "Sovereign LORD, what can you give me since I remain childless and the one who will inherit my estate is Eliezer of Damascus?" And Abram said, "You have given me no children; so a servant in my household will be my heir."

Then the word of the LORD came to him: "This man will not be your heir, but a son who is your own flesh and blood will be your heir."

GENESIS 15:2−4

Abram's intimacy with God is demonstrated vividly in this prayer. He bared his soul before God. He told God how life looked from his perspective and how he felt about it. He even had complained that God's blessings were not enough! Most of us wouldn't feel comfortable laying out our whole case before God in this way. But because Abram believed God and came to the Lord with his requests, Abram was rewarded with a promise — that his own son would be his heir.

Are there circumstances in your life that don't seem fair? Are there longings that have gone unfulfilled for long periods of time? Abram's example can encourage you to tell God about them. Don't be afraid to reveal your deepest desires to the Lord. Bring your longings to him. Trust in him; he will answer. Sometimes, he answers in ways we can't even imagine. ❖

PRAYER

O Sovereign Lord, what good are all your blessings when . . .

july**30**

TRUSTING IN GOD'S UNFAILING LOVE

"Here now is the man
who did not make God his stronghold
but trusted in his great wealth
and grew strong by destroying others!"
But I am like an olive tree
flourishing in the house of God;
I trust in God's unfailing love
for ever and ever.
For what you have done I will always praise you
in the presence of your faithful people.
And I will hope in your name,
for your name is good.

PSALM 52:7–9

Where do you place your trust? Without being aware of it, many of us start hoping that our plans may succeed, that our family and friends may provide us support, or that our wealth may give us the security we need. Yet in the long run, all of these will fade away. Our plans are easily disrupted. Our wealth can be siphoned away. Our clothes, cars, and home will begin to deteriorate. Even our friends or family members can abandon us. In the end, God is the only one who can provide true security. Those who place their trust in him will not be dismayed, for they will receive an eternal inheritance that can never be destroyed. God will never abandon them. He will always love them.

As you approach God in prayer today, express your complete dependence on him and your trust in him. Ask him to show you his good plan for your life. ✤

PRAYER

Dear Lord, I trust in God's unfailing love forever and ever ...

THE LORD, MY STRONGHOLD

I love you, LORD, my strength.

> *The LORD is my rock, my fortress and my deliverer;*
>   *my God is my rock, in whom I take refuge,*
>   *my shield and the horn of my salvation, my stronghold.*
> *I called to the LORD, who is worthy of praise,*
>   *and I have been saved from my enemies.*

PSALM 18:1-3

Most of us don't depend on fortresses or strongholds to protect us much less a shield or a boulder. But for David, such places of safety were often very important factors in his survival. When Saul's army pursued him, David hid behind rocks; but he reminded himself that the Lord was his true rock—his true source of protection from his enemies. He also hid in fortresses; but he reminded himself that God was his true fortress in the barren wilderness. He used his shield to withstand the blows of his enemies; but he reminded himself that God was his true, impenetrable shield.

What do you depend on for security? Is it a large retirement account? A good-paying job? A family member or friend? Acknowledge to God that he is your ultimate source for security and protection. ✤

PRAYER

I love you, Lord, my strength . . .

BOLDLY PROCLAIMING GOD'S GREATNESS

> *Give praise to the LORD, proclaim his name;*
> *make known among the nations what he has done.*
> *Sing to him, sing praise to him;*
> *tell of all his wonderful acts.*
> *Glory in his holy name;*
> *let the hearts of those who seek the LORD rejoice.*
> *Look to the LORD and his strength;*
> *seek his face always.*
> *Remember the wonders he has done,*
> *his miracles, and the judgments he pronounced.*

1 CHRONICLES 16:8 – 12

After his army soundly defeated the Philistines, David paraded the symbol of God's presence—the Ark of the Covenant—throughout the city of Jerusalem. He established its new resting-place in a temporary tent in Jerusalem. In honor of their victory, David's priestly choir sang out their praise in this prayer to "make known among the nations what he has done." It was a momentous day for the people of Jerusalem; and David made sure that everyone knew it by loudly praising God, their Victor.

Do people know the magnitude of God simply by the praise we give to him? In a day when an order of French fries is tagged "super-sized," we too often offer pint-sized praise to our magnificent God. Boldly proclaim God's greatness, today. ✤

> **PRAYER**

Dear Lord, I give thanks to you and proclaim your greatness . . .

TRUSTING WHEN OVERWHELMED BY TROUBLES

Listen to my prayer, O God,
do not ignore my plea;
hear me and answer me.
My thoughts trouble me and I am distraught....
But you, God, will bring down the wicked
into the pit of decay;
the bloodthirsty and deceitful
will not live out half their days.
But as for me, I trust in you.

PSALM 55:1–2, 23

Do you ever wish you could fly like a bird away from your problems? David did. He was completely overwhelmed by his troubles: his enemies had surrounded him and were shouting and making loud threats; even a friend had betrayed him in his hour of need. With his world falling apart, David was terrified that death might overpower him; and he wished he had the wings of a dove so he could fly away from his troubles to a quiet place, where he could rest. Even in his worst difficulties, David called upon God to rescue him.

Are you overwhelmed by troubles? Give your burdens to the Lord, and determine today to trust the Lord to save you. ✤

PRAYER

O Lord, I'm overwhelmed by my troubles. Listen to my cry for help. I need you, and I am trusting you to save me ...

august3

BEGGING TO BE SPARED

Let the priests, who minister before the LORD,
weep between the portico and the altar.
Let them say, "Spare your people, LORD.
Do not make your inheritance an object of scorn,
a byword among the nations.
Why should they say among the peoples,
'Where is their God?'"
Then the LORD was jealous for his land
and took pity on his people.

JOEL 2:17–18

When we are in trouble, we easily cry out, "Save me" or "Spare me." Sometimes those words, however, roll off our tongues too easily. Although Joel did encourage the Israelites to ask the Lord to "spare" them, he first told them how they could approach God. Their pleas for mercy had to be accompanied with genuine repentance. They couldn't simply demonstrate grief over their sins by outwardly tearing their clothes; they had to have broken hearts for offending God. They were to approach him with fasting, weeping, and mourning. God was eager to forgive his people in those days, and he will be merciful to us as well when we repent of our sins.

Praise God for his abundant mercy and great compassion for sinners. Ask him to help you reflect his mercy to others. ✣

PRAYER

O Lord, spare me ...

august4

TAKING TIME TO HOPE IN THE LORD

"Show me, LORD, my life's end
and the number of my days;
let me know how fleeting my life is.
You have made my days a mere handbreadth;
the span of my years is as nothing before you.
Everyone is but a breath,
even those who seem secure.
"Surely everyone goes around like a mere phantom;
in vain they rush about, heaping up wealth
without knowing whose it will finally be.
"But now, Lord, what do I look for?
My hope is in you."

PSALM 39:4−7

We all know people who are married to their job, not their spouse. Their best friend may be a laptop or a cell phone. They spend hour after hour at work; and their bosses certainly reward them for it. They accumulate big bank accounts; but their obsession with work leaves them emotionally and spiritually bankrupt. Tragically, these driven personalities often burn out in their prime and leave their fortunes for others to enjoy. This passage comments on how foolish it is to waste one's efforts on gaining material wealth that soon will pass away. In this prayer, David laments that his time on earth was brief. "Surely everyone goes around like a mere phantom," he said, "in vain they rush about, heaping up wealth without knowing whose it will finally be" So what are we to do? In what or in whom should we put our hope? David gives us the answer: "But now, Lord, what do I look for? My hope is in you."

Today in prayer, place your hope in God alone. ✤

PRAYER

Dear Lord, I know my life on earth is brief and my busy rushing will end in nothing if I don't place my hope in you ...

PRAYING FOR THE HELPLESS

Arise, LORD! Lift up your hand, O God.
Do not forget the helpless....
But you, God, see the trouble of the afflicted
you consider their grief and take it in hand.
The victims commit themselves to you;
you are the helper of the fatherless....
You, LORD, hear the desire of the afflicted;
you encourage them, and you listen to their cry,
defending the fatherless and the oppressed,
so that mere earthly mortals
will never again strike terror.

PSALM 10:12, 14, 17–18

David had seen a lot of injustice in his life, but he never got used to it. In this prayer, David was angry with the wicked man, who was "like a lion in cover he lies in wait. He lies in wait to catch the helpless; he catches the helpless and drags them off in his net" (10:9). His heart was full of compassion for the oppressed, the widows, the orphans, the poor, the weak, and the innocent. He saw the injustice of how they were treated and pleaded for God to come to their defense.

Do you still get angry at the injustice in the world? Do you plead with God to come to the defense of the oppressed and the helpless? Has your heart become cold and indifferent? Ask God to give you a compassion heart. Pray for God to bring justice to this world. ♣

PRAYER

Dear Lord, do not forget the helpless ...

august**6**

THIRSTING FOR GOD

You, God, are my God,
*   earnestly I seek you;*
I thirst for you,
*   my whole being longs for you,*
in a dry and parched land
*   where there is no water.*

PSALM 63:1

Anyone who has ever been in the desert for a long time knows what thirst can do. Your mouth gets as dry as cotton, your throat hurts, and soon you begin imaging a tall, cold glass of water sparkling in the sun. Oh, how good it looks! You can almost taste it! David had experienced that kind of thirst when he stayed in the wilderness of Judah, a "a dry and parched land where there is no water." In this prayer, he compared that type of thirst with his desire for God. He was agonizing, searching for the Lord with all his might. His soul thirsted and his body longed for God.

When have you longed for the Lord that way, so much that you actually *thirst* for him? During your time in prayer, express your desire for God. ✣

PRAYER

Dear Lord, my soul thirsts for you ...

august7

A PRAYER FOR MAKING AN IMPORTANT DECISION

Then they prayed, "Lord, you know everyone's heart. Show us which of these two you have chosen to take over this apostolic ministry, which Judas left to go where he belongs." Then they cast lots, and the lot fell to Matthias; so he was added to the eleven apostles.

ACTS 1:24–26

The big decisions—what job offer we should take, what person we should marry, or where we should live—are the ones that produce the most anxiety. We spend hours agonizing over the pros and cons of each choice. The early church had such an important decision before them. Who would replace Judas among the Jesus' disciples? This wasn't a popularity contest. These early Christians wanted God's choice, so they prayed. As a group, they nominated two men who appeared to be genuine followers of Christ to them. But they realized they couldn't test the hearts of both individuals—only God could do that. So they submitted the choice to God in prayer.

What decision do you need to submit to God? Ask God to guide you in making your decision. Ask him to reveal his choice for you. ✤

PRAYER

Dear Lord, you know my heart. Show me what you have chosen for me ...

august**8**

HONORING GOD AS KING OF THE UNIVERSE

Praise the LORD, my soul.

> *LORD my God, you are very great;*
>   *you are clothed with splendor and majesty.*
> *The LORD wraps himself in light as with a garment;*
>   *he stretches out the heavens like a tent*
>   *and lays the beams of his upper chambers on their waters.*
> *He makes the clouds his chariot*
>   *and rides on the wings of the wind.*
> *He makes winds his messengers,*
>   *flames of fire his servants.*

PSALM 104:1 – 4

Every once in a while, our natural surroundings surprise us. A sudden clap of thunder startles us. Or the beauty of a field of multicolored wildflowers amazes us. Too often, we pass by natural wonders—fields full of grain, towering oak and walnut trees, and the expansive blue sky above—rushing from task to task. We don't take time to thank God for the beautiful environment in which he has placed us. This prayer takes cues from the wonders in nature to magnify and exult God.

At times, the awe-inspiring forces of nature have a way of making us feel small and powerless. Who can stand in the face of the winds of a hurricane? But to God, these are only the tools and trappings of his kingship over the universe. Praise God for his power and wisdom by listing the ways you have witnessed his work in what he has created. ❖

PRAYER

O Lord my God, how great you are! ...

august9

REMINDING ONESELF THAT GOD IS AT WORK

> *The poor will see and be glad—*
> *you who seek God, may your hearts live!*
> *The LORD hears the needy*
> *and does not despise his captive people.*
> *Let heaven and earth praise him,*
> *the seas and all that move in them,*

PSALM 69:32–34

Sometimes when we are in our deepest depression, we despair of anyone hearing our cries for help. David felt this way. "I am worn out calling for help," he said (69:3). His enemies had surrounded him and were even gloating over him. Yet towards the end of this prayer, David reminded himself that God does hear "the needy." He does work out his good plan for his people. One day, the humble will rejoice in the Lord's work. In spite of his circumstances, David reminded himself how faithful God was. He knew the Lord heard his cries and would answer him. In this, he could rejoice. He knew he would see God at work.

During these days of summer, you may find your inner joy being sapped away by some difficult situation. Remind yourself of God's ability to hear your cry for help. Look for ways God is already working in your church and in your community. "The poor will see and be glad." ✣

PRAYER

Dear God, I am glad you are at work in this world . . .

august**10**

A PLEA FOR GOD'S PROTECTION

Then Jacob prayed, "O God of my father Abraham, God of my father Isaac, LORD, you who said to me, 'Go back to your country and your relatives, and I will make you prosper,' I am unworthy of all the kindness and faithfulness you have shown your servant. I had only my staff when I crossed this Jordan, but now I have become two camps. Save me, I pray, from the hand of my brother Esau, for I am afraid he will come and attack me, and also the mothers with their children. But you have said, 'I will surely make you prosper and will make your descendants like the sand of the sea, which cannot be counted.'"

GENESIS 32:9–12

Jacob had reason to be afraid of his brother Esau. Jacob had tricked his brother out of his birthright and the blessing of their father Isaac. Jacob had to leave home because Esau was going to kill him because of his trickery. Years later, after marrying and acquiring wealth in a foreign land, Jacob headed home. On his way home, he heard Esau was coming to greet him. What worried Jacob was that an army of four hundred men accompanied Esau! Convinced his brother was coming to kill him, Jacob earnestly prayed for God to protect him. His prayers were answered when Esau, instead of being angry, greeted his brother with hugs and tears.

We may not fear for our life, but there are times when we fear for our livelihood or for the welfare of our families. At such times, we can remind God, as Jacob did, of his promises to take care of us as his children. ✤

PRAYER

Dear God, you have promised us that if we believe in you, you will preserve us. Lord, I need your protection . . .

august**11**

THE PRAYER OF AN ELDERLY MAN

Even when I am old and gray,
do not forsake me, my God,
till I declare your power to the next generation,
your mighty acts to all who are to come.
Your righteousness, God, reaches to the heavens,
you who have done great things.
Who is like you, God?
Though you have made me see troubles,
many and bitter,
you will restore my life again;
from the depths of the earth
you will again bring me up.
You will increase my honor
and comfort me once more.

PSALM 71:18–21

Whether our days on earth are few or many, God never abandons us. The writer of this psalm had lived a long life. In his old age, he felt abandoned by his friends and family. Yet in his despair, he turned to God, asking the Lord to never abandon him. As this man surveyed his life, he realized how God had worked through the hardships he had suffered and through the difficult circumstances of his life. Because the Lord had always restored him, he wanted to tell the next generation how amazing God was.

In what ways has God restored you to life? How has he lifted you up? Determine today to tell someone else about how God has restored and encouraged you. ❖

PRAYER

Dear Lord, you have done such wonderful things. Let me proclaim your power to this new generation . . .

august**12**

ENTRUSTING ONE'S REPUTATION TO GOD

In you, LORD my God,
I put my trust.
I trust in you;
do not let me be put to shame,
nor let my enemies triumph over me.
No one who hopes in you
will ever be put to shame,
but shame will come on those
who are treacherous without cause.

PSALM 25:1–3

One of our greatest fears in this life is disgrace. We dread a loss of honor in the eyes of other people—whether they are friends or foes. Our natural instinct is to cover up our mistakes and protect our reputations. King David understood that his honor was ultimately in the hands of God. God is able to keep us from disgrace. He is also able to lift us up from the disgraces we bring on ourselves. But dishonor will fall on those who deceive others to enhance their own reputations.

Instead of worrying about your reputation, your success or failure, trust in God for protection. Pray for courage to live with honesty and integrity. ✤

PRAYER

Dear Lord, do not let me be disgraced. No one who trusts in you will ever be disgraced . . .

august**13**

A PLEA FOR HELP

Then Asa called to the LORD his God and said, "LORD, there is no one like you to help the powerless against the mighty. Help us, LORD our God, for we rely on you, and in your name we have come against this vast army. LORD, you are our God; do not let mere mortals prevail against you."

2 CHRONICLES 14:11

King Asa was one of the few kings of Judah who feared God and banned idolatry among God's people. God rewarded him with ten years of peace, although it was not as if his kingdom's tranquility was never threatened. When Zerah, the king of Ethiopia, assembled a huge army against him, Asa saw it as an opportunity to trust God. Rather than jumping first to analyze his options and muster his resources, his first instinct was to entrust the whole situation to God. Because he understood it to be God's battle, not his own, he knew that God's resources were at his disposal. It was not a matter of national or ethnic honor: *God's* honor was at stake. He asked God for help and, then, acted in God's name, trusting the Lord because he had proven himself trustworthy at so many other critical junctures in Asa's life.

You may face overwhelming situations in your life today. Commit those situations to God, and pray that he would use those situations to demonstrate his power and bring honor to his name. ✤

PRAYER

Help me, O Lord my God, for I trust in you alone ...

august**14**

THANKING THE LORD FOR BEING A TRUSTWORTHY ALLY

Praise be to the LORD my Rock,
*   who trains my hands for war,*
*   my fingers for battle.*
He is my loving God and my fortress,
*   my stronghold and my deliverer,*
my shield, in whom I take refuge,
*   who subdues peoples under me.*
LORD, what are human beings that you care for them,
*   mere mortals that you think of them?*

PSALM 144:1–3

When a nation is considering going into battle against a formidable enemy, it sends diplomats to its allies to solicit support—whether it's financial, military, or logistical in nature. No one wants to go into battle without someone to back them up. In this prayer, David proclaimed the Lord God as his only ally. He called God his "Rock," "fortress," "loving God," "stronghold," and "deliverer." He thanked the Lord for training him in the skills needed in combat and for giving him the strength to fight. In the confusion of the battlefield, David could rely on God to help him triumph over his enemies. Yet he still marveled at God's willingness to come to his rescue. "LORD, what are human beings that you care for them?"

When have you needed God as an ally? Today, thank him for the times he has rescued you. ❖

PRAYER

Dear Lord, thank you for being my loving ally and my fortress . . .

august15

MEDITATING ON GOD'S UNFAILING LOVE

Within your temple, O God,
we meditate on your unfailing love.
Like your name, O God,
your praise reaches to the ends of the earth;
your right hand is filled with righteousness.

PSALM 48:9–10

The attributes of power and love appear to be opposites. We often picture a powerful ruler as a dictator or tyrant—someone who uses his power to oppress. We often imagine a loving person as gentle and kind-hearted—someone who would never exercise power over anyone else. But Scriptures describes God as being both powerful and loving. He uses his power in a loving way, by protecting his people, while punishing those who persist in evil ways. In the end, he will ultimately conquer all those who oppose him. Meanwhile, he lovingly gives everyone the opportunity to come to him for salvation. This prayer is a meditation on God's unfailing love. God *will* be honored and praised, for he *will* triumph over his enemies. We have the privilege of joining our voices to that worship *now*—regardless of our circumstances.

Meditate on God's unfailing love for you; and make a commitment this week to tell someone else what he has done for you. ❖

PRAYER

O God, we meditate on your unfailing love as we worship in your Temple ...

PRAISING GOD FOR KEEPING HIS PROMISES

> *I will praise the LORD all my life;*
> > *I will sing praise to my God as long as I live.*
> *Do not put your trust in princes,*
> > *in human beings, who cannot save....*
> *Blessed are those whose help is the God of Jacob,*
> > *whose hope is in the LORD their God.*
> *He is the Maker of heaven and earth,*
> > *the sea, and everything in them—*
> > *he remains faithful forever.*

PSALM 146:2 – 3, 5 – 6

All of us have been let down by someone. A friend or family member may have broken an important promise. A respected church leader may have fallen into sin. Many of us learned early that we can't depend completely on other people — sometimes they don't follow through on their promises. The writer of this prayer declared to God that his confidence wasn't in people. His trust was only in God, for the Lord is always faithful. The sky above and the earth below are tokens of God's unfailing love for his people. God cares enough to keep the earth spinning on its axis and the cosmos in its place for yet another day. No other person deserves our trust more than God.

Take a few minutes to render praise to God for being faithful to you. ❖

PRAYER

Dear Lord, you are the one who keeps every promise forever ...

august 17

BOWING BEFORE THE THRONE

All the angels were standing around the throne and around the elders and the four living creatures. They fell down on their faces before the throne and worshiped God, saying:

> *"Amen!*
> *Praise and glory*
> *and wisdom and thanks and honor*
> *and power and strength*
> *be to our God for ever and ever.*
> *Amen!"*

REVELATION 7:11–12

This excerpt from the book of Revelation gives us a glimpse of God's heavenly throne room. In John's vision, he saw both resurrected believers and awesome heavenly creatures bowing face down before God's throne, praising the Lord for all that he had done. Such profound reverence for God contrasts with the great familiarity with which we often relate to God. No one would approach a president or a head of state with a flippant, "What's up?" In a similar way, we need to remember to whom we're speaking when we pray. As we approach in God in prayer, remember that he is the ruler of the universe. We dare not be too casual with the Holy One.

The angelic beings of Revelation expressed their humility and reverence for God by bowing face down before him. In your prayer today, join these angelic beings in giving deepest respect to your Maker. ✤

PRAYER

Praise and glory and wisdom and thanks and honor and power and strength be to our God for ever and ever ...

august**18**

ASKING FOR PROTECTION

I call on you, my God, for you will answer me;
turn your ear to me and hear my prayer.
Show me the wonders of your great love,
you who save by your right hand
those who take refuge in you from their foes.
Keep me as the apple of your eye;
hide me in the shadow of your wings

PSALM 17:6–8

Our eyes are extremely sensitive. People react swiftly and instinctually to anything heading toward their eyes. In this prayer, David asked the Lord to guard him as if he were the apple or pupil of God's eye. David's request reveals much about his intimate relationship with God. He asked to be guarded in such a way because he believed God would answer him: "I call on you, my God, for you will answer me." He envisioned God, gentle and interested, bending down to listen to his prayer. He believed that God would use his great strength to protect him. With his eyes fixed expectantly on his loving Lord, David received the shelter he desperately sought.

Use David's prayer to remind yourself that God is powerful: He is the only One who can truly guard and protect you. Commit your worries to him in prayer. ✤

PRAYER

Dear Lord, keep me as the apple of your eye. Hide me in the shadow of your wings . . .

BRINGING TRIBUTE TO GOD

> *You are radiant with light,*
> *more majestic than mountains rich with game.*
> *It is you alone who are to be feared.*
> *Who can stand before you when you are angry?*
> *From heaven you pronounced judgment,*
> *and the land feared and was quiet . . .*
> *Make vows to the* LORD *your God and fulfill them;*
> *let all the neighboring lands*
> *bring gifts to the One to be feared.*

PSALM 76:4, 7–8, 11

Anyone who has spent time in the mountains develops an admiration for the forces in nature. We naturally feel small next to massive formations of earth and rock. Though these mountains may seem immovable, their appearance can be radically altered by rock slides, avalanches, earthquakes, and volcanoes. God has given these impressive landscapes to us as clues to his power. This prayer asks, "Who can stand before you when you are angry?" If the whole earth remains silent and trembling before God's awesome power, how much more should we pray with awe and holy respect? We wouldn't want to be counted among his enemies when he renders judgment!

In prayer, praise the Lord for how powerful he is. Give to God the honor and glory we owe him. Commit today to bring tribute—whether it is a portion of your material resources or of your time—to the awesome King of kings. ✤

PRAYER

O God, you are glorious and more majestic than the everlasting mountains. I bring my tribute to you . . .

BLESSING THE LORD

> *Praise be to the LORD God, the God of Israel,*
>   *who alone does marvelous deeds.*
> *Praise be to his glorious name forever;*
>   *may the whole earth be filled with his glory.*
>   *Amen and Amen.*

PSALM 72:18–19

The word *bless* is more likely to enter our prayer vocabulary when we ask God to bless ourselves or others. But Solomon in this prayer called his fellow worshipers to *bless* God. He meant that they should praise and glorify God for all that he had done for them. He *blessed* the God of Israel "who alone does marvelous deeds." This blessing crowns a prayer where Solomon had asked God to bless his nation and his reign. How fitting it is that Solomon, who had received so much from the Lord, should express his indebtedness to God by blessing God's name throughout his life.

As you ask God to bless you and your family, why not bless God for the wonderful ways he continually helps you. ✤

PRAYER

Bless the Lord God, the God of Israel, who alone does such wonderful things …

JESUS' THANKS FOR ANSWERED PRAYER

So they took away the stone. Then Jesus looked up and said, "Father, I thank you that you have heard me. I knew that you always hear me, but I said this for the benefit of the people standing here, that they may believe that you sent me."

JOHN 11:41–42

The story of Jesus raising Lazarus from the dead gives us a unique glimpse into the prayer life of Jesus. So confident was Jesus in the power at his disposal that he went to the tomb of a man who had been dead for four days and ordered the people to roll aside the stone. As the tomb lay open, Jesus thanked God out loud for answering his prayers—not so much to reassure himself that God had heard his prayer, but to demonstrate to his followers that God had sent him. He was confident God would answer him because he prayed in accordance with God's will—believing and not wavering. So when he commanded Lazarus to come out, he wasn't surprised that Lazarus stood up and walked towards him. But those who gathered at the tomb were astonished: How could this be? Jesus' prayer answered their questions. God the Father had sent Jesus to them. Lazarus was physical proof of Jesus' divine power.

Jesus' prayer is for our benefit as well. In prayer today, reaffirm your belief in Jesus' divine power over death. Praise and give him thanks for answering your prayers. ✤

PRAYER

Dear Jesus, I believe God sent you to this earth. Thank you for hearing me . . .

august**22**

SINGING JOYFULLY TO THE LORD

> *Come, let us sing for joy to the LORD;*
> *let us shout aloud to the Rock of our salvation.*
> *Let us come before him with thanksgiving*
> *and extol him with music and song.*
> *For the LORD is the great God,*
> *the great King above all gods.*
> *In his hand are the depths of the earth,*
> *and the mountain peaks belong to him.*
> *The sea is his, for he made it,*
> *and his hands formed the dry land.*

PSALM 95:1–5

In the days when the world was ruled by monarchs, it was not uncommon for people to praise the king aloud on the streets. People would draw attention to the impressive monuments that demonstrated the king's power—such as the king's palace and the extent of his land. This prayer draws attention to the natural monuments that point to God's power—immovable mountains, vast seas, and rich plains. The boundaries of God's kingdom are unmatched—he owns "the depths of the earth" and "the mightiest mountains." Not only does he reign over the whole earth today, he formed it out of nothing in the first place. Our God existed before this earthly kingdom was created to proclaim his greatness. No power on this earth can compare to our Creator.

Think about the natural monuments you have seen that proclaim God's power. Join your voice with all his faithful people in heartfelt praise. ✤

PRAYER

Come, let us sing to the Lord! Let us give a joyous shout to the rock of our salvation!...

LONGING FOR GOD'S WORD

Your statutes are wonderful;
therefore I obey them.
The unfolding of your words gives light;
it gives understanding to the simple.
I open my mouth and pant,
longing for your commands.
Turn to me and have mercy on me,
as you always do to those who love your name.
Direct my footsteps according to your word;
let no sin rule over me.

PSALM 119:129–133

There are times in life when we long for guidance. We want someone who can clearly see the road ahead to guide us — to show us where the pitfalls and dead-ends are. This is the type of longing that the psalmist had for God's word. He yearned for God's word to guide his every step, for he knew that it would lead him to true joy. "Your statutes are wonderful; therefore I obey them," he wrote. In our individualistic society, it is easier to imagine longing for God's freedom than for his commands. But the psalmist understood that in them was to be found life in all its fullness.

Reaffirm your desire for God's word to guide your life. Pray that God might help you resist an evil habit that has been tempting you recently. ✣

PRAYER

Dear Lord, I long for your commands. Guide my steps by your word . . .

PUBLISHING GOD'S GLORIOUS DEEDS

Sing to the LORD, praise his name;
proclaim his salvation day after day.
Declare his glory among the nations,
his marvelous deeds among all peoples.
For great is the LORD and most worthy of praise;
he is to be feared above all gods.
For all the gods of the nations are idols,
but the LORD made the heavens.
Splendor and majesty are before him;
strength and glory are in his sanctuary.

PSALM 96:2-6

Early every morning—Monday through Sunday, brand-new newspapers are distributed throughout cities, towns, and neighborhoods. Or, readers can greet the day by perusing the daily news via the Internet. If only the Good News that Jesus came to save sinners were published and distributed just as widely as the dismal news of our daily newspapers! The psalmist committed himself to publishing the great deeds of God each day—just like a daily newspaper. As God's people, we need to hear again and again about God's saving grace; and the world around us needs to know why they should join us in worshiping and serving God.

Determine to start every morning by thinking of something God has done for you—how he created a brand-new day for you to enjoy, how he has saved you and given you food and shelter. Then find a way that day to publish God's wonderful deeds—to tell someone else about what he has done. ✤

PRAYER

Dear Lord, I will declare your glory among the nations. I will tell everyone about the amazing things you have done . . .

PRAISE TO THE ALL-KNOWING GOD

Where can I go from your Spirit?
Where can I flee from your presence?
If I go up to the heavens, you are there;
if I make my bed in the depths, you are there.
If I rise on the wings of the dawn,
if I settle on the far side of the sea,
even there your hand will guide me,
your right hand will hold me fast.

PSALM 139:7–10

David knew that it is both a wonderful and a fearful thing to realize that God is everywhere. We will never escape his presence. Sometimes, in our human weakness, we actually might try. Perhaps it is because we have a guilty conscience or feel inadequate to a task to which he has called us. Like Jonah, we seek to run away. But no one can run from the omnipresent God. Even if we were to travel to "the depths," God would be there. There is no life circumstance too dark for the light of God to penetrate. David realized he could travel far away; but God's hand would still be there to guide him. God is not limited like we are. No matter where the consequences of our sins might take us, we can never travel beyond the range of his love. To have this Lord on our side, to align our lives with his ways, is true security.

Praise the Lord for being with you right now. Ask him to guide you into his righteous ways. ✤

PRAYER

Dear Lord, I can never get away from your presence. Guide me into your truth ...

august26

RECALLING GOD'S ANSWER TO PRAYER

Let the redeemed of the LORD *tell their story—*
those he redeemed from the hand of the foe,
those he gathered from the lands,
from east and west, from north and south.
Some wandered in desert wastelands,
finding no way to a city where they could settle.
They were hungry and thirsty,
and their lives ebbed away.
Then they cried out to the LORD *in their trouble,*
and he delivered them from their distress.

PSALM 107:2–6

Hungry. Thirsty. Hopelessly lost. Not many of us have experienced the hunger pains caused by starvation, but we all know what it is like to be thirsty and hungry. We know what it is like to be lost—not knowing where to go or to whom we should turn for help. In such a state, we quickly become irritable and confused. When we finally find someone who can help us and supply us with food and drink, a profound sense of relief washes over us. In this prayer, the psalmist described the people of Israel as being hungry and lost. They called on God for help, and miraculously he answered. What a relief! The psalmist expressed his gratitude by praising God for answering their prayers and calling on everyone who was saved to speak out. "Let the redeemed of the LORD tell their story."

Has the Lord redeemed you? Are you excited about it? Take to heart these words of this psalm. Thank the Lord! Speak out! Tell others! ✤

PRAYER

O Dear Lord, thank you for redeeming me. I will speak out about what you have done . . .

august**27**

A PLEA FOR GOD TO LISTEN

Hear my prayer, LORD;
let my cry for help come to you.
Do not hide your face from me
when I am in distress.
Turn your ear to me;
when I call, answer me quickly.
For my days vanish like smoke;
my bones burn like glowing embers....
But you, LORD, sit enthroned forever;
your renown endures through all generations.

PSALM 102:1 – 3, 12

Like a page ripped out of a diary, this prayer gives us a glimpse into the prayer life of someone in great suffering. Many believe these are the journaled thoughts of an Israelite who was exiled to the wicked city of Babylon. The heartbeat of this prayer is simple: "Let my cry for help come to you." The author of this prayer asked God to "turn your ear" down to earth to hear him whisper his needs. No pretenses. No attempts to sound brave. The author of this prayer was devastated, so he cried out to God, begging him to hear his requests.

Go to your Father with your needs today. Ask for his ear to listen and his hand to comfort you as you lay out your concerns before him. ✤

PRAYER

Dear Lord, hear my prayer and listen to my plea ...

FINDING JOY IN THE MIDST OF STRESS

You are righteous, LORD,
  and your laws are right.
The statutes you have laid down are righteous;
  they are fully trustworthy....
Your righteousness is everlasting
  and your law is true.
Trouble and distress have come upon me,
  but your commands give me delight.
Your statutes are always righteous;
  give me understanding that I may live.

PSALM 119:137–138, 142–144

When facing great difficulties in life, have you ever wondered how God's ways fit into the pressures and stresses of real life? It is only normal, given our partial understanding of God, that we would encounter such questions. This prayer provides a wonderful model for bringing those issues truthfully before the Lord. The psalmist began his prayer by reminding himself of God's fairness and trustworthiness. When we make God's power and holiness a starting point for prayer, our daily struggles come into proper perspective. There is only one place to turn when nothing seems to make sense: God and his ways. "Trouble and distress have come upon me, but your commands give me delight," the psalmist declared. What was the source of the psalmist's joy? It was his belief that God is always fair, that he has ordered this world according to his decrees.

Commit the problems and difficulties you will face today to God. Ask him to help you joyfully follow his ways. ✣

PRAYER

Dear Lord, as pressure and stress bear down on me, I find joy in your commands ...

august29

THE ELDERS' PRAISE FOR GOD

Whenever the living creatures give glory, honor and thanks to him who sits on the throne and who lives for ever and ever, the twenty-four elders fall down before him who sits on the throne and worship him who lives for ever and ever. They lay their crowns before the throne and say:

> *"You are worthy, our Lord and God,*
> *   to receive glory and honor and power,*
> *for you created all things,*
> *   and by your will they were created*
> *   and have their being."*

REVELATION 4:9–11

Some people may have had the opportunity to see the riches of a king's palace, but none of us can imagine what God's throne room will be like. Revelation provides us with a picture of it—a brilliant throne made of gemstones, a shiny sea of crystal-like glass, and a rainbow-like glow filling the entire place. Yet what is central to John's description of God's throne room is the people's praise for God. Elders, angelic beings, and exotic living beings covered with eyes join their voices in an unending chorus glorifying God. As the elders lay their golden crowns before the throne, they shout out how worthy God is and how the entire cosmos was made for his pleasure. When we ponder this world—the heights of its mountains, the depths of its seas—we are awed beyond words. How much more, then, will we be overwhelmed to witness what John saw briefly: the whole range of creation, including angelic beings, praising God.

If the universe exists for God's pleasure, our part is clear. We should give God the adoration he deserves. Join your voice with the heavenly host today with these timeless words of praise. ✤

PRAYER

You are worthy, O Lord our God, to receive glory and honor and power . . .

DECLARING GOD AS ONE'S HELP

Do not withhold your mercy from me, LORD;
  may your love and faithfulness always protect me.
For troubles without number surround me;
  my sins have overtaken me, and I cannot see.
They are more than the hairs of my head,
  and my heart fails within me....
But as for me, I am poor and needy;
  may the Lord think of me.
You are my help and my deliverer;
  you are my God, do not delay.

PSALM 40:11 – 12, 17

As the king over all of Israel, David had a mountain of riches — jewels, money, gold, and numerous servants to do his bidding. Yet, David came to a place in his life where he proclaimed that God alone was his "help and ... deliverer." We don't know the specific situation for which this prayer was written — what troubles this prayer addressed. But we can imagine it was a landmark in David's life. What does it take for you to claim God as your "help"? What would make you look solely to God instead of more money, status, or friends to solve your problems? There is promise and power in a prayer like David's.

Think back to a difficult time in your life when the Lord was your only hope. Present your present troubles to God in prayer. Then declare to God that you are trusting him to rescue you. ✤

PRAYER

Dear Lord, my only hope is in your unfailing love. Don't hold back your tender mercies from me ...

august**31**

WORSHIPING THE LORD WITH GLADNESS

Shout for joy to the LORD, all the earth.
    Worship the LORD with gladness;
    come before him with joyful songs.
Know that the LORD is God.
    It is he who made us, and we are his;
    we are his people, the sheep of his pasture.

PSALM 100:1 – 3

Joy. Pleasure. Delight. Too often, we associate these emotions with earthly pleasures — such as enjoying fancy hotels, getting a designer dress or purse, owning a brand-new car or home, or savoring fine food. The author of this prayer, however, associated joy and delight with worshiping God and learning more about his ways. He called upon God's people to "worship the LORD with gladness." Our heartfelt joy in all God has given us — in all he has done for us — is like beautiful, harmonious music drifting back to God's ears. God finds pleasure in those who rejoice in what he has given them and thank him for it.

Find a new way today to express your happiness to God. Rejoice in what God has given you and share your joy with your acquaintances and coworkers. ♣

PRAYER

Dear Lord, I am yours. I come before you with shouts of joy . . .

PRAISE FOR THE GOD WHO GIVES SUCCESS

> *He raises the poor from the dust*
> *and lifts the needy from the ash heap;*
> *he seats them with princes*
> *and has them inherit a throne of honor.*
> *"For the foundations of the earth are the LORD's;*
> *on them he has set the world.*
> *He will guard the feet of his faithful servants,*
> *but the wicked will be silenced in the place of darkness.*
> *"It is not by strength that one prevails;*
> *those who oppose the LORD will be broken.*
> *The Most High will thunder from heaven;*
> *the LORD will judge the ends of the earth.*
> *"He will give strength to his king*
> *and exalt the horn of his anointed."*

1 SAMUEL 2:8–10

Who would ever guess these were the words of a mother who had just given her baby boy to God to be a priest? Instead of despairing over her child, Hannah praised God for blessing her with a son in the first place. In spite of the pain of giving up her child, joy filled her prayers. Her sacrifice was success in her eyes because she was committed to following God.

Success often occurs because of some type of sacrifice, and joy often follows a period of suffering. Let Hannah's prayer remind you of the faith needed when you encounter hardship and suffering in your life. God will transform your suffering into success, your weakness into strength. Hand over your suffering, hardships, and weaknesses to God in prayer. Ask him to use those difficulties in your life to help others. ❖

PRAYER

Dear Lord, I know no one will succeed by strength alone. You give mighty strength to your people . . .

september**2**

A PRAYER FOR GOD'S GUIDANCE

Be good to your servant while I live,
that I may obey your word.
Open my eyes that I may see
wonderful things in your law.
I am a stranger on earth;
do not hide your commands from me.
My soul is consumed with longing
for your laws at all times....
Your statutes are my delight;
they are my counselors.

PSALM 119:17–20, 24

In September, the cool winds begin to blow; and red and orange leaves begin to fall. September marks the end of the lazy days of summer—a time when we begin to concentrate fully on our tasks at work or at school. Life's pace quickens; and more than ever, we need to consult God's Word to find out how we should live. The author of this prayer saw himself as a "stranger on earth"—as someone who lived according to a higher purpose than simply accomplishing the various tasks of each day. He lived to please God and follow his commands. In them he found wise advice; and he prayed that God might reveal to him more of his wonderful truths in Scripture as he studied it. What treasures would we find in God's laws if we only prepared ourselves for reading it by praying!

The next time you set aside time to study Scripture, pray first. Ask God to help you apply the truths of Scripture to your life. ❧

PRAYER

Dear Lord, open my eyes to see the wonderful truths in Scripture. Help me to obey your laws ...

september3

PRAYING FOR VICTORY

May the LORD answer you when you are in distress;
may the name of the God of Jacob protect you.
May he send you help from the sanctuary
and grant you support from Zion.
May he remember all your sacrifices
and accept your burnt offerings.
May he give you the desire of your heart
and make all your plans succeed.
May we shout for joy over your victory
and lift up our banners in the name of our God.
May the LORD grant all your requests.

PSALM 20:1–5

Imagine the tips of sharpened weapons gleaming in the early morning sun as God's people, armed for battle, encouraged their king with their prayers. As they assembled themselves to march out against Israel's foes, they shouted this prayer under the direction of David's director of music.

Who knows what battles the people you love might be facing today? As you think of friends and family members, pray for their protection and for victory in their lives. Ask God to answer their prayers. Picture them assembling themselves for battle—getting ready for the new school year, going to work, mulling through what they must accomplish that day. Then pray for victory in what they must do. Pray that their accomplishments might bring glory to God; and, then, pray the same for yourself. ❖

PRAYER

Dear Lord, I pray that you will fulfill all the plans of . . .

september**4**

ASKING GOD WHICH WAY TO TURN

But I, by your great love,
   can come into your house;
in reverence I bow down
   toward your holy temple.
Lead me, LORD, in your righteousness
   because of my enemies—
   make your way straight before me.

PSALM 5:7–8

David wrote these words amid controversy and confusion. His enemies often tried to harass him with evil rumors and outright lies, as the rest of this psalm indicates. In those difficult and unsettling times, David immediately turned to God for direction. Surrounded by lies, David desired truth. Confronted with choices, David sought to choose the one right path.

Express your desire for God to guide you—especially during those times when life has offered you a confusing array of choices. Ask God to dispel your confusion by helping you decide which way to turn. Pray that God might help you make right choices today. ✣

PRAYER

Dear Lord, tell me clearly what to do. Show me which way to turn...

september5

JESUS' PRAYER FOR HOLY LIVING

They are not of the world, even as I am not of it. Sanctify them by the truth; your word is truth. As you sent me into the world, I have sent them into the world. For them I sanctify myself, that they too may be truly sanctified.

JOHN 17:16–19

Jesus prayed these words the night of his arrest. What is significant about this prayer is its focus. As he faced his final days when he would suffer the most, Jesus' concern was not for his own well-being. He was most concerned about his followers, whom he would leave behind. In front of his disciples, Jesus poured his heart out in prayer. He prayed for their purity and holiness in a world filled with betrayal, revenge, and lies. Jesus' prayer is for us as well. He longs for us to be his pure and holy people in a culture that revels in sexual immorality, greed, and self-centeredness. These words were among the last things Jesus said to his disciples before leaving them. Last words are important words. They indicate how much Jesus prized the purity and holiness of his disciple's lives.

Make Jesus' words your prayer. Pray that you may live a pure and holy life so that you may bring honor to him. ✤

PRAYER

Dear Lord, make me pure and holy by teaching me your words of truth ...

september**6**

THE LORD'S PRAYER

"This, then, is how you should pray:

> *'Our Father in heaven,*
> *hallowed be your name,*
> *your kingdom come,*
> *your will be done,*
> > *on earth as it is in heaven.*
> *Give us today our daily bread.*
> *And forgive us our debts,*
> > *as we also have forgiven our debtors.*
> *And lead us not into temptation,*
> > *but deliver us from the evil one."*

MATTHEW 6:9–13

When you go to a restaurant, you don't just order some food, you make specific requests. When asking for directions to a location, you wouldn't be satisfied with generalities. In the same way, Jesus' prayer reminds us to be specific when we ask God for something. Christ tells us to pray for the food we will eat that day, for forgiveness of our sins, and for protection from temptation.

Too often we pray in generalities. Instead, we can use the Lord's prayer as a guide. Start your prayer by acknowledging whom you're approaching—the almighty God, the one whose name should be honored by everyone everywhere. Recommit yourself to his Kingdom and his purposes. Confess your sins, and pray that the Lord would protect you from succumbing to any further temptations. And finally, ask the Lord for what you need that day. Tell him about your concerns and your needs. God is waiting to pour out his blessing and resources on you—if you only will ask. ✤

PRAYER

Dear Lord, may your will be done . . .

PRAYING FOR KINDNESS AMONG BELIEVERS

I pray that your partnership with us in the faith may be effective in deepening your under-standing of every good thing we share for the sake of Christ. Your love has given me great joy and encouragement, because you, brother, have refreshed the hearts of the Lord's people.
PHILEMON VV. 6–7

Under Roman law, a runaway slave could face death if he was caught. But despite that dire possibility, Paul sent Onesimus—a runaway slave who had converted to Christianity under Paul's teaching—back to his Christian owner, Philemon. Paul, in chains himself for the gospel, didn't want the Romans to have any reason to condemn his or Onesimus's actions. Yet, he prayed that Onesimus wouldn't suffer for what he had done. He prayed that Philemon would welcome Onesimus as a Christian brother—not as a rebellious slave. This was a potentially explosive situation between two believers. Paul faced it head-on first with fervent prayer and then by encouraging those involved to be kind to each other.

When have you faced an explosive situation among your Christian friends? Today, pray for a believer with whom you are having difficulties. Then make an effort this week to praise one admirable character trait in that person. ❖

PRAYER

Dear Lord, help me to be kind to other believers. I am praying for ...

september**8**

A SYMPHONY OF PRAISES

Praise the LORD from the earth,
you great sea creatures and all ocean depths,
lightning and hail, snow and clouds,
stormy winds that do his bidding,
you mountains and all hills,
fruit trees and all cedars,
wild animals and all cattle,
small creatures and flying birds,
kings of the earth and all nations,
you princes and all rulers on earth,
young men and women,
old men and children.

PSALM 148:7 – 12

This earth is filled with all types of intriguing creatures. All you have to do is turn on a nature program to see everything from giant squids to fuzzy koala bears. As the cameras of these naturalists go to the depths of the oceans and the unexplored jungles, they find more and more exotic creatures. The extent of God's creation stretches our imaginations. Meditating on how God reigns over this amazing diversity leads to heartfelt praise. This prayer calls upon all of God's creation— lions and tigers, bulls and cows, sparrows and pigeons—to sing their praises to God. It encourages the forces of nature—lightning and hail; snow and clouds; stormy winds—to join in. No manmade instrument can equal the chorus of God's creation. Every person—both old and young, great and small—can sing their praises to their Creator. He is the one who creates and sustains each of us. At every stage of life, no matter our station, he is worthy of our praise.

Meditate on the extent of God's creation and offer the Lord your praise. ✤

PRAYER

Dear Lord, I praise you . . .

september**9**

ASKING TO BE LED ALONG GOD'S PATH

Show me your ways, LORD,
teach me your paths.
Guide me in your truth and teach me,
for you are God my Savior,
and my hope is in you all day long.

PSALM 25:4–5

Sometimes we're faced with several options, and we don't know which way to go. In this psalm, David asked God for guidance. Perhaps he remembered when, as a shepherd boy, he had to show the right path to his sheep who were wandering away. Just as he knew which path would lead to safety for his sheep, God knew the path that would lead to everlasting life. "Good and upright is the LORD; therefore he instructs sinners in his ways" (25:8). David proclaimed. Just as those sheep who looked to him for direction were in the least danger, so David knew he needed to look to God for direction. He prayed, "Show me the ways," and "teach me your paths."

Today, God still leads us by his truth — the Word. Are you not sure which path to take? Pray like David did. Ask God to show you the right road to follow. ✤

PRAYER

Dear Father, show me the path where I should walk ...

september**10**

JEHOSHAPHAT'S CRY FOR HELP

When the chariot commanders saw Jehoshaphat, they thought, "This is the king of Israel." So they turned to attack him, but Jehoshaphat cried out, and the LORD helped him. God drew them away from him.

2 CHRONICLES 18:31

During battle, the wicked King Ahab of Israel disguised himself as a foot soldier. This cowardly act left his ally, a brightly robed King Jehoshaphat, a sitting duck for their common enemy, the Arameans. Although God had warned Jehoshaphat about allying with Ahab, Jehoshaphat did so anyway. Despite his error, Jehoshaphat knew where to turn when he was in trouble. He cried out to God. His story should soften our pride—especially when we try to cling to our own faulty decisions. His prayer becomes our own when we have the courage to ask God for help, despite our rebellion.

Aren't you glad you never encounter "I told you so" in prayer? Turn to God for help when you know you need it—even when you don't deserve it. ❖

PRAYER

Dear Lord, forgive my pride and sinfulness. Come save me . . .

september11

PRAYING FOR SPIRITUAL WISDOM

For this reason, since the day we heard about you, we have not stopped praying for you. We continually ask God to fill you with the knowledge of his will through all the wisdom and understanding that the Spirit gives.

Colossians 1:9

A mother with a newborn daughter showers an extraordinary amount of attention on her young child, and justifiably so. She keeps the child near by and answers her every cry. Paul treated the Colossians as if he was their parent. Although he was under house arrest in Rome, his concern for their spiritual upbringing was evident in the tender way in which he pleaded with God the Father on their behalf. Of all the things he could have desired for these new believers, he chose understanding and spiritual wisdom as the focus of his prayers. Obtaining spiritual wisdom is not dependent upon on any earthly experience—such as family upbringing, higher education, or some specialized training. It is entirely a gift from God.

Like Paul, we also can ask for wisdom for ourselves and the ones we love. Let Paul's love for the Colossians inspire you to pray for other believers who need God's wisdom in the situations they are facing. ✤

PRAYER

Dear Lord, give spiritual wisdom to ...

september**12**

WAITING ON THE LORD IN THE MORNING

Answer me quickly, LORD;
my spirit fails.
Do not hide your face from me
or I will be like those who go down to the pit.
Let the morning bring me word of your unfailing love,
for I have put my trust in you.
Show me the way I should go,
for to you I entrust my life.
Rescue me from my enemies, LORD,
for I hide myself in you.
Teach me to do your will,
for you are my God;
may your good Spirit
lead me on level ground.

PSALM 143:7–10

It's autumn; and there's a wonderful crispness in the air. The mornings are brisk and invigorating; and it's delightful to walk through the leaves while they're still damp from the dew. On such a morning, it's easy to feel God's nearness. It may have been a morning like this when David prayed, "Let the morning bring me word of your unfailing love, for I have put my trust in you. Show me the way I should go, for to you I entrust my life." David longed to have fellowship with God early in the morning, and he didn't even want to take a step without the Lord's direction. He wanted God's Spirit to lead him to a path where he could find a firm footing.

Determine to start each morning with the Lord. At that time, ask God to direct your every step throughout the day. ❧

PRAYER

Dear Lord, let me hear of your unfailing love to me in the morning. Show me where to walk today . . .

september13

COMMITTING ONE'S CAUSE TO GOD

But you, LORD Almighty, who judge righteously
and test the heart and mind,
let me see your vengeance on them,
for to you I have committed my cause.

JEREMIAH 11:20

Everyone has a *cause* today. We constantly receive mail and phone calls from organizations asking us to give money and time to support their cause. The prophet Jeremiah also had a cause: to deliver God's message, to call the people of Israel to repent and turn to God. Jeremiah's enemies, however, were plotting to kill him. They wanted to silence him and his message. Jeremiah asked the Lord to intervene and take vengeance against those enemies, reminding God that he had committed his cause to him long ago.

If our cause honors God and if we have committed it to him, we can be sure he will honor and bless our efforts. Pray today that you're supporting the right cause. Then, ask for God's blessing on it. ✤

PRAYER

Dear Lord, you know my deepest thoughts. I commit my cause to you . . .

september**14**

SEEKING GOD'S CONFIRMATION

Gideon said to God, "If you will save Israel by my hand as you have promised—look, I will place a wool fleece on the threshing floor. If there is dew only on the fleece and all the ground is dry, then I will know that you will save Israel by my hand, as you said." And that is what happened. Gideon rose early the next day; he squeezed the fleece and wrung out the dew—a bowlful of water.

JUDGES 6:36–38

There are times when we simply can't believe what God is asking us to do. Gideon found himself in such a situation. Although God had told Gideon that he was to rescue Israel from the Midianites and even promised to be with him, Gideon still couldn't believe it. He asked for a sign to confirm God's call. He asked God to make the wool fleece wet by morning, while making the ground around it bone dry. When that happened just as he asked, he was still not convinced. Gideon asked for yet another sign: this time a dry fleece on wet ground. Finally convinced, Gideon obeyed. He led an army of Israelites against the Midianites. God gave him a miraculous victory over them, just as he had promised to do. God is so patient with us, even when we doubt and "put out our own fleece" before we believe and act.

If you believe God is asking you to do something, go to him in prayer. Ask for his confirmation, then act upon it. ✢

PRAYER

Dear God, confirm to me what you want me to do ...

september15

PRAYING FOR SUCCESS

"Lord, let your ear be attentive to the prayer of this your servant and to the prayer of your servants who delight in revering your name. Give your servant success today by granting him favor in the presence of this man."
   I was cupbearer to the king.

NEHEMIAH 1:11

Success is often elusive. It depends on numerous factors, including your boss's mood for that day. Nehemiah understood this, so he approached God in prayer asking for success in what he wanted to do. Nehemiah, the cupbearer for King Artaxerxes, had heard that the people back in Judea were suffering and that the walls of Jerusalem had been torn down. Upon hearing that bad news, he wept, fasted, and prayed. He asked God to send him to Judea to rebuild Jerusalem's walls. He knew the success of his plans would depend on God influencing the heart of the king. Later, Nehemiah boldly presented his plan to the king and asked for permission to return to Jerusalem and rebuild its walls. "Because the gracious hand of my God was on me, the king granted my requests," Nehemiah wrote (2:8).

God knows our needs, and wants us to succeed in those plans that honor him. Take your plans to God in prayer. Ask that you might honor his name through your plans; and, then, pray that God might grant you success. ✤

PRAYER

Dear Lord, I delight in honoring you. Please grant me success ...

september**16**

PRAISING GOD FOR HIS VICTORY

> *Sing to the LORD a new song,*
>   *for he has done marvelous things;*
> *his right hand and his holy arm*
>   *have worked salvation for him.*
> *The LORD has made his salvation known*
>   *and revealed his righteousness to the nations.*
> *He has remembered his love*
>   *and his faithfulness to Israel;*
> *all the ends of the earth have seen*
>   *the salvation of our God.*

PSALM 98:1–3

Singing—both what we sing and how we sing—says a lot about the way we feel. Singing can communicate volumes. A downcast face or halfhearted voice can make joyful lyrics sound weak and flat. A smiling and cheerful singer can liven up almost any song. Talking and thinking about what God has done for us gets our hearts focused on what is good, true, and beautiful. Yet when we sing to him, we offer God something that pleases him greatly: heartfelt sacrifices of praise and thanksgiving. This psalm calls on people everywhere to offer these sacrifices to God by lifting their voices in praise of him. It calls us to join this noisy and joyous celebration of Almighty God.

In your prayer time today, open up a hymnal or praise book. Find a song that celebrates God's power, and use it to praise your Father in heaven. ✦

PRAYER

Dear Lord, I know you have done wonderful deeds. I will sing a new song to you . . .

september**17**

PRAYING FOR OPPORTUNITIES TO SHARE CHRIST

And pray for us, too, that God may open a door for our message, so that we may proclaim the mystery of Christ, for which I am in chains. Pray that I may proclaim it clearly, as I should.
COLOSSIANS 4:3–4

If telling your acquaintances about Christ sometimes seems a daunting task, remind yourself that the apostle Paul found it challenging as well. That is why Paul asked the Christians at Colosse to pray that he would have opportunities to preach the gospel and that he would proclaim the message as clearly as he should. Whether he felt he was lacking in courage or skill or something else, he knew he needed God's Spirit to work through him; and he knew that God would honor the prayers of other believers.

Today, pray for your unbelieving friends and acquaintances. Pray that you may have the opportunity to share with them the message that Christ died for their sins succinctly and clearly. ❖

PRAYER

Dear Lord, help me to proclaim the gospel as clearly as I should . . .

september18

A PRAYER FOR THE PEOPLE'S FAITHFULNESS

And may these words of mine, which I have prayed before the LORD, be near to the LORD our God day and night, that he may uphold the cause of his servant and the cause of his people Israel according to each day's need, so that all the peoples of the earth may know that the LORD is God and that there is no other. And may your hearts be fully committed to the LORD our God, to live by his decrees and obey his commands, as at this time.

1 KINGS 8:59–61

Solomon prayed these words at a moment of great rejoicing. The Temple stood before them in all its magnificence—finally, completed! Golden altars. Towering stone pillars. The smell of incense in the air. It was a day to celebrate. Peace and prosperity reigned under Solomon's watchful eye. But Solomon didn't take this for granted. He knew that if his people were unfaithful, it could be gone in a moment. He knew that in order for them to enjoy God's blessing they would need to be faithful to God. They had to take to heart the commandments God had given them for their own good.

We, too, even in moments of great elation, need to remember to pray that we will be faithful, through good times and bad. ✤

PRAYER

Dear Lord, I always want to be faithful to you . . .

september**19**

KEEPING ONE'S PROMISES TO GOD

Truly I am your servant, LORD;
I serve you just as my mother did;
you have freed me from my chains.
I will sacrifice a thank offering to you
and call on the name of the LORD.
I will fulfill my vows to the LORD
in the presence of all his people,
in the courts of the house of the LORD—
in your midst, Jerusalem.

Praise the LORD.

PSALM 116:16–19

Today, we don't hear too much about slavery—even though people still enslave others in many parts of the world. In ancient times, a debt could cause a person to be sold into slavery. The author of this prayer compared his spiritual walk with God with being liberated from the cruelty of slavery. He responded to God by offering a sacrifice of thanksgiving. He expressed his joy by returning a gift to his Liberator, by vowing to call on his Deliverer at all times, and by vowing to keep his promises to God. He honored the Lord for the great gift he had received. Many of us naturally thank and praise Jesus for saving us. But often we don't realize Jesus expects us to go further. He wants us to follow him, offering our lives to him as pure living sacrifices.

Thank God for saving you from your sin, by committing yourself to following him every day. ✤

PRAYER

Dear Lord, I will keep my promises to you in the presence of all your people . . .

september**20**

ELIJAH'S PRAYER FOR A CHILD'S LIFE

Then he cried out to the LORD, "LORD my God, have you brought tragedy even on this widow I am staying with, by causing her son to die?" Then he stretched himself out on the boy three times and cried out to the LORD, "LORD my God, let this boy's life return to him!"

The LORD heard Elijah's cry, and the boy's life returned to him, and he lived.

1 KINGS 17:20–22

The widow of Zarephath had taken Elijah in as an extra mouth to feed during a time of famine. Though she had nothing to feed herself and her son, she trusted God to provide. And indeed, God saw them through. Later, the woman's son became ill and died. The woman couldn't understand why God would protect her son and then let him die. Elijah turned immediately to the Lord. He knew that life and death are in God's hands. So Elijah pleaded for the child's life. God heard and answered Elijah's bold yet simple plea. God didn't raise from the dead a very important person of Elijah's day—a king or a priest—only a poor widow's son. Every individual is important in the eyes of God.

Take some time to pray for someone who is experiencing heartache or tragedy in his or her life. Pray that God may apply his life-giving power to that situation. We can pray for anyone—no matter how poor, no matter how important—for God cares about that person. ✤

PRAYER

O Lord, why have you brought tragedy on . . .

september21

ASKING FOR GOD'S FAVOR

The LORD bless you
  and keep you;
the LORD make his face shine on you
  and be gracious to you;
the LORD turn his face toward you
  and give you peace.

NUMBERS 6:24–26

What are the signs of favor? Smiles and pats on the back are signs. A mother's smile can produce giggles in an infant. A pat on the back tells the person that he or she did well. These signs express love, affection, approval, and support. In this blessing that God gave to Moses, the Lord taught Moses and the Levites to pray for his favor: "to make his face shine on you and be gracious to you." What a picture of God! He teaches us to ask him to protect and bless us. These requests address some of the most fundamental needs of people.

Take the words of this ancient, God-given prayer, and use it to pray for someone you know. ✤

PRAYER

Dear Lord, please grant me your favor . . .

september**22**

LEAVING OUR LIVES IN HIS HANDS

Come and see what God has done,
his awesome deeds for mankind!
He turned the sea into dry land,
they passed through the waters on foot—
come, let us rejoice in him.
He rules forever by his power,
his eyes watch the nations—
let not the rebellious rise up against him.
Praise our God, all peoples,
let the sound of his praise be heard;
he has preserved our lives
and kept our feet from slipping.

PSALM 66:5−9

Some of the prayers in the Psalms are proclamations shouted from the place of worship for all the faithful to hear. Indeed, if they could, the worshipers would proclaim God's greatness to the whole world—to young and old, to the sea and to the mountains. The author of this prayer invites everyone to celebrate God: "Come, let us rejoice in him." What is there to celebrate? God and his care for them. He has performed miracles for his people. By his great power, he rules forever. No one can succeed in rebelling against him. At the right time, the whole world will bless our God for he holds everyone in his hands—yes, even our lives are in his loving hands. He keeps our feet from stumbling. God is worthy of our praise.

Let us join our voices with his faithful people from the past, praising him for who he is and trusting him with our lives. Thank him for keeping you from stumbling. ✤

PRAYER

Dear Lord, my life is in your hands, and you keep my feet from stumbling . . .

september**23**

PRAISE FOR THE GOD WHO NEVER CHANGES

He also says,

> *"In the beginning, Lord, you laid the foundations of the earth,*
> *and the heavens are the work of your hands.*
> *They will perish, but you remain;*
> *they will all wear out like a garment.*
> *You will roll them up like a robe;*
> *like a garment they will be changed.*
> *But you remain the same,*
> *and your years will never end."*

HEBREWS 1:10−12

The marvels of nature—the astounding heights of mountains, the extent of the oceans and the cosmos beyond—have long inspired people everywhere. The writer of Hebrews offered praise to Jesus, the creator of all this. Jesus had "laid the foundations of the earth" and stretched out the heavens. Yet, the author of Hebrews wrote that even these impressive aspects of creation would eventually be peeled off and thrown away like old, worn-out clothing. Only God himself is permanent. No matter how enduring nature might seem, it cannot compare with God's perfection and permanence. God "remain[s] the same."

How comforting to know that our Creator, the one on whom we depend to sustain our lives, is *unchanging!* Though we ourselves are fickle, changeable and, most of all neglectful of our relationship with him, he will never change in his love for us. Though we age and become feeble, God's power never fades. Turn to the Unchanging One with all your needs. ✤

PRAYER

Dear Lord, you are always the same . . .

september24

A PETITION FOR BLESSING

Jabez cried out to the God of Israel, "Oh, that you would bless me and enlarge my territory! Let your hand be with me, and keep me from harm so that I will be free from pain." And God granted his request.

1 Chronicles 4:10

One name stands out in the genealogy in 1 Chronicles—Jabez. His mother named him "Distress" because her labor was so difficult. Often in Scriptures, a person's life conforms to the meaning of his name. But Jabez, when he reached adulthood, literally appealed to a higher authority. In the histories of many peoples, individuals are mentioned for their great deeds, but Jabez is mentioned for his *prayer*. His requests were ordinary enough—who would not wish for prosperity and the absence of trouble! But Jabez trusted God enough to ask God for these things. History records that God granted his request; and obviously Jabez told everyone about God's answer to his prayer.

Imitate the faith Jabez had in God. Boldly ask the Lord to bless you—to be with you in whatever you do and wherever you go. ❖

PRAYER

Dear God, please be with me in all that I do . . .

PRAISING THE LORD FOR HOW GOOD HE IS

Praise the LORD.

> *Praise the name of the LORD;*
>> *praise him, you servants of the LORD,*
> *you who minister in the house of the LORD,*
>> *in the courts of the house of our God.*
> *Praise the LORD, for the LORD is good;*
>> *sing praise to his name, for that is pleasant.*

PSALM 135:1–3

God's goodness is evident in every aspect of our lives. Our friends, family, and children are gifts from the Lord. Our possessions are from God's hands. For these reasons, some of our prayer time should be devoted to rejoicing in his goodness. The author of this prayer did just that. He called upon all God's people gathered in the Temple for worship to praise the Lord for his goodness. The very organization of the Temple, with its regal decoration and its hallowed chambers, was designed to inspire awe and praise for God. Entire clans were dedicated to magnifying God Almighty—generation after generation. Some celebrated the feasts and sacrifices. Others were trained musicians, leading the people in song. This prayer calls upon all of these people—and the common people as well—to celebrate God's goodness.

Make certain that some of your prayers this coming week are devoted to praising God for his goodness to you and your family. ✦

PRAYER

Dear Lord, I praise you, for you have been good to me . . .

september**26**

PRAISING THE GOD WHO KNOWS US

You have searched me, LORD,
  and you know me.
You know when I sit and when I rise;
  you perceive my thoughts from afar.
You discern my going out and my lying down;
  you are familiar with all my ways.
Before a word is on my tongue
  you, LORD, know it completely.

PSALM 139:1–4

One of the greatest desires of the human heart is that of intimacy: knowing and being known. Our relationship with God is unique in that he alone knows us completely. David honored this relationship in grateful prayer. It is an act of worship and submission to admit that God knows *everything* about us. Regardless of where we may find ourselves, regardless of what time, day, or year, God knows our every thought. More than that, he can *direct* us, telling us where to go and even when to rest in him. Incomprehensible as it may be to our finite minds, God's knowledge is not limited to the past and the present. To use David's words, "Before a word is on my tongue. you, LORD, know it completely." That is how intimately God knows and understands you. That is how much he loves you.

In prayer today, answer God's love for you with joyful praises to the one who knows you so well. ✣

PRAYER

O Lord, you have examined my heart and know everything about me . . .

PRAISING GOD FOR SAVING US

> *A glorious throne, exalted from the beginning,*
> *   is the place of our sanctuary.*
> *LORD, you are the hope of Israel;*
> *   all who forsake you will be put to shame.*
> *Those who turn away from you will be written in the dust*
> *   because they have forsaken the LORD,*
> *   the spring of living water.*
> *Heal me, LORD, and I will be healed;*
> *   save me and I will be saved,*
> *   for you are the one I praise.*

> JEREMIAH 17:12–14

Jeremiah had the daunting task of warning God's rebellious people that there will be consequences to their disobedience, idolatry, and self-seeking behavior. After announcing God's judgment to the people, he turned to God in prayer, naming the Lord as the only source of his hope. Turning from all the greed, injustice, and unrighteousness around him, he meditated on God's "glorious" throne. He reiterated in conversation with God the truths he had been proclaiming—that those who turn from him would one day be disgraced. Death and the grave are the natural consequences of refusing God's "spring of living water." Jeremiah, in contrast, declared his dependence on God. Having reminded himself of these eternal truths, how could he not praise the only true God?

We, too, should remember who has saved and healed us. Again and again, we need to remind ourselves in prayer of how much God has done for us. ✤

PRAYER

O Lord, you alone can heal me; you alone can save . . .

september**28**

OFFERING ONE'S LIFE TO GOD

Then I heard the voice of the Lord saying, "Whom shall I send? And who will go for us?"
And I said, "Here am I. Send me!"
He said, "Go and tell this people:

"'Be ever hearing, but never understanding;
be ever seeing, but never perceiving.'"

ISAIAH 6:8 – 9

"Here am I. Send me!" Isaiah's response to God's call was eager enthusiasm. The kind of enthusiasm a young child shows for baking cookies with mom or cleaning the garage with dad—an eagerness to do new things, even though the tasks are considered work. After being cleansed of his sins with a burning coal, Isaiah was anxious to show his gratitude to God in tangible ways. When God asked "Whom shall I send? And who will go for us?" Isaiah responded with a zeal that comes from intense gratitude. Once he had been justified in the presence of the Holy One, he held nothing back from God. God revealed a need for someone to go as a messenger to his people. Isaiah offered the only thing he had—himself; and God accepted his offering.

Are you eager to respond to God's call? In prayer, imitate Isaiah's attitude by offering your life to God. ✤

PRAYER

Dear Lord, I'll go! Send me . . .

september29

GLAD TO BE IN GOD'S PRESENCE

May God arise, may his enemies be scattered;
may his foes flee before him.
May you blow them away like smoke —
as wax melts before the fire,
may the wicked perish before God.
But may the righteous be glad
and rejoice before God;
may they be happy and joyful.
Sing to God, sing in praise of his name,
extol him who rides on the clouds;
rejoice before him — his name is the LORD.

PSALM 68:1 – 4

Too often, we approach our prayer time with a familiar reluctance. It is almost as if we are saying, "Not again. I'm too busy to find time to talk to God." As this prayer indicates, David cultivated an attitude of joy when he approached God in prayer. He understood what a privilege it was to talk to the Almighty. God's enemies wouldn't even be able to stand in the Lord's presence. They would quickly melt away like wax in a furnace. Though David was astonished by God's power, he was filled with joy because he was allowed to enter God's presence. He counted himself among the godly — those who reverence God and obey his laws. They were God's children and were allowed to enter his magnificent throne room, enjoy his gifts, and thank and praise him.

When you enter God's presence today in prayer, thank God for listening to you. Rejoice in the gifts he has given you. ✤

PRAYER

Dear God, I am glad to be in your presence. I am filled with joy . . .

september**30**

PONDERING GOD'S AMAZING DEEDS

Praise the LORD.

> *I will extol the LORD with all my heart*
> *   in the council of the upright and in the assembly.*
> *Great are the works of the LORD;*
> *   they are pondered by all who delight in them.*
> *Glorious and majestic are his deeds,*
> *   and his righteousness endures forever.*
> *He has caused his wonders to be remembered;*
> *   the LORD is gracious and compassionate.*
> *He provides food for those who fear him;*
> *   he remembers his covenant forever.*
> *He has shown his people the power of his works,*
> *   giving them the lands of other nations.*

PSALM III:I–6

Our minds naturally go back again and again to the things we don't understand—pondering them, trying to make sense of them. The psalmist encourages believers to reflect on the amazing deeds of their God. We should express our thanks to God publicly as well as privately, letting other believers be encouraged by our reports of God's goodness to us. Everything God does reveals something about him—his love and compassion, his power and glory. God feeds us; he never forgets his covenant with us; he demonstrates his love and power to us by giving us all types of gifts—including land, houses, vineyards, and other possessions. "Glorious and majestic are his deeds."

Add your own testimony to this chronicle of God's faithfulness in both your private prayers and before the people in your church. ✤

PRAYER

Dear Lord, how amazing are your deeds! You have shown me the power of your works...

october1

A PRAYER THAT GOD WOULD PROVE HIMSELF

At the time of sacrifice, the prophet Elijah stepped forward and prayed: "LORD, the God of Abraham, Isaac and Israel, let it be known today that you are God in Israel and that I am your servant and have done all these things at your command. Answer me, LORD, answer me, so these people will know that you, LORD, are God, and that you are turning their hearts back again."

1 KINGS 18:36–37

In a moment of crisis in Israel, the prophet Elijah set up a showdown—a duel between the living God and the false god Baal. The priests of Baal had led so many Israelites astray that Elijah thought it was time to expose their sham—Baal didn't exist. Elijah challenged the Baal priests to pray that Baal might set fire to their sacrifice. They cried out to Baal. No response. They shouted louder. Again, no response. In desperation, they cut themselves. No answer. Just silence. Then came Elijah's turn. He prepared his sacrifice by drenching it with gallons of water. Only when the altar was soaked and the trench around it was overflowing did Elijah pray to God. He asked God to prove himself to these doubting people. God had no obligation to prove himself once again to these people; but Elijah asked that he would so the Israelites would repent of their ways and glorify him. Elijah's simple prayer was answered with fire raining down from heaven, consuming the entire altar. One prayer. One unmistakable answer. No need for questions anymore.

Think of some of your friends and acquaintances who are not certain whether they should follow God. Ask God to prove himself to them by answering your prayers. ✤

PRAYER

Dear Lord, answer me so these people will know that you, O Lord, are God . . .

october2

EXALTING THE GOD OF CREATION

The heavens declare the glory of God;
the skies proclaim the work of his hands.
Day after day they pour forth speech;
night after night they reveal knowledge.
They have no speech, they use no words;
no sound is heard from them.
Yet their voice goes out into all the earth,
their words to the ends of the world.
In the heavens God has pitched a tent for the sun.
It is like a bridegroom coming out of his chamber,
like a champion rejoicing to run his course.

PSALM 19:1–5

The starry nighttime sky. The brilliant blue heavens. For David, the moon and the sun, the stars and the planets were all reminders of what a remarkable craftsman God was. He had created those starry heights and had set them into motion. In this prayer, David focused on the sun. He didn't worship the sun as his pagan neighbors did. No, he saw the sun itself as worshiping its Creator by doing what it was made to do—joyfully shining down on the earth. David believed that the sun—and indeed the entire heavens—were rejoicing in God. If only our ears could hear the pitches at which all creation sings out God's praises! Though to our ears they seem silent, their message rings out throughout the whole world.

Take some time to ponder the intricate details in the natural world around you. Join your voice with the "voices" of the heavens in praise of your Creator. ✤

PRAYER

Dear God, the heavens tell of your glory ...

october**3**

QUIET BEFORE GOD

My heart is not proud, LORD,
*   my eyes are not haughty;*
I do not concern myself with great matters
*   or things too wonderful for me.*
But I have calmed and quieted myself,
*   I am like a weaned child with its mother;*
*   like a weaned child I am content.*

PSALM 131:1–2

We have all seen it. A small child climbs up in her mother's arms. Full of trust and love, she is content to rest there—leaving behind her tears, worries, and even her desires. She lies content in her mother's embrace. In this prayer, David described himself as being like such a child—content to rest in God's embrace. David quieted his soul before God enough to accept his circumstances, the difficulties that were beyond his control. He left those "great matters or things too wonderful for me" to God. He simply trusted that God—someone wiser and more powerful than he— was looking after his needs.

Quiet your soul before God in your prayer time as David did. Leave your life in his hands. ❖

PRAYER

Dear God, I have quieted myself, just as a weaned child is quiet with its mother . . .

october4

HONORING THE GOD OF ALL GLORY

LORD, our Lord,
how majestic is your name in all the earth!
You have set your glory
in the heavens.
Through the praise of children and infants
you have established a stronghold against your enemies,
to silence the foe and the avenger.

PSALM 8:1−2

The glory an athlete enjoys after winning a race or the glory a millionaire enjoys because of his wealth can't compare to God's glory. Were we to try to measure his glory, it would be greater than all of the universe combined. Yet, one sort of praise begins to adequately express God's glory. It is the praise from the lips of children and infants. Indeed, David imagined that these young ones had learned to sing praises from God himself. Their simple prayers of praise shame the prayers of adults. Often with their sincere faith in God, they understand what sophisticated adults are unable to embrace. In fact, Jesus encourages us to become like little children in order to enter God's kingdom (Matthew 18:3). In God's marvelous economy, the praises of children can silence God's enemies. How can anyone contradict a simple, yet miraculous prayer from a small child's lips?

This week, find some time to listen to children praying. Let their simple prayers inspire you to express in prayer a childlike trust in God. ♣

PRAYER

Dear Lord, your name fills the earth. You have taught children and nursing infants to give you praise . . .

october5

HAVE MERCY ON US

As Jesus went on from there, two blind men followed him, calling out, "Have mercy on us, Son of David!"

When he had gone indoors, the blind men came to him, and he asked them, "Do you believe that I am able to do this?"

"Yes, Lord," they replied.

Then he touched their eyes and said, "According to your faith let it be done to you"

MATTHEW 9:27–29

"Have mercy on me." This is the basic Christian prayer. "Jesus, show mercy to me—a sinner." Though these two blind men couldn't see their surroundings, they could see that Jesus could help them and so they asked for one thing—his mercy. By calling Jesus the "Son of David," they showed that they believed Jesus was the Messiah, God's Son. Everyone in Israel knew that the Messiah was to be a direct descendant of David, Israel's greatest king. To use that title was to acknowledge him as Lord. That is why these men were persistent. They didn't just cry out as Jesus passed by, giving up when his group traveled on past them. They followed him into the house where he was staying. Though the crowd shoved and jostled them, they persistently felt their way towards Jesus' voice. They didn't care what others thought of them. They pursued Jesus because they knew he alone was the answer to their needs.

May our own prayers be full of the faith and fervency of those two blind men, who asked for and received mercy from God. ✤

PRAYER

O Son of David, have mercy on me ...

october**6**

ADMIRING GOD'S CREATION

How many are your works, LORD!
In wisdom you made them all;
the earth is full of your creatures.

PSALM 104:24

A famous artist will be admired and remembered because of the scope and variety of his or her work. How much more should we admire God for the incredible variety of his creation. Whether we set out to study biology, geology, or astronomy, variety is one of the first lessons we learn. There are oaks and elms, red and black ants, beagles and elkhounds, sparrows and cardinals. When we consider the vast differences in climate around the world and the diversity it engenders, we are dumbfounded. God's wonderful creation inspires us to praise him. Just as we are gratified when others applaud us for the work of our hands, God finds pleasure in those who appreciate his creation and thank him for it.

Let the endless variety of God's creation be the starting point for your meditation and praise today. ❧

PRAYER

O Lord, what a variety of things you have made ...

PRAISING GOD'S TRUSTWORTHINESS

Sing joyfully to the LORD, you righteous;
it is fitting for the upright to praise him.
Praise the LORD with the harp;
make music to him on the ten-stringed lyre.
Sing to him a new song;
play skillfully, and shout for joy.
For the word of the LORD is right and true;
he is faithful in all he does.
The LORD loves righteousness and justice;
the earth is full of his unfailing love.

PSALM 33:1–5

What does it mean to be trustworthy and true? In a society that insists that all truth is relative, many people have given up looking for truth much less basing their lives on it. But Scripture declares that there is something that is completely true—no matter what angle you look at it, no matter what perspective you come from. God and his word are true; and he will always remain true. This prayer celebrates God's truthfulness. God will never change. He will always be trustworthy; his word is always true. This psalm encourages believers everywhere to shout for joy, for their lives are securely established on God's eternal truths.

Praise God for remaining trustworthy and true. Then, commit some time this week to study Scripture, asking him to reveal his eternal truths to you. ✤

PRAYER

Dear God, your word holds true, and everything you do is worthy of my trust . . .

october8

EXPRESSING WHAT ONE WANTS IN LIFE

Look and see, there is no one at my right hand;
no one is concerned for me.
I have no refuge;
no one cares for my life.
I cry to you, LORD;
I say, "You are my refuge,
my portion in the land of the living."
Listen to my cry,
for I am in desperate need;
rescue me from those who pursue me,
for they are too strong for me.

PSALM 142:4−6

Difficult circumstances have a remarkable way of revealing what is most important in our lives. In the case of King David, his situation looked completely hopeless without God's help. He had fled into a cave because Saul wanted to take his life. Nobody cared about his plight or gave him a passing thought. It was only at this low point that David understood most clearly that God himself is all he could ever want or need. Granted, taking refuge in the Lord doesn't mean that all of our problems will be solved instantaneously. But knowing that God is with us in our trying times should comfort us and give us the strength to go on.

In those situations when it seems like the whole world is crashing down on you, can you sincerely pray, with David, "You are all I really want in life"? Seek God and draw from the strength he provides for his children. ♣

PRAYER

Dear Lord, you are my place of refuge. You are all I really want in life ...

DECLARING THE WONDER OF HIS NAME

He says,

> *"I will declare your name to my brothers and sisters;*
> *in the assembly I will sing your praises."*

<small>HEBREWS 2:12</small>

Our senses can become deadened by the continual bombardment of images from the screens of televisions, movie theaters, and computers. After staring hour after hour at images dancing across the screen, we tend to lose our sense of wonder for the real world—for the brilliant autumn colors across our landscape, for the sturdy oaks whose branches reach up to the sky. But more troubling than that is we may stop looking for the way God works wonders in our lives—the way he strengthens and provides for us, the way he rescues us from all sorts of predicaments, and the fact that he has saved us from our sin. One reason Jesus came to earth was to point out God's wonders. His prayer was that he would "declare your name to my brothers and sisters." With his life, death, and resurrection, Jesus did just that, inspiring his followers to declare the wonders of God's name as well.

Determine to whom you are going to tell this week how wonderful God has been to you and your family. ✤

PRAYER

Dear Lord, I will declare the wonder of your name to my brothers and sisters . . .

october**10**

A PRAYER FOR FORGIVENESS AND MERCY

For the sake of your name, LORD,
  forgive my iniquity, though it is great....
Turn to me and be gracious to me,
  for I am lonely and afflicted.
Relieve the troubles of my heart
  and free me from my anguish.
Look on my affliction and my distress
  and take away all my sins.

PSALM 25:11, 16–18

Have you ever felt like your life was like a series of dominos? One domino falls down, and it sets off a chain-reaction that knocks down the rest of the dominoes. Likewise, one small mistake can lead to a multitude of problems, leaving our lives in disarray. David felt that his problems were going from bad to worse—his enemies had begun to surround him, waiting for his ultimate demise. David could see no way out. But even in his despair, he knew there was one whom he could always trust to help him. He turned to God, confessed his sins, asked for forgiveness, and pleaded for mercy: "For the sake of your name, LORD, forgive my iniquity, though it is great."

When we feel the loneliness of separation from God because of our sins, we can come to him and ask for help. We must first repent of our sins and ask for forgiveness. Then, with a clean heart, we can come before him and ask for help. He will hear and answer us "for the sake of his name." ❖

> **PRAYER**

Dear God, for the sake of your name, please forgive my many sins and have mercy on me ...

AN APPEAL FOR GUIDANCE

Send me your light and your faithful care,
let them lead me;
let them bring me to your holy mountain,
to the place where you dwell.
Then I will go to the altar of God,
to God, my joy and my delight.
I will praise you with the lyre,
O God, my God.
Why, my soul, are you downcast?
Why so disturbed within me?
Put your hope in God,
for I will yet praise him,
my Savior and my God.

PSALM 43:3 – 5

Have you ever been so lost that you were encompassed by total darkness? The psalmist felt this way—lost in darkness, surrounded by enemies, and discouraged. He didn't know which way to turn. But he did know to whom he should cry out for help. He asked God to show him the way, to guide him in the truth, and to lead him to the Lord's holy mountain. Only in God's presence would he feel safe. Only there could he burst forth with joyful praises for his Deliverer. When we are surrounded by liars, oppressors, and enemies, we must focus on God's ability to guide us into the truth, allowing him to comfort our discouraged soul with the prospect of his deliverance.

Pray that God would guide your steps with his light and truth. Set your sights on your final destination—God's dwelling place—and encourage yourself with the prospect of living joyfully in the Lord's presence. ✤

PRAYER

Dear God, send out your light and your truth; let them guide me . . .

october**12**

FINDING NO RECORD OF SINS

> *Lord, hear my voice.*
> *Let your ears be attentive*
> *   to my cry for mercy.*
> *If you, LORD, kept a record of sins,*
> *   Lord, who could stand?*
> *But with you there is forgiveness,*
> *   so that we can, with reverence, serve you.*
> *I wait for the LORD, my whole being waits,*
> *   and in his word I put my hope.*
> *I wait for the LORD*
> *   more than watchmen wait for the morning,*
> *   more than watchmen wait for the morning.*

PSALM 130:2–6

In our society, we dread the tax auditor. Even those with good financial records don't want to go through the ordeal of a tax audit. They don't want to have to justify every tax receipt. People don't want someone scrutinizing their entire financial life. The psalmist rejoiced that God didn't keep a record of his wrongs. What a relief to know that God wouldn't ask him to account for every sin he had committed! God forgives us if we repent of our sin—no record of wrongs, no accounting needed. Of all the works of God, one that should strike amazement in us is God's willingness to forgive. God is absolutely holy and just; and human beings are, without exception, prone to sin. But we can still cry out to God because God graciously offers us forgiveness. God is waiting to hear from us, to forgive and to restore.

Thank God today for not keeping a record of your sins. ♣

PRAYER

Dear Lord, if you kept a record of our sins, who could ever survive? But you offer forgiveness ...

PRAYING WHEN ALL HOPE IS LOST

When my life was ebbing away,
I remembered you, LORD,
and my prayer rose to you,
to your holy temple.
Those who cling to worthless idols
turn away from God's love for them.
But I, with shouts of grateful praise,
will sacrifice to you.
What I have vowed I will make good.
I will say, "Salvation comes from the LORD."

JONAH 2:7–9

This amazing prayer was prayed by the prophet Jonah from the belly of the great fish that had swallowed him! Deep down, Jonah must have known that it was fruitless to try to escape God's call. On a ship headed *away* from where God had told him to go and preach, Jonah got caught in a storm that endangered his life as well as many innocent people. He knew that he was the reason for the impending disaster and eventually asked to be thrown overboard to spare the others. Instead of requiring his life, God ordered a huge fish to swallow him. Jonah wasted no time. From within its belly he began to praise God, recognizing that salvation could come from no one else. Although his feet still were not on dry land, he trusted that God, in his own extraordinary way and in his own timing, was working out Jonah's deliverance.

Turn your thoughts to God as Jonah did in his moment of distress. Reaffirm your dependence on God for salvation. ✤

PRAYER

Dear Lord, I turn my thoughts to you for salvation comes from you alone . . .

october**14**

TRUSTING IN GOD

Be merciful to me, LORD, for I am in distress;
my eyes grow weak with sorrow,
my soul and body with grief.
My life is consumed by anguish
and my years by groaning;
my strength fails because of my affliction,
and my bones grow weak....
But I trust in you, LORD;
I say, "You are my God."
My times are in your hands;
deliver me from the hands of my enemies,
from those who pursue me.

PSALM 31:9–10, 14–15

Suffering and pain are inevitable features of the human life. Careless words, financial obligations, and situations at work can sap the strength out of an otherwise productive existence. In this prayer, David told God about the misery and suffering he had faced. His grief and sadness had weakened him, leading him to say, "My strength fails because of my affliction, and my bones grow weak." Yet even in his struggles, David found strength in the Lord by placing his future in God's hands. We too can trust the Lord's plans for our lives to give us hope and a future.

What are the situations in your life that cause you anguish and misery? As you spend time in prayer, commit those situations to him. Ask him to take control of your future. ✤

PRAYER

Dear God, you are my God! My future is in your hands ...

october15

PLACING ONE'S HOPE IN GOD'S WORDS

I call with all my heart; answer me, LORD,
and I will obey your decrees.
I call out to you; save me
and I will keep your statutes.
I rise before dawn and cry for help;
I have put my hope in your word.
My eyes stay open through the watches of the night,
that I may meditate on your promises.

PSALM 119:145–148

We tend to turn to God for help when our backs are against the wall—when nothing is going right, when our world is falling apart. We might even try to strike deals with God, making promises to obey him if he only will deliver us from our current predicament. In this prayer turning to God was not a last resort. God was the *only* solution the psalmist ever tried. He even got up early in the morning to meditate on God's promises and ask for the Lord's help. If his nights were sleepless, he focused his thoughts on what is holy and true. It was that type of commitment to God and his words that helped him get through times of difficulty.

Determine how you can make God's words a central part of your everyday life. Should you set aside a certain time during the week to study Scripture? Should you commit to read Scripture in the morning and in the evening? Ask God to help you focus on his life-giving words this week. ❖

PRAYER

Dear Lord, I rise early to place my hope in your words. I will obey your principles . . .

october**16**

CONFESSING OUR SINS

Then the Israelites cried out to the LORD, "We have sinned against you, forsaking our God and serving the Baals." ...

But the Israelites said to the LORD, "We have sinned. Do with us whatever you think best, but please rescue us now." Then they got rid of the foreign gods among them and served the LORD. And he could bear Israel's misery no longer.

JUDGES 10:10, 15–16

It takes more than words to convince others of a change of heart. A repeat offender has to prove himself. They have to back up their words with action. The Israelites were in such a situation with God. Again and again, they had adopted the gods of the pagan nations around them. God grew angry with the Israelites, allowing their pagan neighbors to attack them. So when the Israelites cried out to God for deliverance, they realized that confession wasn't enough. They had to back up their prayers with action. They had to tear down their idols and begin serving the Lord. How God responded to them gives us wonderful insight into the heart of God. The passage says "he could bear Israel's misery no longer." God will respond in the same compassionate way, if we tear down our idols—our worship of material wealth, fame, or power—and depend on him for our needs.

Search your heart for the things you depend on—for the things to which you sacrifice your time and money. Those are the idols in your life. Tear them down and affirm your allegiance to God alone. ✤

PRAYER

Dear Lord, I have sinned. I yield to your will. Please rescue me ...

PRAISING GOD FOR HIS PROTECTION

I lift up my eyes to the mountains—
where does my help come from?
My help comes from the LORD,
the Maker of heaven and earth.
He will not let your foot slip—
he who watches over you will not slumber;
indeed, he who watches over Israel
will neither slumber nor sleep.
The LORD watches over you—
the LORD is your shade at your right hand.

PSALM 121:1–5

The role of security guards is important for protecting buildings from intruders. If guards do not pay attention to their surroundings, they could allow an intruder to sneak in undetected. That is why they closely watch everything during their shift. In the same way, the psalmist describes the Lord as one who "will neither slumber nor sleep." He stands beside us to make sure we don't stumble and fall. Our God is always paying attention and will be our "shade" day in and day out. No wonder the psalmist said, "My help comes from the LORD, the Maker of heaven and earth."

In your prayer time, remember that God never tires of watching over you. ❖

PRAYER

Dear Lord, I know you are watching over me . . .

october**18**

A PLEA TO GOD

Answer me when I call to you,
my righteous God.
Give me relief from my distress;
have mercy on me and hear my prayer.

PSALM 4:1

"Hey, did you hear what so-and-so did yesterday? Well, let me tell *you* ..." Gossip and malicious slander can be destructive to the person it's directed at, ruining relationships and destroying a person's confidence. Many times, we're tempted to counter gossip with destructive words of our own. However, David offers us a better solution than slandering another person. In this psalm, he faced individuals who had falsely accused him. But David doesn't retaliate. Instead, he praised God for declaring him innocent. Likewise, we have confidence that God will declare us innocent when we face our accusers. We can have this confidence because Jesus died for our sins. Surely the God who redeemed us from the bondage of sin and death will hear our cries of distress, have mercy, and answer our prayers.

Spend time today thanking God for declaring you innocent. ✤

PRAYER

Dear Lord, you have declared me innocent. Hear my prayer and have mercy on me ...

TAKING COURAGE IN GOD

> *How abundant are the good things*
> *that you have stored up for those who fear you,*
> *that you bestow in the sight of all,*
> *on those who take refuge in you.*
> *In the shelter of your presence you hide them*
> *from all human intrigues;*
> *you keep them safe in your dwelling*
> *from accusing tongues....*
> *Be strong and take heart,*
> *all you who hope in the LORD.*

PSALM 31:19–20, 24

Hurricanes are one of the most devastating forces in nature. People caught in them run to structures that will shield them against the fierce winds and torrential rain associated with such storms. In this prayer, David described God as a shelter that protects him from the dangers of this world—his enemies, harmful lies, and conspiracies. As King of Israel, David would have had the nation's might at his command. Yet at the same time, he would have been the target of all kinds of attacks. David wisely sought God's protection. He knew God protected and blessed those who run to him for safety. He took courage in the fact that God would shield him from any danger he would encounter.

In prayer, ask God to protect you and your family with his presence. Pray that his protection might give you the courage to do the tasks before you. ♣

PRAYER

O God, I will take courage for you have done so much for those who come to you for protection ...

HUMBLING ONESELF BEFORE GOD

Then Job replied to the LORD:

> *"I know that you can do all things;*
> *no purpose of yours can be thwarted.*
> *You asked, 'Who is this that obscures my plans without knowledge?'*
> *Surely I spoke of things I did not understand,*
> *things too wonderful for me to know.*
> *"You said, 'Listen now, and I will speak;*
> *I will question you,*
> *and you shall answer me.'*
> *My ears had heard of you*
> *but now my eyes have seen you.*
> *Therefore I despise myself*
> *and repent in dust and ashes."*

JOB 42:1–6

When we complain to God, we may speak without thinking and have to take back our words. Job had plenty of time to think, yet he still had to repent for his lack of humility. The Lord listened to Job's complaints, criticisms, and questions. But after letting Job speak, he didn't answer his questions. Instead, God soundly rebuked him: "Who is this that obscures my plans without knowledge?" Chastened and humbled by God, Job immediately repented of what he said and asked the Lord to forgive him. "I spoke of things I did not understand," he said. We may not openly challenge God as Job did, but sometimes we may doubt God's care for us. He wants us to come to him with our doubts and pray for answers. By faith we know that God's plan is good, just, and loving.

Ask for faith to overcome your doubts. Trust God and leave your complaints in his hands. ♣

PRAYER

Dear God, I know that you can do anything, and no one can stop you . . .

october21

CRYING OUT TO THE LORD

I cry aloud to the LORD;
I lift up my voice to the LORD for mercy.
I pour out before him my complaint;
before him I tell my trouble.
When my spirit grows faint within me,
it is you who watch over my way.
In the path where I walk
people have hidden a snare for me.
Look and see, there is no one at my right hand;
no one is concerned for me.
I have no refuge;
no one cares for my life.

PSALM 142:1–4

Have you ever been overwhelmed by your troubles and uncertain which way you should turn? Wherever David went, his enemies set traps for him. He searched for someone to help him, but no one gave him a passing thought. No one would help him. No one cared a bit about what was happening to him. Sound familiar? Sometimes we need to vent our frustrations about a distressing situation that has no apparent solution. Like David, we lament, "No one is concerned for me. I have no refuge; no one cares for my life."

When you're feeling discouraged and low, seek the Lord. Pour out your complaints before him, and tell him all your troubles. God is big enough for your problems. He can show you the way you should go. ❖

PRAYER

Dear God, I am overwhelmed. You alone know the way I should turn . . .

october**22**

A PRAYER FOR FORGIVENESS

> *Return, Israel, to the LORD your God.*
> > *Your sins have been your downfall!*
> *Take words with you*
> > *and return to the LORD.*
> *Say to him:*
> > *"Forgive all our sins*
> *and receive us graciously,*
> > *that we may offer the fruit of our lips.*
> *Assyria cannot save us;*
> > *we will not mount warhorses.*
> *We will never again say 'Our gods'*
> > *to what our own hands have made,*
> > *for in you the fatherless find compassion."*

HOSEA 14:1–3

One of the main goals in today's society is to be the strongest, the wealthiest, or the most skillful at something. Some people will do whatever it takes to accomplish these lofty objectives. In doing so, the goal can become an idol that takes the place God rightly deserves. After describing God's fierce anger over Israel's idols, the prophet Hosea made it clear that God would still welcome them if they returned to him in humility and repentance. Hosea even taught the Israelites the prayer they should use when they returned to God. They were to verbally tear down their old idols. They were to admit to God that their own strength, skill, and wealth couldn't save them; their powerful neighbors couldn't save them; their wooden, lifeless idols couldn't save them. Only the Almighty could save. Only the Lord deserved their adoration and worship.

When we are brought low by our sin, when we are tempted to trust in our own strength, skill, and wealth, let us come to God in humility. May we pray that God may forgive and graciously receive us. He promises to answer such a prayer. ✤

PRAYER

Dear Lord, forgive all my sins and graciously receive me, so that I may offer you a sacrifice of praise . . .

THANKING GOD IN ALL CIRCUMSTANCES

My God, whom I praise,
  do not remain silent,
for people who are wicked and deceitful
  have opened their mouths against me;
  they have spoken against me with lying tongues.
With words of hatred they surround me;
  they attack me without cause.
In return for my friendship they accuse me,
  but I am a man of prayer ....
With my mouth I will greatly extol the LORD;
  in the great throng of worshipers I will praise him.
For he stands at the right hand of the needy,
  to save their lives from those who would condemn them.

PSALM 109:1–4, 30–31

In good and bad times, when we are flush with success and also when we brought low by failure—we are to praise God. As believers, we know that our present circumstances shouldn't affect our allegiance to him. In this prayer, David confessed that he was in deep trouble: the wicked were slandering him and telling lies about him. They were all around him with their hateful words. They returned evil for good and hatred for his love. His enemies tried to destroy him even as he prayed for them. Yet in such a predicament, David said, "With my mouth I will greatly extol the LORD; in the great throng of worshipers I will praise him."

Whatever your circumstances today, you should offer your thanks and praise to God, for he is the one who sustains you. ✣

PRAYER

Dear Lord, no matter what circumstances I am in, I will give repeated thanks to you ...

october24

A PRAYER FOR GOD TO REMEMBER HIS PROMISE

But in your great mercy you did not put an end to them or abandon them, for you are a gracious and merciful God.

Now therefore, our God, the great God, mighty and awesome, who keeps his covenant of love, do not let all this hardship seem trifling in your eyes — the hardship that has come on us, on our kings and leaders, on our priests and prophets, on our ancestors and all your people, from the days of the kings of Assyria until today.

NEHEMIAH 9:31–32

Fifty-two days after they started, the people of Israel completed rebuilding the walls of Jerusalem. For the next several weeks Nehemiah and the priests led the people in confession and in the reading of the Law. He asked them to renew their commitment to God and offer their worship to him. Nehemiah recounted how God had delivered the people time after time, and how the people had, in turn, disobeyed the Lord. Today's passage features Nehemiah's prayer for the people. He asked God to spare his people in spite of their disobedience. He asked for mercy and reminded God of his promises. Before the people, Nehemiah praised God as the "the great God, mighty and awesome, who keeps his covenant of love."

God does keep his promises. Like Nehemiah, let us pray and thank him for that great gift. ✤

PRAYER

Dear God, what a gracious and merciful God you are! In your great mercy, you did not abandon me forever ...

PRAYING THROUGH SORROW

How long, LORD? Will you forget me forever?
How long will you hide your face from me?
How long must I wrestle with my thoughts
and day after day have sorrow in my heart?
How long will my enemy triumph over me?
Look on me and answer, LORD my God.
Give light to my eyes, or I will sleep in death....
But I trust in your unfailing love;
my heart rejoices in your salvation.
I will sing the LORD's praise,
for he has been good to me.

PSALM 13:1−3, 5−6

Does it ever seem to you as if God has forgotten you? Have you prayed and prayed and seemingly received no response? David, despite his intimate relationship with God, felt that way more than once. But he didn't wallow in self-pity and hopelessness. He took those feelings of abandonment directly to God. He was honest before the Lord. He expressed his impatience: "How long must I wrestle with my thoughts?" As he bared his soul to God, a change began to take place in him. He remembered God's faithfulness to him in the past. His cries of distress turned into songs of praise.

When you enter God's presence with all of your complaints, you will undergo a similar change. Rather than feeling forgotten, you will understand the extent of God's faithfulness to and love for you. ✦

PRAYER

Dear Lord, how long must I wrestle with my thoughts? But I will trust in your unfailing love ...

MOSES' PRAYER FOR ISRAEL

Surely it is you who love the people;
all the holy ones are in your hand.
At your feet they all bow down,
and from you receive instruction,

DEUTERONOMY 33:3

Just before his death, Moses gathered the people of Israel together and blessed each one of the tribes. For the tribe of Reuben, Moses prayed that they might "live and not die" (33:6); for Levi, he prayed that they might "[teach] your precepts to Jacob and your law to Israel" (33:10); for Ephraim and Manasseh, he prayed that their land might blessed their land "with the precious dew from heaven above and with the deep waters that lie below" (33:13). Moses shared his prayer for each one of the tribes of Israel. But the grand theme of all his prayers appears in his introduction. He prayed that God would continue to "love the people," and in turn, Israel would accept God's instructions and follow in the Lord's steps. Moses' prayer teaches us also. The Lord does love those who believe in him and holds them safely in his hands. It is our responsibility to accept his instruction and follow in his steps.

Thank God for loving you and holding you in his hands. Then, ask him for strength to follow in his steps. ✤

PRAYER

Dear Lord, thank you that we are safe in your hands. Help us to follow in your steps and accept your instruction . . .

OBSERVING GOD'S POWER IN ACTION

> *Some went out on the sea in ships;*
> *they were merchants on the mighty waters.*
> *They saw the works of the LORD,*
> *his wonderful deeds in the deep.*
> *For he spoke and stirred up a tempest*
> *that lifted high the waves....*
> *Then they cried out to the LORD in their trouble,*
> *and he brought them out of their distress.*
> *He stilled the storm to a whisper;*
> *the waves of the sea were hushed.*
> *They were glad when it grew calm,*
> *and he guided them to their desired haven.*

PSALM 107:23 – 25, 28 – 30

When we've safely gone through a dramatic experience—from barely missing a collision with another car to suffering a terrible bout with the flu—the whole world seems fresh and new. We have a new appreciation for the gift of health and life. This prayer described the exiles as experiencing such a feeling. After fearing for their lives when their ships were at the mercy of fierce winds and relentless waves, God had calmed the wind in answer to their cries for help. We can only imagine how those windblown exiles rejoiced over that safe harbor. They would never take God's protection for granted again. With this renewed sense of God's work in their lives, the exiles praised and thank God for all he had done for them.

Recount the ways God has worked powerfully in your life. Praise him for bringing you through the trials and hardships you have experienced. Then, ask him to help you now and in the future. ✤

PRAYER

Dear Lord, I have seen your power in action. Lord, help me ...

october28

RELYING ON GOD IN TIMES OF HARDSHIP

And the God of all grace, who called you to his eternal glory in Christ, after you have suffered a little while, will himself restore you and make you strong, firm and steadfast. To him be the power for ever and ever. Amen.

1 PETER 5:10–11

Circumstances in our lives can change without a moment's notice. A spouse is fired from their job for no apparent reason. A close relative is diagnosed with an incurable disease. A common response to situations such as these is, "Why is there suffering in the world? And why is it happening to me?" Although we may have to wait until heaven to find the answer, we can be encouraged by Peter's benediction. Without explaining the reason *why* we suffer, he assures the reader that God has called believers to his eternal glory through Jesus Christ. He reassures us that after we have suffered for a while, the Lord will restore, support, and strengthen us. He will one day place us on a firm foundation.

Are you going through suffering of some kind? Are you wondering why God allows it to occur? Whatever the reason, God will help you through it and bring you out stronger on the other side. Join Peter in proclaiming the power of the Almighty and in trusting him for the strength to endure your trials. ✤

PRAYER

Dear Lord, all power is yours forever. Restore, support, and strengthen me. Place me on a firm foundation . . .

A PRAYER FOR A CLEAN HEART

> *But who can discern their own errors?*
> *Forgive my hidden faults.*
> *Keep your servant also from willful sins;*
> *may they not rule over me.*
> *Then I will be blameless,*
> *innocent of great transgression.*
> *May these words of my mouth and this meditation of my heart*
> *be pleasing in your sight,*
> *LORD, my Rock and my Redeemer.*
>
> PSALM 19:12–14

The closer we get to God, the more we become aware of our own sin and our own unworthiness. David starts out this prayer by proclaiming the greatness of the Lord: "The heavens declare the glory of God; the skies proclaim the work of his hands. Day after day they pour forth speech; night after night they reveal knowledge" (19:1–2). As he praises God, David senses the sin that exists in his life. He asks the Lord to cleanse him and keep him from all sins—even those that are hidden deep in his own heart. In spite of his weaknesses and failures, David wants his entire life, even what he says and thinks, to be pleasing to God.

Start your prayer time today by meditating on God's perfection and how much he dislikes sin. Then, confess your sins to God. Ask him to cleanse your heart, pointing out the sins buried deep in your lifestyle. ✣

PRAYER

Dear God, how can I know all the sins lurking in my heart? Cleanse my heart. Make the words of my mouth and the thoughts of my heart pleasing to you ...

JESUS' PRAYER FOR OUR PROTECTION

I am coming to you now, but I say these things while I am still in the world, so that they may have the full measure of my joy within them. I have given them your word and the world has hated them, for they are not of the world any more than I am of the world. My prayer is not that you take them out of the world but that you protect them from the evil one.
JOHN 17:13–15

After their Last Supper together, Jesus was with his disciples in the upper room. Jesus knew that his "time had come." So he prayed for his disciples and asked God the Father to protect them and keep them safe from Satan. Jesus also prayed for those "those who will believe in me through their message" (17:20). That includes us! Jesus, in the last few minutes before he faced his trial and death, prayed for his disciples' protection—and also for ours! That should be a great comfort to us. It should free us from anxiety, uncertainty, and fear. After all, if God is for us, who can be against us?

Pray that God may protect you from those who want your demise. Ask the Lord to keep you from all evil. He will certainly answer your prayers. ♣

PRAYER

Dear Lord, I don't belong to the world. Please keep me safe from the evil one ...

october31

PRAISE FOR GOD'S ENCOURAGING WORD

LORD, you understand;
remember me and care for me.
Avenge me on my persecutors.
You are long-suffering—do not take me away;
think of how I suffer reproach for your sake.
When your words came, I ate them;
they were my joy and my heart's delight,
for I bear your name,
LORD God Almighty. . . .

Therefore this is what the LORD says:

"If you repent, I will restore you
that you may serve me;
if you utter worthy, not worthless, words,
you will be my spokesman.
Let this people turn to you,
but you must not turn to them.

JEREMIAH 15:15–16, 19

Words can be used powerfully in both positive and negative ways. With uncaring, thoughtless words, we can hurt and humiliate other people. On the other hand, words of encouragement can be incredibly powerful when a person is going through a difficult situation. In today's prayer, the prophet Jeremiah asked God to punish his persecutors and give them what they deserve. He then tells the Lord, "When your words came, I ate them; they were my joy and my heart's delight." God's encouraging words helped to sustain him during the persecution he was enduring.

In response to his prayer, God told Jeremiah to do the same—to "utter worthy, not worthless, words." His words were to influence the people of Israel. Think of some ways that you can use words for good and not evil. Ask the Lord for opportunities to be his spokesman. ✣

PRAYER

Help me as your spokesman, O Lord, to speak words that are worthy . . .

november1

THANKING GOD FOR A FRIEND

Grace and peace to you from God our Father and the Lord Jesus Christ.

I always thank my God as I remember you in my prayers, because I hear about your love for all his holy people and your faith in the Lord Jesus.

PHILEMON VV. 3 – 5

We are often drawn to prayer by tragedies and difficult circumstances in our lives. We tell God all about our problems and ask for his help — and rightly so. Paul was certainly in difficult circumstances when he wrote this letter to Philemon. He was under house arrest in Rome, awaiting a trial before Caesar. Roman guards watched his every move; and Paul's opponents were gathering their case against him. He certainly had much to pray for. But his attention in prayer was also focused on others — on those who were miles away and who were enduring a different set of problems. Philemon was one person Paul lifted up in prayer. In his letter to Philemon, Paul didn't forget to tell Philemon that he was praying for him — that he was thanking God because of him. Perhaps, Philemon felt insignificant. Yet Paul told Philemon that he was appreciated, loved, and prayed for. What an encouragement that must have been!

Are there brothers or sisters in Christ who have encouraged you? Have you told them how much you appreciate them and that you are praying for them? Resolve to tell them how much they mean to you. ✤

PRAYER

Dear Lord, thank you for . . .

november2

MOSES' INTERCESSION FOR HIS PEOPLE

So Moses went back to the LORD and said, "Oh, what a great sin these people have committed! They have made themselves gods of gold. But now, please forgive their sin—but if not, then blot me out of the book you have written."

EXODUS 32:31–32

Moses had every reason to be upset with the people of Israel. While he was meeting with God on the mountain to obtain God's law, they had fashioned a golden calf and begun to worship it. By doing so, they were not only breaking their promise to worship the living God alone, but they were also rejecting Moses' spiritual leadership. Moses could have easily asked God to destroy them on the spot. Instead, he pleaded for God's mercy on them. Yes, they had committed a terrible sin. "But now," Moses prayed, "please forgive their sin—but if not, then blot me out of the book you have written." Despite the fact that they had rebelled against his authority, Moses loved the Israelites so much he was willing to die for their sake. God wants those types of leaders—self-sacrificial leaders, not self-centered ones.

Among your family, friends, coworkers, and acquaintances, are you a self-sacrificial leader? Are you concerned about the best interests of others? Go to the Lord; ask him to have mercy on those who least deserve it. ✤

PRAYER

Dear God, we have committed terrible sins. But now, please forgive us . . .

november3

A PRAYER FOR HARMONY IN THE CHURCH

May God, who gives this patience and encouragement, help you live in complete harmony with each other—each with the attitude of Christ Jesus toward the other. Then all of you can join together with one voice, giving praise and glory to God, the Father of our Lord Jesus Christ.

Romans 15:5–6

Worshiping in a congregation whose members are excited about what God is doing is thrilling. In contrast, worshiping in a congregation whose members are fighting among themselves for power and credit is depressing. What damages the church's testimony for Christ is the lack of harmony among believers. Jesus told his disciples, "By this everyone will know that you are my disciples, if you love one another" (John 13:35). In his letter to the Romans, Paul prayed that the believers in Rome would "live in complete harmony with each other—each with the attitude of Christ Jesus toward the other." Only when believers live that way will they "join together with one voice, giving praise and glory to God, the Father of our Lord Jesus Christ."

Think what an impact the church could have on a skeptical—but watching—world, if we could live in harmony as the Bible teaches. Pray for that type of harmony in your church community. ✤

PRAYER

Dear Father, help me to live in complete harmony with my fellow believers ...

november**4**

THANKSGIVING THAT GOD IS NEAR

I will praise the LORD, who counsels me;
even at night my heart instructs me.
I keep my eyes always on the LORD.
With him at my right hand, I will not be shaken.

PSALM 16:7–8

Sometimes we try to ride out the storms in our lives—doing this the best we can. We fool ourselves by thinking, "If I can just hang on and be strong, I can get through this." David knew he couldn't make it on his own. In the past, he had found help in the Lord God. And in this prayer, David again sought the Lord's protection: "Keep me safe, my God, for in you I take refuge" (Psalm 16:1). He rejoiced in the guidance and assistance the Lord had given him. Though his enemies were trying to shake and topple him, he stood firm because God was at his "right hand."

In prayer today, acknowledge that God is right beside you—upholding and guiding you. ✤

PRAYER

Dear Lord, I know you are always with me. I will not be shaken, for you are right beside me . . .

november5

A REQUEST FOR GOD TO REMEMBER US

Blessed are those who act justly,
who always do what is right.
Remember me, LORD, when you show favor to your people,
come to my aid when you save them,
that I may enjoy the prosperity of your chosen ones,
that I may share in the joy of your nation
and join your inheritance in giving praise.

PSALM 106:3–5

Feeling forgotten is one of the worst feelings—especially if the people who forgot you are your only ride home or your only hope for help. Samson felt that way when he was languishing in prison—blind and alone. Instead of going over in his mind his mistakes or blaming God for abandoning him, he asked God: "Sovereign LORD, remember me. Please, God, strengthen me just once more" (Judges 16:28). Job felt that same way after enduring multiple personal crises. He prayed, "If only you would set me a time and then remember me!" (Job 14:13). Even the thief on the cross asked Jesus: "Jesus, remember me when you come into your kingdom" (Luke 23:42). These people—along with the psalmist in this prayer—understood that their lives depended on God's loving concern. They quickly learned that the Lord never forgets his own. We are the ones who foolishly wander away from him. God is always ready to welcome those who return to him.

Though you may feel alone, you can always ask God to remember you. ♣

PRAYER

O Father, remember me today. Let me rejoice with your people ...

313

november**6**

JESUS' PRAYER FOR THE CHURCH

I have revealed you to those whom you gave me out of the world. They were yours; you gave them to me and they have obeyed your word. Now they know that everything you have given me comes from you. For I gave them the words you gave me and they accepted them. They knew with certainty that I came from you, and they believed that you sent me.
JOHN 17:6–8

In his last hours on earth, Jesus prayed to his Father on behalf of his disciples, asking the Father to protect them. In this portion of his prayer, Jesus explained to God how he had been obedient to the task the Lord had given him. Certainly God already knew how faithful Jesus had been; but Jesus explained this for the sake of his disciples who were listening to him. God had entrusted Jesus with his words; and Jesus had been faithful in communicating it accurately and clearly to the twelve disciples gathered around him that evening. Jesus' job was done. Now, it was the disciples' turn to share with others God's message. What a rich heritage we have as followers of Christ. Just think of it, the very words of God have been entrusted to us. What a precious treasure that is!

Are we treating God's words as the priceless gift it is? Are we telling others about God's message? Thank God today for giving you his words. ❖

PRAYER

Dear God, thank you for sending Jesus to earth to communicate your word to me. I believe in you and accept your word . . .

november7

ASKING GOD TO HEAR THE PEOPLE'S PRAYERS

When a prayer or plea is made by anyone among your people Israel—being aware of their afflictions and pains, and spreading out their hands toward this temple—then hear from heaven, your dwelling place. Forgive, and deal with everyone according to all they do, since you know their hearts (for you alone know the human heart), so that they will fear you and walk in obedience to you all the time they live in the land you gave our ancestors.
2 CHRONICLES 6:29–31

After the building of the Temple was completed, Solomon gathered the people to dedicate it to God's glory and honor. Then, on a platform in front of all the assembled people, he lifted his hands up to heaven and prayed. Solomon's prayer at this time of celebration gives us a window into Solomon's heart. Though his kingdom was at peace and riches were flowing into his treasury, he knew that God was the source of all these blessings. If the people didn't follow God, they would quickly lose his favor. Solomon didn't pray for more riches and wealth; he prayed for those difficult times when it is hard to trust God. He prayed that God would have compassion on his people and listen to their pleas. What's amazing is God answered Solomon's prayer. Again and again, he came to his people's aid when they cried out to him.

Today God still takes pleasures in answering the prayers of his people. Don't hesitate to turn to him for help. Ask him to hear your pleas and forgive. Ask him for the assistance you need for the troubles and difficulties you face. ✤

PRAYER

Dear God, please hear me and forgive . . .

PRAYING FOR GOD'S VERDICT

> *Vindicate me, LORD,*
> * for I have led a blameless life;*
> *I have trusted in the LORD*
> * and have not faltered.*
> *Test me, LORD, and try me,*
> * examine my heart and my mind;*
> *for I have always been mindful of your unfailing love*
> * and have lived in reliance on your faithfulness.*

PSALM 26:1–3

Not many people enjoy tests. Having someone else examine us to see how much we know isn't pleasant. The fears of test taking are magnified even more when someone puts us on trial. No one wants inquisitive lawyers cross-examining every statement and action. It's a nightmare scenario. But David prayed that God would do just that. He asked the Lord to cross-examine his life. He wanted God to declare him innocent so the accusations of his enemies would be forever silenced. Because he had consistently tried to follow God's ways, David was confident that the Lord would protect him from these accusations. All of us will endure times when we are unjustly accused. If we have been careful to submit our ways to God, we can be confident that God will declare us innocent.

In prayer today, commit your ways to God. Ask the Lord to examine your life and help you change those areas that don't conform to his will. ✤

PRAYER

Dear God, test my motives and affections. Help me to live according to your truth ...

november9

BOWING BEFORE THE KING OF ALL NATIONS

> *From you comes the theme of my praise in the great assembly;*
> *before those who fear you I will fulfill my vows.*
> *The poor will eat and be satisfied;*
> *those who seek the LORD will praise him—*
> *may your hearts live forever!*
> *All the ends of the earth*
> *will remember and turn to the LORD,*
> *and all the families of the nations*
> *will bow down before him,*
> *for dominion belongs to the LORD*
> *and he rules over the nations.*

PSALM 22:25–28

Kings and queens, powerful dictators and tyrants, and presidents and rulers have held the reigns of power for years; but inevitably they lose their power and pass off the scene. After a few generations, they may even be forgotten by most people. Yet, there is one King who will never pass away. He will rule all the nations forever and ever. The whole earth will acknowledge his reign. People from every nation will bow before him, "For dominion belongs to the LORD and he rules over the nations." Every knee will bow; every tongue will confess allegiance to him (Isaiah 45:23). Earthly rulers rise and fall, but our Lord, the King of all nations, reigns forever.

Bow before the King of kings. Worship his holy name. ✤

PRAYER

Dear God, you are King. You rule all the nations. I bow down before you ...

PRAYING IN THE MIDST OF A STORM

Instead, the men did their best to row back to land. But they could not, for the sea grew even wilder than before. Then they cried out to the LORD, "Please, LORD, do not let us die for taking this man's life. Do not hold us accountable for killing an innocent man, for you, LORD, have done as you pleased." Then they took Jonah and threw him overboard, and the raging sea grew calm. At this the men greatly feared the LORD, and they offered a sacrifice to the LORD and made vows to him.

JONAH 1:13 – 16

The sailors were desperate. As the wind and waves grew more fierce, they feared for their lives. They tried everything—taking down the sails, throwing cargo overboard, and praying to false gods. Nothing worked—until Jonah admitted he was running from God. What a way to witness to unbelievers! It was these pagan sailors who encouraged Jonah, a prophet of God, to obey the living God—not the other way around. Yet God not only brought Jonah back to himself, he also demonstrated his power to those unbelieving sailors. They submitted themselves to God's will, prayed that he would spare their lives, and committed themselves to following him.

When the storms of life batter your life, remember that God faithfully works his good purposes through all circumstances. ❖

PRAYER

Dear God, you have sent this storm for your own good reasons. Please spare me . . .

november11

DAVID'S SEARCH FOR GOD'S WILL

In the course of time, David inquired of the LORD. "Shall I go up to one of the towns of Judah?" he asked.

The LORD said, "Go up."

David asked, "Where shall I go?"

"To Hebron," the LORD answered.

2 SAMUEL 2:1

Knowing God's will in life is a struggle many people face. They wonder, "What should I do after college?" "Should I accept this job offer?" "Is this person the one I should marry?" They attempt to find God's will through their circumstances, through the advice of others, or plead with God to reveal his will and then refuse to wait for his answer. In today's prayer, David wanted to know where to begin his reign as the King of Judah. Instead of talking to others about where to go, David asked God what his will was in the situation. And he waited for him to answer his prayer. Although God may not unveil his will to everyone with flashing lights, bells, and whistles, he wants us to stop and listen for his reply.

As you seek God's will in your life, thank him for bringing you to where you are today. Then ask him to show you his will for you, listening for his answer. ✤

PRAYER

Dear Lord, show me where I should go ...

november**12**

REJOICING OVER GOD'S VICTORIES

Then Moses and the Israelites sang this song to the LORD:

> *"I will sing to the LORD,*
>   *for he is highly exalted.*
> *Both horse and driver*
>   *he has hurled into the sea.*
> *"The LORD is my strength and my defense;*
>   *he has become my salvation.*
> *He is my God, and I will praise him,*
>   *my father's God, and I will exalt him."*

EXODUS 15:1 – 2

Moses had just seen the Lord part the Red Sea, protect the Israelites as they passed through on dry ground, and then drown Pharaoh's well-armed soldiers as the Red Sea's waters crashed down upon them. Moses had seen God demonstrate his power in a marvelous way; and he couldn't stand silent. He simply had to announce God's victory: "The LORD is my strength and my defense," he sang, "he has become my salvation."

What victories has God given you? In what ways have you seen God triumph over his enemies? Sometimes we forget that God is fighting with us. We find ourselves fighting the battle in our own strength. Let's remember who is our real victory. Praise the Lord as Moses did, and trust him to become your victory. ❖

PRAYER

Dear Lord, you are my strength and my song. You have become my victory. I will praise you …

november**13**

AN APPEAL FOR JUSTICE

Rescue me, LORD, from evildoers;
protect me from the violent,
who devise evil plans in their hearts
and stir up war every day....
May slanderers not be established in the land;
may disaster hunt down the violent.
I know that the LORD secures justice for the poor
and upholds the cause of the needy.
Surely the righteous will praise your name,
and the upright will live in your presence.

PSALM 140:1 – 2, 11 – 13

Almost daily we hear news reports of cruelty and injustice suffered by innocent people. Sadly, the stories are often of little children who are abandoned or beaten by adults who seemingly have no conscience or remorse. When we hear of such inhuman and unspeakable acts, most of us become angry. We may even ask, "Where is the justice in this situation?" David was concerned about the injustice the poor, innocent, and defenseless suffered. He asked the Lord to help those who are persecuted, to maintain the rights of the poor, and to destroy those who were committing these violent acts.

Take some time today to pray for those suffering in the world today. Ask God to bring justice to that situation. ✤

PRAYER

Dear God, maintain the rights of the poor. Rescue the innocent from evil people ...

TRUSTING GOD TO RESCUE

> *My heart, O God, is steadfast;*
> *I will sing and make music with all my soul.*
> *Awake, harp and lyre!*
> *I will awaken the dawn.*
> *I will praise you, LORD, among the nations;*
> *I will sing of you among the peoples.*
> *For great is your love, higher than the heavens;*
> *your faithfulness reaches to the skies.*
> *Be exalted, O God, above the heavens;*
> *let your glory be over all the earth.*
> *Save us and help us with your right hand,*
> *that those you love may be delivered.*

PSALM 108:1–6

The difference between a team that wins a championship and one that loses is the confidence they have in each other. David in this prayer placed his confidence securely in God. He knew that he couldn't save himself. Only God could rescue him. In prayer, he reminded himself that God's love was higher than the heavens, his glory was evident all over the earth. It is easy for us to forget the extent of God's power and love. We dwell on the problems we are going through, instead of the God who could give us victory.

In prayer today, recount the ways God has saved his people in the past. Use David's words to praise his power and love. ✤

PRAYER

Dear Lord, your unfailing love is higher than the heavens. No wonder I can place my confidence in you . . .

november15

HONOR TO THE TRUE KING OF NATIONS

No one is like you, LORD;
you are great,
and your name is mighty in power.
Who should not fear you,
King of the nations?
This is your due.
Among all the wise leaders of the nations
and in all their kingdoms,
there is no one like you.

JEREMIAH 10:6–7

Throughout history cruel, egotistical dictators have risen to power in nations all over the earth. These despots live in wealth and splendor, while their subjects struggle to survive in poverty and hunger. They act and live as if they were gods and demand love and worship from the people over whom they rule with an iron fist. But the Bible tells us there is only one true King; and Jeremiah says that God alone is worthy of love, adoration and worship. As for the title of "King of the nations," Jeremiah says, "This is your due."

Let us praise and exalt the name of the Lord God, who is not only the King of all the earth, but also the one who causes other kings, presidents, rulers—and dictators—to rise and fall at *his* command. Praise and adore the Lord. There is no one like him. ❧

PRAYER

Dear Lord, there is no one like you. You are the King of the nations . . .

PRAISE TO THE CREATOR OF THE UNIVERSE

But God is my King from long ago;
he brings salvation on the earth.
It was you who split open the sea by your power;
you broke the heads of the monster in the waters.
It was you who crushed the heads of Leviathan
and gave it as food to the creatures of the desert.
It was you who opened up springs and streams;
you dried up the ever-flowing rivers.
The day is yours, and yours also the night;
you established the sun and moon.
It was you who set all the boundaries of the earth;
you made both summer and winter.

PSALM 74:12 – 17

When the forces of nature disrupt our world—whether it's a volcano, earthquake, or a flood—it inspires both awe and fear. No amount of human effort can stop the raging waters of a disastrous flood or the hot lava of a volcano. But God controls even these awesome forces. He was the one who shaped the continents and tamed the ocean waves. He is the one who created the earth, started it spinning on its axis, and determined its place in the solar system. The cycles of the seasons reflect his design. The variety of animal and plant species reflects his creative mind. Yet, God's greatest work is the salvation he provides to those who call on his name.

We do indeed serve an all-powerful God. Offer your praises to him. ✤

PRAYER

Dear God, you are my king from ages past, bringing salvation to the earth ...

november17

ASKING FOR GOD'S PROTECTION

I hear many whispering,
  "Terror on every side!
  Denounce him! Let's denounce him!"
All my friends
  are waiting for me to slip, saying,
"Perhaps he will be deceived;
  then we will prevail over him
  and take our revenge on him."
But the LORD is with me like a mighty warrior;
  so my persecutors will stumble and not prevail.
They will fail and be thoroughly disgraced;
  their dishonor will never be forgotten....
Sing to the LORD!
  Give praise to the LORD!
He rescues the life of the needy
  from the hands of the wicked.

JEREMIAH 20:10–11, 13

At some point in our lives most of us have been threatened by a "bully" of some kind, some*one* who intimidated us, or some*thing* which struck fear in our heart. Those of us who had no big brother, sister, or muscular friend to stand up for us probably longed for a superhero who would come to our rescue and put the bully in his or her place. Jeremiah, who was surrounded by "bullies," had such a hero. "The LORD is with me like a mighty warrior; so my persecutors will stumble and not prevail." God is ready to come to the aid of his children. No matter how big the enemy, "the LORD is with me like a mighty warrior."

Are you facing bullies in your life? Don't try to defeat them in your own strength. Call upon the Lord, and he will come and stand beside you. ✣

PRAYER

Dear God, I know you stand beside me like a great warrior ...

november**18**

PRAISE FOR GOD'S GIFTS

You care for the land and water it;
you enrich it abundantly.
The streams of God are filled with water
to provide the people with grain,
for so you have ordained it.
You drench its furrows and level its ridges;
you soften it with showers and bless its crops.

PSALM 65:9–10

At the end of November, trees have shed their leaves; flowers and plants have died. Crops have been harvested; and perennial plants have gone dormant until next spring. It's the time of year for reflection. We often take for granted the trees and plants that come back every year with new growth and beauty. We plant seeds in the ground and depend upon the rains to come again to water the seeds so they can produce the bountiful harvests which follow in their season. Upon reflection, however, we know nothing would have life without the touch of the one who created it all. God is the Creator of all things, the Giver of life to all human beings—and also to all animals and plants.

Let us not take any of God's gifts for granted. Thank him for the life he gives. ❖

PRAYER

Dear God, thank you for taking care of the earth and making it fertile ...

november**19**

ASKING GOD TO RELIEVE OUR SUFFERING

LORD, see how my enemies persecute me!
Have mercy and lift me up from the gates of death,
that I may declare your praises
in the gates of Daughter Zion,
and there rejoice in your salvation....
Arise, LORD, do not let mortals triumph;
let the nations be judged in your presence.
Strike them with terror, LORD;
let the nations know they are only mortal.

PSALM 9:13–14, 19–20

"See how my enemies persecute me!" Life is difficult enough as it is without people destroying our reputations or causing us to stumble. But as David quickly learned when he became king, the more responsibility and power we are given, the more enemies oppose us. When we are being attacked by our enemies, we instinctually fight back—often ferociously. But as this prayer shows, our first response to opposition should be to bring the situation to God in prayer—asking him to come to our defense and rescue us from our enemies' traps. Instead of plotting how he could destroy his enemies, David identified how his current predicament could bring glory and honor to God. He prayed, "Have mercy and lift me up from the gates of death, that I may declare your praises in the gates of Daughter Zion."

What difficult and troublesome situations have you gone through? Submit those situations to God, and ask him to save you so that you may rejoice in him. ✤

PRAYER

Dear Lord, you know how I am suffering. Please save me so I can rejoice in you ...

JESUS' PRAYER CONCERNING HIS PEOPLE

I pray for them. I am not praying for the world, but for those you have given me, for they are yours. All I have is yours, and all you have is mine. And glory has come to me through them. I will remain in the world no longer, but they are still in the world, and I am coming to you. Holy Father, protect them by the power of your name, the name you gave me, so that they may be one as we are one. While I was with them, I protected them and kept them safe by that name you gave me. None has been lost except the one doomed to destruction so that Scripture would be fulfilled.

JOHN 17:9–12

When we're in need of a person to talk to or desire to spend time with someone, we usually turn to those who care about us. While Jesus was awaiting his arrest by the Pharisees, he took time to give us a glimpse of how much he cares for his people. He prayed for those God had given him, asking his protection on those whom he would die for the next day. Listen to Jesus words: "Holy Father, protect them by the power of your name, the name you gave me, so that they may be one as we are one." Jesus' prayer revealed the tenor of his heart. He cares for us and wants us to spend time with him.

Meditate on how much Jesus cares for you. Jesus is so concerned about you that he is praying for you and interceding on your behalf before God the Father. ✤

PRAYER

Dear Jesus, thank you for caring for me . . .

november21

APPROACHING GOD WITH A HONEST HEART

Hear me, LORD, my plea is just;
  listen to my cry.
Hear my prayer—
  it does not rise from deceitful lips.
Let my vindication come from you;
  may your eyes see what is right.
Though you probe my heart,
  though you examine me at night and test me,
you will find that I have planned no evil;
  my mouth has not transgressed.
Though people tried to bribe me,
  I have kept myself from the ways of the violent
  through what your lips have commanded.
My steps have held to your paths;
  my feet have not stumbled....
As for me, I will be vindicated and will see your face;
  when I awake, I will be satisfied with seeing your likeness.

                         PSALM 17:1–5, 15

Like a child who longs to see his father after he has been away for awhile, David longed to see God face to face. He wanted to thank and praise God who had rescued him. David knew God was holy and that all who enter his presence must come with a honest heart and an upright life. In this prayer, David promised to follow God's ways and even asked the Lord to examine his heart. David had certainly sinned before. At one dark moment in his life, he orchestrated the murder of an innocent man. But David didn't hide his sins; he confessed them to God. He asked God to cleanse him from sin so he could enter the Lord's presence with praise.

   May we ask God to cleanse us from sin as we enter God's presence. ✤

PRAYER

Dear Lord, my prayer comes from a honest heart. Test my thoughts and examine my heart ...

november**22**

THANKS FOR A BOUNTIFUL HARVEST

> *You crown the year with your bounty,*
> *and your carts overflow with abundance.*
> *The grasslands of the wilderness overflow;*
> *the hills are clothed with gladness.*
> *The meadows are covered with flocks*
> *and the valleys are mantled with grain;*
> *they shout for joy and sing.*

PSALM 65:11 – 13

For farmers, harvest is a time to rejoice. The long hours of backbreaking work in the fields finally bear fruit. The acres burst forth with grain; the limbs of trees become weighed down with fruit. It is a time to rejoice in what God has provided, to sing of his goodness. In this prayer, David thanked God for all his blessings on Israel — the meadows were filled with sheep; the pastures were lush; and the fields were filled with grain. The land was so blessed by God that it appeared to be shouting out in joy.

In this month of thanksgiving, we ought to thank the Lord of the harvest in our lives. Harvests of love and friendships. Harvests of blessing, protection, and joy. What makes you want to shout and sing for joy in prayer today? ✤

PRAYER

Dear Lord, you crown the year with a bountiful harvest . . .

november23

HOLY, HOLY, HOLY

Each of the four living creatures had six wings and was covered with eyes all around, even under its wings. Day and night they never stop saying:

> *"'Holy, holy, holy*
> *is the Lord God Almighty,'*
> *who was, and is, and is to come."*

REVELATION 4:8

Can you hear it? Be still and listen closely. There it is again. Over and over. The words ring out over the horizon of time itself—"holy, holy, holy." The first person to hear that heavenly refrain was the prophet Isaiah. He heard those words from the angelic beings who gathered around God's throne. Then, hundreds of years later, John, while exiled on the island of Patmos, was allowed to hear this eternal chorus: "Holy, holy, holy is the Lord God Almighty." When the minutia of life seems to outweigh its eternal meaning, when the ebb and flow of life's routine weighs you down, listen closely for heaven's refrain. "Holy, holy, holy." The prayer of praise rings on.

Today take a moment to join the heavenly chorus in praising God, for he is holy. ✤

PRAYER

Dear Lord, you are holy. You are the Lord God Almighty—the one who always was, who is, and who is still to come . . .

november24

PRAISE FOR BLESSINGS THAT OVERFLOW

> *You prepare a table before me*
> *in the presence of my enemies.*
> *You anoint my head with oil;*
> *my cup overflows.*
> *Surely your goodness and love will follow me*
> *all the days of my life,*
> *and I will dwell in the house of the LORD*
> *forever.*

PSALM 23:5-6

Though wolves and foxes might roam the countryside, a loyal shepherd would always protect his sheep. He would lead them to lush pastures and flowing streams, watch for predatory animals, and then guide them back to a place of safety. David thought of God as his loyal shepherd, providing for and protecting him. Yet, God did even more than any shepherd would do. He didn't simply provide food; he arranged a feast for David in front of his enemies' jealous eyes. God didn't simply allow him to attend this feast; he treated David as his guest. God didn't merely give him gifts; he gave him a cup overflowing with all sorts of blessings.

Think of the ways in which God has provided for you and blessed you more than you deserve. ❖

PRAYER

Dear Lord, you have made my cup overflow with blessings. I want to live in your house forever ...

november25

THANKS TO GOD ALONE

> *Give thanks to the Lord of lords:*
> > *His love endures forever.*
> *to him who alone does great wonders,*
> > *His love endures forever.*
> *who by his understanding made the heavens,*
> > *His love endures forever.*
> *who spread out the earth upon the waters,*
> > *His love endures forever.*
> *who made the great lights—*
> > *His love endures forever.*
> > > PSALM 136:3–7

Whether it's the air we breathe or the sand under our feet—the entire earth is God's gift to us. We owe him our thanks for his many gifts to us. In this corporate prayer, a worship leader calls on the people to thank God for one aspect of his creation. The people respond with the refrain: "His love endures forever."

Let this ancient worship leader guide your thanks to God today. Look at God's creation around you—the sky above, the sparkling stars that shine down, the soil beneath you. Let those aspects of God's creation remind of how faithful God has been to you, how he has provided you with what you need—food, clothes, and shelter. ✣

PRAYER

Dear Lord, your faithful love endures forever. I thank you for . . .

GIVING THANKS FOR GOD'S GOODNESS

> *Enter his gates with thanksgiving*
> *and his courts with praise;*
> *give thanks to him and praise his name.*
> *For the LORD is good and his love endures forever;*
> *his faithfulness continues through all generations.*

PSALM 100:4–5

Imagine yourself entering the gates at the entrance to the Temple alongside a throng of people gathering to praise the Lord. As you near the courts of the Temple, you are swept up in the words of this prayer uttered by all those around you: "Enter his gates with thanksgiving." This prayer functioned as a call to worship for people entering the Temple. It helped the people to focus their thoughts on God and his good gifts to them. It set a tone of thankfulness for the worship service that would follow.

Let the words of this prayer focus your thoughts on God's goodness to you. Come into his presence with thanksgiving and praise on your lips. ♣

PRAYER

Dear Lord, I enter into your presence with thanksgiving and praise, for you are good . . .

november**27**

DRINKING FROM THE FOUNTAIN OF SALVATION

With joy you will draw water
from the wells of salvation.

In that day you will say:

"Give praise to the LORD, proclaim his name;
make known among the nations what he has done,
and proclaim that his name is exalted.
Sing to the LORD, for he has done glorious things;
let this be known to all the world."

ISAIAH 12:3 – 5

This excerpt is a pause of joyful praise in an otherwise frightful prediction from God's prophet Isaiah concerning Israel's disobedience. It is the prayer Israelites will offer to God after he saves them from their sins. Isaiah compared their change of heart to quenching one's parched throat at a water fountain. Isn't it amazing how experiencing the dreadful results of sin brings a new appreciation of the joys of obeying God? The hearts of these newfound believers overflow with thanksgiving for God for all he has done.

In prayer, thank God for saving you. Ask him to satisfy your parched soul and renew your spirit. ❖

PRAYER

Dear Lord, I thank you and praise your name. You have done wonderful things . . .

THANKSGIVING FOR ANSWERED PRAYER

> *Open for me the gates of the righteous;*
>   *I will enter and give thanks to the LORD.*
> *This is the gate of the LORD*
>   *through which the righteous may enter.*
> *I will give you thanks, for you answered me;*
>   *you have become my salvation.*

PSALM 118:19–21

This psalm pictures a victorious yet battle-weary king at the helm of a throng of grateful people entering the gates of the Temple to thank God for saving them. During those times, the Temple represented God's presence—the place where his followers would go to pray to the Lord. Today, we enter into God's presence in a car, at work, or in the aisles of a grocery store—wherever we take time to pray to him. We can be sure God hears our prayer and answers each one wherever and whenever they are uttered. And by doing so, he gives us even more reasons to pray.

Just like the victorious king in this psalm, we should enter God's presence by thanking him for answering our prayers. For what answers to prayer are you thankful today? ❖

PRAYER

Dear Lord, I thank you for answering my prayers ...

november**29**

A PRAYER FOR GOOD MOTIVES

I know, my God, that you test the heart and are pleased with integrity. All these things I have given willingly and with honest intent. And now I have seen with joy how willingly your people who are here have given to you. LORD, the God of our fathers Abraham, Isaac and Israel, keep these desires and thoughts in the hearts of your people forever, and keep their hearts loyal to you. And give my son Solomon the wholehearted devotion to keep your commands, statutes and decrees and to do everything to build the palatial structure for which I have provided."

Then David said to the whole assembly, "Praise the LORD your God." So they all praised the LORD, the God of their fathers; they bowed down, prostrating themselves before the LORD and the king.

1 CHRONICLES 29:17–18, 20

David's prayer comes at a pinnacle moment in his reign as king—the dedication of gifts for the building of the Temple. As the people entered a new era in their relationship with the living God, David prayed that their motives would be pure. He knew that God was more concerned about the condition of people's hearts than the silver and gold they were giving away. Even with all the authority he possessed as king, David could not accurately judge the motives behind the Israelites' gifts. Only God could examine his heart and theirs. He prayed that God would find in their hearts integrity and a willingness to obey.

Follow David's example. Ask God to make you a person of integrity—a person who willingly obeys. ✤

PRAYER

Dear Lord, examine my heart. May you find integrity there…

ASKING FOR GOD'S HELP

> *I have chosen the way of faithfulness;*
> *I have set my heart on your laws.*
> *I hold fast to your statutes, LORD;*
> *do not let me be put to shame.*
> *I run in the path of your commands,*
> *for you have broadened my understanding.*

PSALM 119:30–32

Asking for help is something we as humans don't like to do. We tend to think we don't need any help. "I can handle things myself," we say to ourselves. In today's prayer, the desire of the psalmist is to be faithful to God. But he confesses that he can't follow the commands of God on his own. What humility to say that only with God's divine assistance was obedience possible for him! We may not like to ask for help, but our Father informs us that we need his guidance to make it through each day.

Express to the Lord your desire to follow him with all your heart, soul, and mind. Then commit yourself to asking him for his guidance and assistance in the situations you face in life. ✤

PRAYER

Dear Lord, if you will help me, I will follow your commands today . . .

december1

REJOICING OVER ETERNAL BLESSINGS

You, my God, have revealed to your servant that you will build a house for him. So your servant has found courage to pray to you. You, LORD, are God! You have promised these good things to your servant. Now you have been pleased to bless the house of your servant, that it may continue forever in your sight; for you, LORD, have blessed it, and it will be blessed forever.

1 CHRONICLES 17:25–27

One evening at the end of his reign, God spoke to David through a prophet and promised him an eternal dynasty. His descendants would reign as kings forever and forever. David's immediate response to such wonderful news was to thank God. He shouted a resounding "yes" to God's marvelous promise. "Yes, do as you say. Establish my family for all of eternity," David, in effect, said. He immediately noticed what was unique about God's promise. It would last for all eternity. His family would not only enjoy blessings in this world, they could look forward to an eternal inheritance.

Are your prayers too often confined to earthly joys? Consider widening the scope of your prayers to eternal blessings as well. Like David, you can look forward to an eternal inheritance. In this month when we focus on the birth of our Savior, thank God for the eternal inheritance you have in Jesus Christ, God's Son. ❖

PRAYER

Dear Lord, when you grant a blessing, it is an eternal blessing. Thank you for an eternal inheritance . . .

december**2**

PRAISE FOR THE VICTORY OF THE ANOINTED

The LORD is the strength of his people,
a fortress of salvation for his anointed one.
Save your people and bless your inheritance;
be their shepherd and carry them forever.

PSALM 28:8–9

Everyone wants to be around winners, whether it's the person who wins that all-important contract or the sport team that wins the championship. In David's time, winning military victories was critical for the survival of the nation of Israel. If David didn't triumph over his enemies, conquering armies would ravage the nation. David trusted God to give him—the one whom God had anointed as king—victory. The Hebrew word for *anointed* is *Messiah;* and so David's psalm is also a victory celebration of the Messiah who was to come—Jesus Christ, the ultimate Anointed One. Jesus is the Victor! He has defeated on the cross the devil and death itself. His victory is also ours, for he defeated the sin that enslaved us.

Think of the ways Christ has enabled you to conquer those sins that used to control you. In your prayer time today, celebrate Christ's victory over sin. ✤

PRAYER

Dear Lord, you have given victory to your Anointed One ...

december3

THE JOYS OF THOSE WHO TRUST IN HIM

Taste and see that the LORD is good;
blessed is the one who takes refuge in him.
Fear the LORD, you his holy people,
for those who fear him lack nothing.
The lions may grow weak and hungry,
but those who seek the LORD lack no good thing.

PSALM 34:8 – 10

David invites us all to "taste and see that the LORD is good." David had recently seen God's goodness at work in his life when he wrote this prayer. Even though King Saul had sought David's death and Abimelech was considering whether he should execute David, God had spared David's life by allowing him to escape from them both. David's heart was bursting with joy because he had just experienced God's power at work in his life. Yet in his celebration, he didn't forget to invite others to find their joy in God as well—to "taste and see that the LORD is good."

How has God showed his goodness to you? What good things has God given you? Let David's prayer inspire you to find joy in the Lord. ❖

PRAYER

Dear Lord, I have tasted and seen that you are good. Because I trust in you, I will lack nothing . . .

december4

THANKSGIVING FOR GOD'S PROMISES

Then King David went in and sat before the LORD, and he said:

"Who am I, Sovereign LORD, and what is my family, that you have brought me this far? And as if this were not enough in your sight, Sovereign LORD, you have also spoken about the future of the house of your servant—and this decree, Sovereign LORD, is for a mere human!

"What more can David say to you? For you know your servant, Sovereign LORD. For the sake of your word and according to your will, you have done this great thing and made it known to your servant.

"How great you are, Sovereign LORD! There is no one like you, and there is no God but you, as we have heard with our own ears."

2 SAMUEL 7:18–22

"Who am I, Sovereign LORD, and what is my family, that you have brought me this far?" This was David's response to God after hearing that the Lord was going to make his family into an eternal dynasty. God's plans for David were impressive—more than David could ever imagine. Not only would David's descendants reign as kings on this earth; but his family dynasty would last throughout eternity as well. The eternal King of kings, Jesus Christ himself, would one day come from David's royal line. There was nothing that David could have done to deserve such an honor, for God knew what David's heart was really like. Such a wonderful blessing could only come from God's inscrutable and merciful will.

What blessings have you enjoyed from God's hand? List the ways he has blessed you beyond your wildest dreams. ❖

PRAYER

Dear Lord, who am I that you have brought me this far?...

december5

SHOUTING FOR JOY

I will praise you with the harp
  for your faithfulness, my God;
I will sing praise to you with the lyre,
  Holy One of Israel.
My lips will shout for joy
  when I sing praise to you—
  I whom you have delivered.
My tongue will tell of your righteous acts
  all day long,
for those who wanted to harm me
  have been put to shame and confusion.

PSALM 71:22–24

"My lips will shout for joy when I sing praise to you." Does this sound like the words of an elderly man? A typical retirement home isn't filled with shouts and loud, joyful songs. Usually it's a solemn and quiet place. Yet after surveying his life in prayer, this elderly person was filled with joy. He sang God's praises for everything God had done for him. It was the Lord who had redeemed him and brought him through all the troubles of his life. He promised to tell others about God's righteous deeds as long as he lived.

Picture the robust praises of this aged man, as he told all who would listen what God had done for him. Let this man's enthusiasm inspire you to offer your own praises to God and resolve to tell others about the Lord's wonderful deeds. ✤

PRAYER

Dear Lord, I will shout for joy and sing your praises today ...

december**6**

PAUL'S PRAYER FOR THE EPHESIANS

I pray that the eyes of your heart may be enlightened in order that you may know the hope to which he has called you, the riches of his glorious inheritance in his holy people, and his incomparably great power for us who believe. That power is the same as the mighty strength
EPHESIANS 1:18–19

While the believers in Ephesus enjoyed the luxuries and wealth available in a cosmopolitan city located on major sea and land trade routes, Paul was confined to a small room in Rome, under the constant watch of a Roman guard. But who would ever guess from Paul's prayer that he was deprived of anything? Paul's confident description of God's power in this prayer does not betray a hint of hopelessness—something we might expect from a person in such a situation. Instead, Paul speaks of the rich inheritance and wonderful future he would have in heaven. Paul's future on the earth was in the hands of Caesar. Yet Paul's ultimate hopes weren't set on this world; his hopes were set on heaven and on eternity.

In your prayers, place your hopes on your eternal inheritance in heaven, just as Paul did. Pray that God might help you understand how powerful he is. ✜

PRAYER

Dear Lord, help me to understand the wonderful future you have promised to me . . .

PRAISE FOR GOD'S MIGHT

The seas have lifted up, LORD,
the seas have lifted up their voice;
the seas have lifted up their pounding waves.
Mightier than the thunder of the great waters,
mightier than the breakers of the sea—
the LORD on high is mighty.
Your statutes, LORD, stand firm;
holiness adorns your house
for endless days.

PSALM 93:3–5

People throughout the ages have admired God's handiwork when they come to the coast. There, a vast body of water, constantly in flux, meets the stability of the ground. When angry, churning ocean waves break violently upon the cliffs and shoals of a shoreline, they display the great power of these immense bodies of water. Yet, as great as these forces may be, the power of the Creator exceeds any forces found in nature. The energy found in roaring ocean waves, violent earthquakes, or volcanic eruptions can't compare to God's strength.

If God's power exceeds these natural forces, he certainly can handle our troubles. Don't allow the deafening roar of discouraging circumstances disrupt your confidence in God's power. As you pray today, picture mighty waves tumbling upon the shore and imagine how mightier God is compared to those waves. ✤

PRAYER

Dear Lord, I praise you for being mightier than all of creation . . .

december**8**

MAY GOD'S PROMISE LAST FOREVER

And now, LORD, let the promise you have made concerning your servant and his house be established forever. Do as you promised, so that it will be established and that your name will be great forever. Then people will say, "The LORD Almighty, the God over Israel, is Israel's God!" And the house of your servant David will be established before you.

1 CHRONICLES 17:23–24

In a world where little can be enjoyed "forever," David praised God for giving him an everlasting promise. His family would reign forever on Israel's throne. One can imagine David's delight when he realized that this promise would be fulfilled by the birth of the Messiah, Jesus Christ. Born in David's royal line, Jesus was the King of kings, who at the end of this age will reveal his eternal reign over all of creation.

Generations later, we too are moved to prayer when we consider God's eternal promises to us. Favorite sweaters. Middle school romances. Nothing in this world really lasts forever, except for the promises we have in God's word. May David's words help us thank God for his eternal promises — our salvation and our eternal inheritance in heaven. Spend some time thanking God for his promises that will last forever. ✤

PRAYER

Dear Lord, do as you have promised to me. May your promises last forever ...

december9

PRAISE FOR THE KING FROM EVERLASTING PAST

> *The LORD reigns, he is robed in majesty;*
>   *the LORD is robed in majesty and armed with strength;*
>   *indeed, the world is established, firm and secure.*
> *Your throne was established long ago;*
>   *you are from all eternity.*
>
> PSALM 93:1–2

According to Jewish tradition, this psalm hints at the arrival of a Messiah, who will save God's people. Its opening lines describe the incomparable royalty of this King who would come—King Jesus. This King is from everlasting past; and his throne is from time immemorial. No wonder this King's majestic robe inspires such praise from the psalmist.

Our image of God can directly affect the nature of our prayers. Sometimes the image of God the Father suits our prayer for guidance. At other times, we are reminded of God as our closest friend. As you pray throughout this day, let this psalm help you picture Jesus as King "robed in majesty and armed with strength." Let your imagination ignite your praises for the King. ✤

PRAYER

Dear Lord, I praise you for you are robed in majesty and armed with strength . . .

december**10**

GLORY TO THE GOD BEYOND UNDERSTANDING

Oh, the depth of the riches of the wisdom and knowledge of God!
How unsearchable his judgments,
and his paths beyond tracing out!
"Who has known the mind of the Lord?
Or who has been his counselor?"
"Who has ever given to God,
that God should repay them?"
For from him and through him and for him are all things.
To him be the glory forever! Amen.

ROMANS 11:33–36

After contemplating God's mercy in his letter to the Romans, Paul burst forth with this prayer of praise for God. "Oh, the depth of the riches of the wisdom and knowledge of God!" His wisdom holds this world together. His knowledge exceeds that of any scholar. His riches are far more glorious than that of any king or queen. "How unsearchable his judgments, and his paths beyond tracing out!" In this doxology full of praise for God, Paul focused on God's unique qualities—his wisdom, power, and greatness.

In a similar manner, we ought to praise God for being the one friend and counselor, who is beyond any earthly comparison. In prayer today, forget trying to understand God completely. Simply rejoice in God's unique standing. ✤

PRAYER

Oh, what a wonderful God I have! How great are his riches and wisdom and knowledge! . . .

december**11**

GRATITUDE FOR GOD'S GIFTS

Wealth and honor come from you;
you are the ruler of all things.
In your hands are strength and power
to exalt and give strength to all.
Now, our God, we give you thanks,
and praise your glorious name.

"But who am I, and who are my people, that we should be able to give as generously as this? Everything comes from you, and we have given you only what comes from your hand."
1 CHRONICLES 29:12 – 14

Although God prevented King David from building the great Temple in Jerusalem, the king gathered some materials so that his son Solomon could build the Temple easily. The people gave generously for the future building of the Temple. David was touched by their generosity and expressed his praise to God in prayer.

At this time of the year, when people express their generosity by giving gifts to each other, David's words can help us remember that everything we have comes from God. Genuine giving expresses gratitude to God. We give in response to God's gifts to us. ❧

PRAYER

Dear Lord, everything I have comes from you, and I give you only what you have already given me . . .

december**12**

DANIEL'S CONFESSION FOR HIS PEOPLE

I prayed to the LORD my God and confessed:

"Lord, the great and awesome God, who keeps his covenant of love with those who love him and keep his commandments, we have sinned and done wrong. We have been wicked and have rebelled; we have turned away from your commands and laws. We have not listened to your servants the prophets, who spoke in your name to our kings, our princes and our ancestors, and to all the people of the land.

"Lord, you are righteous, but this day we are covered with shame—the people of Judah and the inhabitants of Jerusalem and all Israel, both near and far, in all the countries where you have scattered us because of our unfaithfulness to you.... The Lord our God is merciful and forgiving, even though we have rebelled against him."

DANIEL 9:4–7, 9

Daniel had already lived a full life. He had already survived the lion's den. Now, his days were filled with startling visions of God's future plans for the world. As he read the predictions of the prophet Jeremiah, he was overwhelmed with how faithful God was and how faithless the Israelites were, how just God's judgments were and how wicked the Israelites were. He realized he was living in a foreign land because of the mistakes of his ancestors. This prayer was Daniel's confession for his people.

One of the ways we know we are reading God's word attentively is by how much our conscience is affected by what we read. We should be moved to praise or repentance when we read Scripture. Like Daniel, we will discover how great and awesome God is and how merciful and forgiving he is to those who turn to him. ❖

PRAYER

O Lord, you are a great and awesome God! You are merciful and forgiving . . .

december13

FINDING HOPE IN THE HEIR TO DAVID'S THRONE

And again,

> *"Praise the Lord, all you Gentiles;*
> *let all the peoples extol him."*

And again, Isaiah says,

> *"The Root of Jesse will spring up,*
> *one who will arise to rule over the nations;*
> *in him the Gentiles will hope."*

May the God of hope fill you with all joy and peace as you trust in him, so that you may overflow with hope by the power of the Holy Spirit.

ROMANS 15:11–13

"May the God of hope fill you with all joy and peace as you trust in him." What a wonderful blessing for a Christmas card! Paul wrote this prayer for the Romans, after contemplating how Jesus came to this earth to save all people—both Jews and Gentiles. That is why Isaiah predicted that Gentiles would one day place their hopes on Jesus—the great heir to David's throne. We fulfill Isaiah's prediction when we, Gentiles, sing the words of the Christmas carol, "O Little Town of Bethlehem" by Phillips Brooks: "The hopes and fears of all the years are met in thee tonight." We honor the birth of David's heir, our Lord and Savior Jesus Christ, when we place all of our hopes in Jesus for our salvation. As Christmas approaches, pray that your friends and acquaintances may find their hope and peace in Jesus alone. ✤

PRAYER

Dear Lord, please give hope, happiness, and peace to ...

JOB'S PRAISE TO GOD

At this, Job got up and tore his robe and shaved his head. Then he fell to the ground in worship 21 and said:

> *"Naked I came from my mother's womb,*
>   *and naked I will depart.*
> *The LORD gave and the LORD has taken away;*
>   *may the name of the LORD be praised."*

> *In all this, Job did not sin by charging God with wrongdoing.*

JOB 1:20–22

Job had lost everything—all of his animals, his servants, and even all of his children. Yet in the midst of such tragedy, Job realized everything he had was from God. Even his children were gifts from God, and so there was still reason to say "may the name of the LORD be praised."

The tragedies of this life are not lessened by our hope in God. Losses still hurt. Our bond with Job's suffering is simply the bond of a shared humanity. What is amazing, however, is that God allowed his Son to come to this earth to suffer. God not only gives us everything we have, he gives us his Son to redeem us from our sins. Praise the name of the Lord! ✤

PRAYER

Dear Lord, you gave me everything I have. Praise the name of the Lord . . .

december15

HANNAH'S PRAISE TO THE LORD

Then Hannah prayed and said:

> *"My heart rejoices in the LORD;*
> *in the LORD my horn is lifted high.*
> *My mouth boasts over my enemies,*
> *for I delight in your deliverance.*
> *"There is no one holy like the LORD;*
> *there is no one besides you;*
> *there is no Rock like our God."*

1 SAMUEL 2:1–2

During this Advent season you will probably hear a reading of Mary's prayer, in which she thanks and praises God for allowing her to bear Jesus, God's Son (Luke 1:46–55). Her ancestor Hannah had the same feelings of gratitude towards God and shared the same prayer. Both of them were linked across the centuries as women who gave birth to special babies—the prophet Samuel to infertile Hannah, and Jesus to the virgin Mary. Hannah's prayer rings with amazement over God's miraculous intervention in her life. Her celebration of God in prayer was her answer to her enemies—the Lord himself had answered her request for a son.

In our prayers, we should imitate Hannah's example by looking for the ways God has blessed us. Our praise for God's work in our lives is the best testimony to others. What will capture people's attention is not the size of God's answers, but the fact that God does answer prayer. Find ways this week to tell others how God has answered your prayers. ♣

PRAYER

Dear Lord, oh how you have blessed me! My heart rejoices in you . . .

december16

WAITING FOR GOD

Listen to my words, LORD,
consider my lament.
Hear my cry for help,
my King and my God,
for to you I pray.
In the morning, LORD, you hear my voice;
in the morning I lay my requests before you
and wait expectantly.

Psalm 5:1 – 3

We can be in deep trouble and not realize it. Values from our culture can present themselves with such insidious attractiveness that we fail to see how they distort our lives. Our lack of discernment leaves us vulnerable. Scripture, however, tells us of God's unfailing love. God is faithful to us even when we forget him. When our ship of life runs aground, we may feel like God has deserted us. But God doesn't hide from us; instead it's our selfishness that prevents us from recognizing him. And when, in a moment of insight, we understand our predicament, we have God's promise that when we call on him and wait for him, he will hear us.

When we are experiencing difficulties in this life, it's certainly hard to wait on God. The Israelites, who were suffering under Roman rule, felt the same way. They couldn't wait for their Savior. But after centuries of waiting, their hopes were fulfilled in the baby born in Bethlehem. God did send his Son to save the world; all they had to do was wait for his timing. ✤

PRAYER

Dear Lord, I wait expectantly on you. Answer my prayers, O Lord …

december**17**

JESUS' PRAYER FOR THE UNITY OF BELIEVERS

My prayer is not for them alone. I pray also for those who will believe in me through their message, that all of them may be one, Father, just as you are in me and I am in you. May they also be in us so that the world may believe that you have sent me.

JOHN 17:20–21

In this month when we celebrate Jesus coming to this earth, we should remember Jesus' purpose in coming. Shortly before his arrest, Jesus expressed what he hoped his life would achieve. He prayed that those who believed in him would become united in their love for God and each other. Only then would the world believe God had sent Jesus to the earth to save all of humanity from their sins. Christian unity has many imitators. For some, unity means uniformity—every believer marching in lockstep whether in doctrine, worship, or church order. For others, unity is turned into expediency, as significant issues are swept aside and superficial unity is proclaimed. But in this prayer, Jesus explained what real Christian unity is: it imitates the intimate communion the Father and the Son share. It is a dynamic unity—a complementary relationship of give-and-take, a sharing of life and purpose. This is the union that Jesus prayed for his disciples—interceding with the Father both then and now.

Jesus' prayer is answered whenever we show love to our fellow believers, in matters both great and small. ❖

PRAYER

Dear Father, with Jesus your Son, I pray that I might be one with other believers so that the world will believe in you . . .

december**18**

REALIZING NOTHING IS TOO HARD FOR GOD

Ah, Sovereign LORD, you have made the heavens and the earth by your great power and outstretched arm. Nothing is too hard for you. You show love to thousands but bring the punishment for the parents' sins into the laps of their children after them. Great and mighty God, whose name is the LORD Almighty, great are your purposes and mighty are your deeds. Your eyes are open to the ways of all mankind; you reward each person according to their conduct and as their deeds deserve.

JEREMIAH 32:17–19

Jeremiah bought some land even when times were bleak, and smart people were investing in liquid valuables—gold and cash. Even so, God told his prophet to invest in real estate. Although God's people would be sent into exile, their return to the land was guaranteed by God. "Once more fields will be bought in this land" (32:43). Jeremiah banked on God's faithfulness. Having put his money on the line, Jeremiah added today's prayer. In it, he reflected on God's faithfulness to his people. He voiced a thought we need to remember when we face difficult times— "Is anything too hard for the LORD?" (Genesis 18:14).

When we've thought through all the possibilities and think our situation is hopeless, we make a huge mistake if we discount God's power. The past has demonstrated God's power over hopeless situations. Though Jesus was born in a manager, God lifted him up to become a light to all the nations. Though Jesus' life ended with his suffering on a cross, God empowered him to conquer both sin and death. Though your present circumstances may be challenging your trust in God, place your hopes in God. Your hope will be rewarded in wonderful and surprising ways. ✤

PRAYER

Dear Lord, nothing is too hard for you. You are great and powerful . . .

december**19**

PRAISE FOR JESUS' COMING

For I tell you that Christ has become a servant of the Jews on behalf of God's truth, so that the promises made to the patriarchs might be confirmed and, moreover, that the Gentiles might glorify God for his mercy. As it is written:

> *"Therefore I will praise you among the Gentiles;*
> *I will sing the praises of your name."*

Again, it says,

> *"Rejoice, you Gentiles, with his people."*

ROMANS 15:8–10

"Rejoice, you Gentiles, with his people." To us, this statement might not seem so radical. But to Jews of Paul's day, it was like saying, "Let the Iraqis and the Americans have a party together." Jews and Gentiles were enemies in Paul's day. But because Christ had come to this earth to save both Jews and Gentiles, Paul encouraged them to accept each other and even to pray together. He asked them to join their voices together in praising Jesus, their Savior. Certainly, the angelic announcement of Jesus' birth included all of us, for the angel said, "I bring you good news that will cause great joy for all the people" (Luke 2:10). Jesus' birth should inspire joy in "all the people"—even in the hearts of those people who are completely different from us.

Rejoice in your Savior. Determine today to set aside time during this busy season to celebrate with other believers the birth of your Savior. ♣

PRAYER

Dear Lord, I too want to add my voice to those who sing praises to your name . . .

december**20**

ISAIAH'S PRAYER FOR A REDEEMER

For our offenses are many in your sight,
  and our sins testify against us.
Our offenses are ever with us,
  and we acknowledge our iniquities:
rebellion and treachery against the LORD,
  turning our backs on our God,
inciting revolt and oppression,
  uttering lies our hearts have conceived....
"The Redeemer will come to Zion,
  to those in Jacob who repent of their sins,"
  declares the LORD.

ISAIAH 59:12–13, 20

When the bills pile up—when the dishes in the sink pile up—we start feeling guilty about not attending to our responsibilities. But Isaiah prayed about something far more serious. He described Israel's sins as piling up—sins that offended God and deserved punishment. Israel couldn't do anything to clean up this pile; but God could. Though the Israelites had rebelled against God, though they had turned their backs on the Almighty, God promised to send a Redeemer. Only he could buy them back from their slavery to sin. Only he could save them from their sins. This Redeemer is Jesus—the one whose birth we celebrate on Christmas day. In a sense, Christmas was God's shopping day. God sent Jesus to this earth to "buy back" sinners who turn from their sins and believe in him. The divine shopping trip lasted more than thirty years, and the bill required Jesus' own death.

In prayer today, praise God for sending Jesus to this earth to save us from our sins. ✤

PRAYER

Dear Lord, my sins are piled up. Thank you for buying me back ...

december**21**

HONOR TO THE COMING KING OF KINGS

To keep this command without spot or blame until the appearing of our Lord Jesus Christ, which God will bring about in his own time—God, the blessed and only Ruler, the King of kings and Lord of lords, who alone is immortal and who lives in unapproachable light, whom no one has seen or can see. To him be honor and might forever. Amen.

1 TIMOTHY 6:14–16

"Is it Christmas yet?" The anticipation in children's voices around Christmas reminds us of that "I-can-hardly-wait-until-it-gets-here" feeling. Waiting for Christmas should remind us that we who are trusting in Christ are also waiting— waiting for Jesus' return in glory. Just as the ancient Israelites were waiting for the birth of the coming Messiah, we are waiting for Christ's return. Only God knows the date. Only he will decide the right time. Yet one day he will return in glory.

In the meantime, we are to live as excited children, four days before Christmas. We may not know the date when Jesus will return; but we know the day is coming! We have the right attitude when we ask the Lord with excitement: "Is it Christ's time yet?" ✣

PRAYER

Dear Jesus, I am waiting for the right time when you will be revealed from heaven . . .

december**22**

REJOICING IN OUR SAVIOR

And Mary said:

> *"My soul glorifies the Lord*
>   *and my spirit rejoices in God my Savior,*
> *for he has been mindful*
>   *of the humble state of his servant.*
> *From now on all generations will call me blessed,*
>   *for the Mighty One has done great things for me—*
>   *holy is his name."*

Luke 1:46–49

Several months pregnant, Mary visited the home of her relative, Elizabeth. Elizabeth was about to deliver a surprise baby herself. Her child, the future John the Baptist, jumped in the womb at the sound of Mary's voice. After Elizabeth told Mary what was going on inside her, Mary responded with a song of praise. Not only did Mary understand the greatness of God, she also believed that God had done great things for her. She felt connected. She realized she was part of God's good plan. Neither God's actions in our lives nor through our lives come as a result of personal merit. Mary knew that she didn't deserve the privilege of carrying the Messiah. She expressed her amazement at God's choice.

Mary's role was unique. Only she could bear our Savior. Yet, our role is surprising similar to Mary's. As believers, our lives should be dwelling places for Christ's spirit. ✤

PRAYER

Dear Lord, thanks for taking notice of me. I rejoice in you, my Savior . . .

december23

MARY'S PRAISE FOR GOD'S MERCY

His mercy extends to those who fear him,
from generation to generation.
He has performed mighty deeds with his arm;
he has scattered those who are proud in their inmost thoughts.
He has brought down rulers from their thrones
but has lifted up the humble.
He has filled the hungry with good things
but has sent the rich away empty.
He has helped his servant Israel,
remembering to be merciful
to Abraham and his descendants forever,
just as he promised our ancestors.

LUKE 1:50–55

We all take electricity for granted in a modern society. It assists us in almost everything we do—from writing letters to working to cooking food. Life wouldn't be the same without it. God's mercy is somewhat similar. We take it for granted too often. It's only because God mercifully sends our land rain and good weather that it produces abundant food. It's only because of God's mercy that we enjoy good food, warm clothes, and comfortable homes. We are too often like children, who are only concerned about begging for mercy when they get into trouble. Mary's prayer in this passage reveals that she wasn't as shortsighted as we often are. She remembered to rejoice in God's mercy when she was enjoying his blessing.

Remember how merciful God has been to you and your family—the ways he has lifted you up when you were down. During this wonderful Christmas season, remember how far God was willing to go to display his mercy to a fallen world. ♣

PRAYER

Dear Lord, your mighty arm does tremendous things. You have exalted the lowly ...

december**24**

ZECHARIAH'S PRAISE FOR A FULFILLED PROMISE

Praise be to the Lord, the God of Israel,
because he has come to his people and redeemed them.
He has raised up a horn of salvation for us
in the house of his servant David
(as he said through his holy prophets of long ago),
salvation from our enemies
and from the hand of all who hate us—
to show mercy to our ancestors
and to remember his holy covenant,
the oath he swore to our father Abraham:
to rescue us from the hand of our enemies,
and to enable us to serve him without fear

LUKE 1:68–74

The joy of seeing a promised fulfilled is sometimes unspeakable—even more so if it's a promise that's too good to be true. Think back on how you, as a child, rejoiced when your parents gave you something they had promised—perhaps it was a new bike or a great vacation trip. For Zechariah, it was God's promise to give him a son. Yet on the day of his son's birth, Zechariah had even more to rejoice over. His son's birth was only the beginning. His son—later named John the Baptist—would one day announce the coming of the Messiah—the Savior God had promised to Israel long ago. Another promise kept. Another reason to rejoice. We can only imagine what it was like for Zechariah to watch God's promises being fulfilled before his eyes. His heart must have raced with joy, as he offered his praises to the Lord.

As Christmas is just around the corner, meditate on what it means to you to serve a God who keeps his promises—even if it means sending his only Son to this earth to die for the sins of all. ♣

PRAYER

Dear Lord, I praise you for you have sent us a mighty Savior, just as you promised ...

december25

GLORY TO GOD IN THE HIGHEST HEAVEN

Suddenly a great company of the heavenly host appeared with the angel, praising God and saying,

> *"Glory to God in the highest heaven,*
> *and on earth peace to those on whom his favor rests."*

LUKE 2:13–14

Daily life wasn't all that different on the night Jesus was born. Inns and taverns were busy with their customers. Shepherds gathered around the fire to swap stories as they passed the night, guarding their sheep. But in a secluded corner of Bethlehem, in an out-of-the-way stable, a baby slept in a manger. Although the inns of Bethlehem couldn't find a room for this baby, all of heaven rejoiced. As the shepherd settled down for a quiet night, the angels assembled into a vast choir. All of sudden, the silence of that night was interrupted by loud praises. The sky lit up with the sight of an army of brilliant angels. Imagine the shepherd's response: Shock, fear, and, then, awe. Awe for the one whom this army of angels was praising. They knew that they had to find this extraordinary child whose birth the angels had announced.

As you celebrate Christ's birth on this joyous day, seek out Jesus as the shepherds did years ago. Use this heavenly song to rejoice in Jesus' birth. ✤

PRAYER

Glory to you, God, in the highest, and peace on earth to all whom you favor ...

SIMEON'S PRAISE FOR THE SAVIOR

Sovereign Lord, as you have promised,
*   you may now dismiss your servant in peace.*
For my eyes have seen your salvation,
*   which you have prepared in the sight of all nations:*
a light for revelation to the Gentiles,
*   and the glory of your people Israel.*

LUKE 2:29–32

Old Simeon wasn't some Jewish senior citizen sitting around with waning hopes that the Messiah would come in his lifetime. He was waiting with an attitude: expectant, confident, and ready! His attitude, and that of the prophetess Anna (Luke 2:36–38) was informed by Scriptures. He understood what this tiny baby Mary and Joseph brought to the Temple meant to all the nations. This baby was the Savior of the world.

Today, people are still making the mistake of seeing only the manger and missing the message. They remember the remarkable baby Jesus; but they overlook God's very presence among us. Where others saw a little child, Simeon saw "a light for revelation to the Gentiles." He was ready to see God! Where others may view the Christmas season as a time to celebrate their gifts, we see it as a time to worship the newborn King of kings. ✤

PRAYER

Dear Lord, you have given me a Savior. Jesus is a light to the nations . . .

december27

JESUS' PRAYER THAT THE WORLD MAY KNOW HIM

I have given them the glory that you gave me, that they may be one as we are one—I in them and you in me—so that they may be brought to complete unity. Then the world will know that you sent me and have loved them even as you have loved me.

Father, I want those you have given me to be with me where I am, and to see my glory, the glory you have given me because you loved me before the creation of the world.

JOHN 17:22–24

As we remember Jesus' birth this week, we should remember why Christ came to this earth in the first place—why he, as God's only Son, allowed himself to become a helpless infant. Later, as a grown man, Jesus prayed about his purpose for coming. He prayed that we, who believe in him, would experience both a oneness with God and a oneness with each other. Part of that prayer forms today's meditation. His prayer puts into words what Jesus accomplished with his life—the reestablishment of our relationship with God as well as the possibility of unity between all people. In his last hours, Jesus placed the ultimate fate of his life back into his Father's hands. Jesus became one of us so that we could become one with God. He made the living God accessible as never before. The child whose birth we remember grew into the one who invites us to become children in his heavenly kingdom.

As you contemplate what Jesus' life and death means to you, pray that you may reflect Jesus' love in your life by showing love to others. ✤

PRAYER

Dear Jesus, help me to show God's love so that the world may know God sent you ...

december**28**

ANTICIPATING THE WEDDING FEAST

Then I heard what sounded like a great multitude, like the roar of rushing waters and like loud peals of thunder, shouting:

> *"Hallelujah!*
> *For our Lord God Almighty reigns.*
> *Let us rejoice and be glad*
> *and give him glory!*
> *For the wedding of the Lamb has come,*
> *and his bride has made herself ready.*
> *Fine linen, bright and clean,*
> *was given her to wear."*

(Fine linen stands for the righteous acts of God's holy people.)

REVELATION 19:6–8

In Scriptures, the revelation of God calls forth one of two responses. Either we are to fall silent before the awesome presence of our living Lord, or we are to shout out our praises—to celebrate his rule over all people. The apostle John was witness to both responses. He was granted a vision of a day in the future when God's people—the bride—would celebrate their union with Jesus—the Lamb. In John's vision, a voice from God's throne leads God's people in praise: "Hallelujah! For the Lord God Almighty reigns." This grand celebration in honor of the church's union with Jesus is the ultimate reason Jesus came to the earth. He came to buy his people back from their slavery to sin, so that they could become joyful members of his eternal kingdom.

This vision of our joyful union with Christ should always remain before us, as we serve Jesus on this earth. Even now Jesus, our Bridegroom, is with us. Let the celebration begin! ✤

PRAYER

Hallelujah! You reign, O Lord God. I rejoice and honor you . . .

december**29**

A PRAYER FOR GOD TO ANSWER

Answer me, LORD, out of the goodness of your love;
in your great mercy turn to me.
Do not hide your face from your servant;
answer me quickly, for I am in trouble.
Come near and rescue me;
deliver me because of my foes.

PSALM 69:16–18

Sometimes we're up, and sometimes we're down. The Scriptures, especially the Psalms, reflect the full range of human emotions, and so they can help us to pray whatever our mood is. At times, we perceive the Lord's presence clearly and vividly; at other times, it is shadowy or hidden behind a cloud. Still, God's word stands whatever our circumstances; and we may carry on our conversation with the Lord through thick and thin. Although it may be hard to see our Lord's face, we can be certain he is near. When Jesus left this earth, he said, "I am with you always, to the very end of the age" (Matthew 28:20). Jesus' promise to be with us always is just as true today as it was in the disciples' time. When we pray to him, we can be certain that Jesus will answer us and come to our rescue. ✤

PRAYER

Dear Lord, answer my prayers, for your unfailing love is wonderful. Come and rescue me ...

december**30**

CLOSE TO THE SHEPHERD

> *Even though I walk*
>   *through the darkest valley,*
> *I will fear no evil,*
>   *for you are with me;*
> *your rod and your staff,*
>   *they comfort me.*

PSALM 23:4

A culture that places a high value on success and self-fulfillment finds it difficult to speak of death. The Holy Scriptures, however, never attempt to hide from us the certainty of death. We are told that we shall return to dust, that our existence on earth is a fleeting as vapor. In one sense, the whole of life is merely a prelude for our glorious existence in heaven. In this prayer, David voiced his belief that God was close to him, even in "the darkest valley." He would not be afraid because he knew God was near. As this year of prayer comes to end, we can reflect on the entire year, looking for ways God was near to us in those "dark valleys." Though this year is ending, another year will follow, with new opportunities. And when our earthly days finally have run their course, another life—filled with wonder and excitement—will open up to us. The Lord Jesus will welcome us to our eternal home.

In prayer today, thank the Lord for being near to you in the "dark valleys" of last year. Ask the Lord to be close by your side in the year ahead. ♣

PRAYER

Dear Lord, even when I walk through the dark valley of death, I will not be afraid, for you are close beside me . . .

december31

PRAISE FOR GOD'S WONDERFUL PLAN

LORD, you are my God;
I will exalt you and praise your name,
for in perfect faithfulness
you have done wonderful things,
things planned long ago.

ISAIAH 25:1

Has this year seen the fulfillment of God's purpose in your life, as you have been drawn to him in devotion, praise, and petition? We may not always know how God is going to answer our prayers. God is full of surprises! But we have assurance from God's Word that he is always at work in the lives of those who belong to him—"those who love him, who have been called according to his purpose" (Romans 8:28).

No matter what happens to us, we can praise him and profess, "You are my God," just as Isaiah did. We can begin our annual cycle of prayers with this profession of faith. And we can end the cycle with the same affirmation—now more deeply felt and more clearly understood, for we are closer to learning what it means to be a servant of such a God. And, whether or not mighty works and great deliverances have come to us from the hand of the Lord during these twelve months, one miracle stands: we are here to declare, once again, that "LORD, you are my God." ✣

PRAYER

You are my God, O Lord, and you do such wonderful things ...

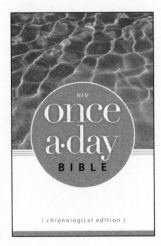

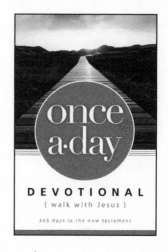